William Gordon Murdoch, William S. Bruce

From Edinburgh to the Antarctic

William Gordon Murdoch, William S. Bruce

From Edinburgh to the Antarctic

ISBN/EAN: 9783743318601

Manufactured in Europe, USA, Canada, Australia, Japa

Cover: Foto ©ninafisch / pixelio.de

Manufactured and distributed by brebook publishing software (www.brebook.com)

William Gordon Murdoch, William S. Bruce

From Edinburgh to the Antarctic

FROM EDINBURGH TO
THE ANTARCTIC

An Artist's Notes and Sketches during

the Dundee Antarctic Expedition of

1892-93

BY W. G. BURN MURDOCH

WITH A CHAPTER BY W. S. BRUCE
NATURALIST OF THE BARQUE 'BALÆNA'

LONDON
LONGMANS, GREEN AND CO.
AND NEW YORK: 15 EAST 16TH STREET
1894

TO

C. J. LONGMAN

WITH THE AUTHOR'S

BEST WISHES

CONTENTS

CHAPTER I

Written in the North-East Trades, recalling our departure from Edinburgh and the University Hall, ... 1

CHAPTER II

In Dundee we sign Articles as Assistant-Surgeon on the Barque *Balæna*, bound for the Antarctic and the Adjacent Seas—We bid farewell to Dundee and sail North to make the Atlantic by the Pentland Firth, ... 14

CHAPTER III

A Short Account of the Origin and Objects of the Dundee Antarctic Expedition—We have a long spell of Heavy Weather in the North Atlantic, ... 23

CHAPTER IV

Further Notes during the Bad Weather, . . . 37

CHAPTER V

Fine Weather at Sea—Life on a Sailing Vessel—Artist's Impressions—Sailors—Sailors' Songs—Willie Watson, ... 42

CHAPTER VI

Old Horse Day—Song, 'The Dead Horse,' . . 74

CONTENTS

CHAPTER VII

An Account of how Two Boys came to Stow away in the *Balena*, written by one of them—Hot Weather and Blue Seas, . . 79

CHAPTER VIII

We run into the North-East Trades—Fishing Bonita—In the Doldrums—Heat, Calms, and Squalls—Yarns, . . 89

CHAPTER IX

We Cross the Line—Neptune comes on Board—A Great Function—Full description of the Actors and Ceremony—'Ships that pass in the Night'—Our Day at Sea—Pleasure and slight Discomforts, 100

CHAPTER X

A Tropical Storm—Grey Sea south of Line—Sea-bird Life south of the Line—Fishing Petrels—The Albatross—Stormy Weather in the Forties—Ossian, ... 120

CHAPTER XI

Albatross Fishing—The Ship's Dog—Gales again—The Doctor visits a vessel in Mid-Atlantic—'A Girl with a Blue Dress on'—Heavy Seas—Whales—Strong Gales in the Forties, . . 130

CHAPTER XII

Changeable Weather—Yarns about Bears—We approach the Falkland Islands—The Watch below—Charlie spins his Yarn, . 146

CHAPTER XIII

The Falkland Islands—Port Stanley—Birds—On Shore again—A Colonial Store and Bar—We go shooting Specimens—The Bagpipes—We stop a Night on Shore with a Family—Notes on the Islands—Trout, People, etc.—Government House—Sir Rodger Tuckworth Goldsworthy—The Dr. and the Upland Goose—Wild Duck—Sea Fishing—Malvina—Interior of an Old Colonial Farm House—Men of the Islands—The Climate—A Gold Digger from 'the Coast,' 164

CHAPTER XIV

Leave the Falklands—The want of proper Pilotage—A Scurvy Ship—On our way South again—A Glimpse of the Polar World—Whales—Fog and Icebergs—The First Blood—The Crow's Nest—The Edge of the Antarctic Ice—'He's a Bowhead!'—Ice of all kinds—Colouring—Bergs and Mist—Mist and Bergs—South Shetland—'A Sail!'—Bergs to Port, to Starboard, Ahead, Astern—A Gale—Berg Thirty Miles long—Swell on the Pack Edge—A Berg breaking up—Land!—White Seals—Penguins—Meet our Consorts *Diana* and *Active* in Erebus and Terror Gulf,   19

CHAPTER XV

Christmas Eve in the Antarctic Ice, .   232

CHAPTER XVI

Christmas Day—Meet Dr. Donald of the *Active*—Sealing—Large Black Seals—In the Engine-Room—Antarctic Fossils—A Visit from Captain Larsen of the *Jason*—Sealing, ...   243

CHAPTER XVII

The Pack-ice that barred the progress of Ross's Sailing Vessels—Approximate Cost of an Exploring Expedition to the Antarctic—The Active Whale—Sealing in Mist—The Norwegians celebrate their King's Birthday—Vive Napoleon!—Whalers' opinion on Nansen's Expedition—In the Norwegian Focsle—Fog, Wind, Snow, Gale—Seals—A long Day in the Boats—Seals on a Berg—Sunshine and Gales—A Gale amongst the Bergs—A Bad Night—A Calm Evening in the Ice—A Mirage—A Yarn from the Arctic—Jammed in the Pack—Roughing it in the Ice—Old Junk—The Doctor's Hair Restorer—Various Incidents, .   269

CHAPTER XVIII

Off to the North again—Open Sea—In the Engine-Room—Notes on Matrimony—The South Shetlands—Out of the Polar World—Cape Horn Sea—Jock Harvey Yarns—The Falklands again,   337

CHAPTER XIX. BY W. S. BRUCE, NATURALIST ON THE 'BALÆNA,'   349

MAPS

CHART SHOWING TRACK OF THE S.S. BALÆNA, *at end of book*

SKETCH CHART OF SOUTH ORKNEYS, SOUTH SHETLANDS, ETC., *at page* 349

FROM EDINBURGH TO THE ANTARCTIC

CHAPTER I

Barque Balæna,
Atlantic, N.E. Trades.

AFTER all, life is not so bad. I had come to the conclusion that it is all vanity and vexation of spirit; but that is a long time ago—nearly six weeks now. At that time all on board the *Balæna*, from the skipper to the stowaway, expressed the same gloomy opinion of life at sea. 'Who would sell a farm and go to sea?' was the most poetical rendering of the common plaint in the cabin. 'Wish a blasted sea would jolly well clear us out,' was what Jack in his wet clothes was growling in the flooded focsle.—We were very miserable! We ought to have had a little fine weather for a new enterprise like ours, but the very worst was served out to us; and when we had made the best of that, and had begun to think our troubles were over, down came another gale on us, worse, if possible, than the one before. Three weeks we lay somewhere off the N.W. of Ireland—where, exactly, nobody knew, for the sun only winked at us once or twice.

At one time we drove north almost on to St. Kilda; at another we were nearly as far west as Rockall, a most objectionable rock rising out in the N.W. Atlantic. The reader perhaps has never heard of it: I certainly never had, and do not wish ever to be near it again. Some of our crew had made its acquaintance before, and survived. They still spoke of it with hushed voices, and open, fearful eyes. On a black winter night they had driven on to it. All hands were saved; but the only passenger, an elderly spinster, was drowned in her cabin! She was said to be coming home with a fortune in specie—the skipper, they told me, never went to sea again, but lived on shore and built himself a splendid house.

But these evil days are past now: we are well into the warm weather, and the N.E. trades send us steadily southwards. Porpoises plunge round our bows, and blue flying-fish with gossamer, dragon-fly wings skip over the sunny waves. If the old pessimist who discoursed so wisely of the vanities were swinging alongside here in the hammock, he would agree that a bundle of cigarettes would make life perfect. . . . . . .

Here it occurs to me that I have begun this log, or narrative, or whatever it may be called, in an unorthodox manner. From a number of volumes I have with me, it appears that the way to begin a book of travel is to give first the reasons that induced the author to leave his native shores, then detailed accounts of what stores and provisions he laid in, and so on. Such matter may be of service to future travellers, and it has the immediate advantage of filling up the first chapter. With this latter object in view, I shall explain at some length how I come to be writing notes on the heaving bosom of the Atlantic instead of drawing pictures at home.

The writer ought to be drawing in Edinburgh, but that became impossible last August; for the British Association met there, and the people of the University Summer Session gathered from the four corners of the world and brought with them a fever of intellectual life. Even in its outward aspect the town became affected by the influx of wise men and women, and the lonely men in the club windows looked down on a strange and unfamiliar people: blue-veiled Americans, dainty French ladies, festive professors, and blue-stockings crowded the streets where were wont to pace tall Edinburgh beauties and impressive advocates. Up the Castle Hill the intellectual contagion spread, till the artists and students in the highest, quietest rooms of the University Hall were infected, and could no longer do their own work, but went foolishly listening to others.

For months past I had been designing a huge frieze of our Scotch kings on white horses, jogging along in a row, with great men walking beside them on foot. Through winter and spring I worked hard, and drew all day and read old chronicles at night, and the work went on apace. Duncan the Mild and the long line of the children of Banquo had passed in procession; and James the Sixth 'stopped the way,' when the intellectual carnival began.

For the life of me he would not look the least kingly or move on an inch. Just when I was desperate with efforts to work through the distractions of the Summer Session, came my friend Bruce—an old resident in the Hall—saying, 'I'm off to the Antarctic as naturalist and surgeon on the Dundee Antarctic Expedition—will you come?' And I said 'Yes.'

Five minutes after coming to this decision, a hundred and one unanswerable arguments occurred to me in favour of it. I remembered how it had always been my intention to see the polar regions; how, even in nursery days, when we listened to *Fast in the Ice*, I had vowed to bring home white bear-skins to the gentle reader. Such a chance as this might never occur again, I argued, and it is right to see the wonders of the world abroad before one grows old; besides, the frieze would undoubtedly benefit greatly by being laid aside for a time.

Bruce told me he had heard there was a berth to be had on the Balæna, the vessel he was going on, so we straightway wrote to the shipping agent to engage it, and waited as patiently as possible for the answer.

Great was my disgust, after waiting for several days, to hear that there was no berth, not even one foot of spare room on any of the ships, and that therefore the Company could not possibly take a passenger. The situation was distinctly unpleasant: half of my acquaintances had heard of my intention of going south, and, if I did not go, there was the horrible prospect of meeting people for months to come who would make continual inquiries as to when I intended to start for the North Pole.

Aren't you glad you didn't go? and Don't you think you are much better where you are? It would be better, I thought, to sign before the mast than undergo this torture.

The Balæna was to sail in about a week from the day on which I received the agent's letter, so there was little time to try and put matters right. However, I wrote immediately to some friends who took a keen interest in the scientific prospects of the venture, and who were also good enough to believe that my drawings in the southern latitudes would be of value to science, and prayed them to exert their influence in my behalf, and next morning went through to Dundee to try and alter the agent's decision.

Once at Dundee, there is no difficulty in finding the whalers. All Dundonians, from the small boys to the big shareholders, take a proud interest in them. I asked a policeman to direct me to the whaling Company's office; fortunately he could speak pure Scotch—the natives use a *patois* of their own—'Ower yonder, East Whale Lane,' he said, lifting a leg-of-mutton fist in the direction of a blank wall, 'jist gang straicht forrart.' So I went 'straicht forrart,' meditating as I went on the melodious tones of my native Doric. It was a very narrow lane running up from the docks between two high walls, and there was no mistake about its being Whale Lane, the very air was greasy, and the kerbstones were black and oily. There was but one big doorway in the lane: I opened it, and found myself in a yard littered with casks and whale-boats and ship's-gear, and beyond this impedimenta was the office. It was a quaint little place, not at all the sort of place one associates with well-to-do shipping concerns. Round the walls were a few maps, mostly of the Arctic regions, much soiled by many voyages of skippers' fingers. A pile of rusty, greasy rifles, mostly old Henrys, leant against the counter, and in the far corner of the room was a collection of whaling-gear and old ledgers. The agent himself was a pleasant, bright little business man, full of interest in the expedition, and I suppose as well informed about Arctic matters as any of his ships' masters. He seemed willing enough to take a passenger; but the objection remained that there was not an inch of room to spare on the Balæna, or in any other of the three ships. However, his advice was to go down to the docks and have a look round the ships myself. So off I went, and found the Balæna—she had just returned from somewhere beyond 80 north, and as she lay in the dry dock, her iron-wood lining could be seen right down to the keel, scarred with long ragged furrows, which told of late encounters with the ice. The first impression was rather disappointing. Everything about the vessel was in hopeless disorder: aloft, stays were slack, halyards and braces dangled anyhow, and from stem to stern her decks were littered with blocks and tackles, cables and anchors, coal-bags, spare spars, boats, and all sorts of ship's-gear.

On board I found that what the agent had said was quite the case,—every spare corner was filled with stores. The only untenanted bunk was a place about the size of a chest of drawers, next the surgeon's berth, and this

was full of tubs and tinned-meat cans. If it had not
been for these wretched tubs and things, I was told, I
would have been welcome to stow away there, but there
was absolutely nowhere else to put them. This was
poor comfort, and I returned to Edinburgh in a very low
state of mind, and for two or three days laboured at my
frieze, avoided the face of man, and vainly tried to forget
my Antarctic castle in the air. That was impossible.
Bruce was camped in my quarters, and his preparations
for the voyage made me think of the tumbling seas and
glittering green bergs instead of dusty old memories of
dead kings.

Just three days before the Balæna sailed I went through
to Dundee to see for the last time whether a berth could
not be found on one of the ships. The master of the
Balæna was not on board, so I went to the other ships
to find if there was still a berth to be had before the mast.
There was apparently plenty of room there, as it seemed
that it was hard to get hands for the Antarctic, though
there were numbers ready for the Arctic. Before signing the
articles I determined to pay one more visit to the Balæna,
and this time the result was satisfactory; for at last I was
told that the bunk beside the doctor's was mine if he could
put me up in his cabin for the first week at sea—after
that week the bunk would be cleared of the stores that
were then in it. I could scarcely believe my good fortune
—how I hugged myself as I trained home that evening!
The other passengers in the carriage must have wondered
what on earth could make the opposite party look so
happy. A pretty French *bonne*, in charge of two children,

found me beaming vaguely at her corner of the carriage as we came out of a tunnel, and smiled bewitchingly; the children laughed because she laughed; and an old gentleman laughed at the children. The mother looked icy daggers at me, but what did I care! I could have shaken hands all round, and kissed the—children.

The rose-leaf in my happiness was that I knew Bruce was so utterly good-natured that he would never dream of refusing to put me up. How I rushed from the Waverley up the Mound five steps in the stride! Bruce was seated amongst his baggage—coat off—hair on end, utterly distracted between lists of packages and the finances of the Summer Gathering. I put my case before him as he sat there, knowing well what his reply would be: 'Why, of course I'll put you up,' he cried. 'Man, I'll put you up for the whole voyage—there's heaps of room in my berth.' Was there ever such generosity! The berth was about the size of a rabbit-hutch, and into this he had to cram scientific instruments, specimen bottles, camera, clothes, and half a doctor's stock-in-trade. . . . That was settled, and we shook hands over the rampart of baggage, and no more packing was done that night, but we rested and went down to the club and drank whiskies-and-sodas to the success of our voyage. We could look with pity on the poor lawyer-fellows, bound to their desks with golden fetters. They may have the best of it in the long-run, those steady men; but we did not envy them that evening, and the moon never winked down on jollier Bohemians than on us two, as we climbed the Mound, arm-in-arm, in the small hours of the morning.

We had strict injunctions to be on board the Balæna by mid-day on the following Monday, which left me only two days to get my kit together—a short time considering that all my baggage, guns, and artistic properties were distributed all over the town; but it was time enough, and if it had not been limited, I could easily have spent a fortnight collecting baggage, with the result that I would have brought a lot of unnecessary things.

We had been advised by Arctic men to bring our oldest clothes; but I had no time to make any selections —simply bundled what lay nearest into a box and bag, and was ready in no time as regards covering. But laying in a fresh stock of painting and drawing materials took a lot of time, for it was difficult to form any estimate of how much one would be able to use in these unknown parts. There was the same difficulty about ammunition. I had not the least idea whether I might use a few hundred cartridges, or thousands, so I laid in a supply of about one thousand, of different sizes of shot, and took a re-loading and capping machine. A Henry express and a rook-rifle made up my armament. The rifles would have been as well left at home, for there are plenty of old Henrys on board, and shot guns as well.

On Saturday evening we heard from the agent that the date of sailing was postponed from Monday till the following Wednesday, owing to the difficulty in getting hands to sign articles. Though we were both ready to start on Monday, the reprieve of two days was welcome to both of us, as it gave us time to make a few more preparations, and scribble some hasty P.P.C.'s. I sent post-cards, simply illustrated in the style of Phil May or the early cave dwellers. Informal, perhaps, but expressive enough, I fancy.

Then we bade farewell to some of our friends of the Summer Course, who still lingered at Riddle's Court. This Riddle's Court, from which the Doctor and I make our departure for the Antarctic, is quite the centre of the world. There may be those who do not know of it: I would refer all such to the old city records of Edinburgh; there they will find how 'the huise was biggit by ane worthie Bailie M'Morran,' who met his death at the hands of a schoolboy, St. Clair of that ilk, who led his school-fellows in the first recorded lock-out, and who fired a cannon from the High School roof, so that the ball struck the bailie in the 'wameis' so sorely that he died on the spot. That was long ago in the sixteenth century, when the times were lively. Since then Professor Patrick Geddes brought it to light, and tore the newspapers off the groined ceilings and the panelled walls, furnished it, and made it one of the University Halls. Now it is to Edinburgh what the Plantin is to Antwerp, and people come from distant lands to look at it, and wonder at the skill of the old builders; and the city guides tell them curious, untrue tales of the people who once lived in it. One of the guides, a M'Kay—an old, bent man, with a long, white beard—interests me more than the others, he takes such a kind, paternal interest in each of the tourists he brings to see the place, and his grand, proprietorial air makes one think the house belongs to him. Whenever I hear the familiar click of his stick coming into the small court I listen with all my ears. First he tirls the pin on the oak door, and insists on his charges doing the same; then he points out the very spot where the bailie breathed his last, and tells how the old worthy entertained Bonnie Prince Charlie and Queen Mary at right royal entertainments. 'Ye'll hae heard tell o' Mary Queen o' Scots,' he says, 'her as was beheided by Queen 'Liz'beth?' 'Ou ay, we ken a' aboot the jade,' say the country cousins; and 'I guess so,' say the Murricans : they have, in all probability, just bought a pretty picture of her in Princes Street, and 'it is vury like, indeed.' American tourists buy thousands of these photos, always from the picture which represents Queen Mary a pretty, sentimental girl of twenty, in black velvet, with a ruff and prayer-book—and a block in the distance. They do not think the portraits of a middle-aged, broken queen are at all like. Then the old man unbends his back and points up with his stick to a plaster bust of Socrates that a man of unclassical tastes put out in a niche, because there was no place for it in his room. 'Yonder,' he says, 'is the image o' Bailie M'Morran hi'sel'; it's said to be jist a wonerfu' guid likeness,' and the tourists look up open-mouthed at the rain- and soot-streaked ancient, and wonder where the sounds of laughter come from. 'Ou, it's jist they daft student laddies,' says M'Kay; and he tells his charges as they go on to the next show-place of the queer ways of the men of the Hall.

I have made a sketch of one of the rooms as I last saw it. It ought to form a contrast to the drawings I may make in the Antarctic. It was done in the tail of a N.W. gale, with everything pitching about, so much allowance may be made for it. The ladies in the sketch,

I ought to say, are the students who come in August to sit at the feet of Professor Geddes, and who turn us poor men out of Riddle's Court to find shelter in some of the other Halls.

The parting with our friends that evening was quite touching; some sorrowed because they could not come with us, and a few that we were so foolish as to venture on such an expedition from which we would never come back,—the hardships would be far too great for us,—they knew.

Such forebodings gave our prospects quite an artificial zest, and consequently I felt bound to make arrangements against every possible misfortune. To a skilful artist of Dundee I intrusted the finishing of the frieze, and made arrangements for the payments of all legal debts, and with a voice that perhaps betrayed the depth of my emotion, asked a friend to take care of my watch.— Dear old turnip,—my only heirloom,—how you recall the palmy days of my ancestors! Many well-lined fobs have you ticked in, in your time; and now you lie amongst old parchments and family jewels in a lawyer's safe, whilst your poor owner travels the world o'er on a whaler, with a Waterbury—beggarly Waterbury, that broke the first time I wound it up.

After these affecting ceremonies we adjourned to the Club with an old friend, and there Bruce and I saw the last fair meal we were to see for many a day.

How vividly do I now recall that last evening of luxury; the gleaming white linen and silver, and the harvest moon peeping over the Castle, blending her silvery rays in the yellow bubbles of the Heidsieck.

CHAPTER II

T' was late when we made our way back to our Hall; the only people afloat were two soldiers, feeling their way to barracks, and the night policeman. Of course we had forgotten our latch-keys, so we had to pelt the windows till a good professor wakened from the dreams of his youth, and threw down his key wrapped in paper. There was still some more packing and writing to do, so there was no time for sleep, and when the sun rose we were working away, roping, strapping, and hauling our baggage down the spiral staircase.

It was such a beautiful September morning that we felt half sorry to leave Edinburgh. Princes Street and the houses of the new town lay beneath us, still asleep in the violet shadow of the old town, and over in Fife the hills were just touched with the level morning rays; on the Firth the sails of a ship caught the light and gleamed white as a sea-gull's wing, and the grey water changed to vivid, sparkling blue. Beyond the blue rolling pine-woods of the Kinross, the Ochils lit up, and far away over the silvery bends of the Forth, Ben Ledi and Ben Lomond raised their grey heads into the yellow western sky.

As we took our departure at such an early hour, the citizens of Edinburgh did not turn out in force to bid us farewell, but one Hall man, who had been working all night for his final, came out of his lamp-lit room into the daylight as we rattled our boxes down-stairs, and generously said nothing about the horrid racket we must have made all night just above his head, but shook flippers and wished us God-speed. I see him now, a tall, woe-begone figure, in a red and yellow blazer, with a wet towel round his head like a turban. Poor fellow! we felt that he needed good wishes more than we did. We wished to make a sensation somehow or other, so we mentioned in an off-hand way to our jarvie that we were going to the Antarctic, and you should have seen how he stared, and how carefully he hoisted our boxes on to the dickey. He had heard about the expedition in the papers. As it was a long road, we suggested that he had perhaps better hurry a little, and by Jove he did; the way we clattered up Bank Street to Riddle's Court to get the last of our baggage was a thing to be remembered.

The lady students had flown with the summer, and the housekeeper and her maids went about the deserted rooms sweeping up bows, ribbons, etc., making preparations for the return of the winter residents. We wolfed a hurried breakfast there in the common room, bundled into the cab again, and rattled down to the Waverley just in time to catch the first train to Dundee.

So at last we were fairly *en route* for the Antarctic, possibly the South Pole.

... Dundee, like other towns, is a very ugly blot on the beautiful face of Nature. When I left school I had a romantic belief that Bonnie Dundee, who died for the Royal family at Killiecrankie, was in some way connected with the town. But this belief was unfounded, and I have not yet learned that it has ever been connected with any character so picturesque as the Bonnie Lord Viscount. Long ago it used to be considered a safe banking town. The soldier burghers of the towns to the south, when they shut their shops and went to the borders to fight with the English, sent their money-bags to the burghers of Dundee for safe keeping; which was, doubtless, a very good plan.

The American War is partly responsible for the town being what it now is; before that war it was a pleasant, quiet-going weaving town and port. The jute fever came with the cotton famine, and the small independent weavers were brought from the looms in their houses to work in big factories. The organisers of the work became 'the bloated capitalists' that we hear so much about, and the workers went down, and remain down. I have heard an elderly man describe the early days of the 'city's prosperity,' as they are called—its mushroom growth of factories and fortunes, with its stores and flash bars, and the *nouveaux riches*, with their gold and their girls; and it sounded like the rise of a Western mining town rather than the quiet growth of an East Coast seaport.

The jute fever has long since subsided, and the moneyed employer has satisfied all his individual physical wants, and is now trying to gratify his artistic cravings. He has no taste; he is a business man, and taste has not been in his line. This he admits without the least shame, so he goes to the picture dealer and the artistic upholsterer who keep art in stock. These have neither taste nor conscience, still they decorate the manufacturer's house. They dangle the clever things in gold frames from exhibitions over the walls, and fill the rooms with upholstery; with a result that you, the reader, if you are a man of business, could not but fail to realise.

The working classes have, perhaps, as little cultivation as their employers; but want of means prevents them showing an unlimited amount of bad taste. Of necessity they are simple, and simplicity is the *sine qua non* of great art. They show some vitality in music, however. It is only the poorest workman who does not possess a harmonium on which his wife or daughter can play him the air of some soothing popular melody, or one of those martial hymns that have made such a noise in the world since the days of Sankey. Concertinas and melodeons are as common as blackberries, and the twilight hours are filled with their melody, poured forth by the enamoured youth at the stair-foot of his senorita's seven-floor tenement.

Lately the Milo and other beautiful Greek and Egyptian works have been enshrined in a fine Gothic building in the centre of the town. A few people go to look at them, and enjoy them, and wonder why there is no Apollo, and why there should be but one beautiful spot in such a large and wealthy town. But enough of Dundee! Thank heaven if you need not work under its smoky cowl, and pray for the poor souls who think that they must.

After we had taken our traps on board we went down to the shipping office and waited our turn to sign articles. This was quite an impressive function. The clerk and the skipper stood behind a broad counter and both looked very kind; the crew stood in front and looked rather grim. The two parties were separated by a substantial brass lattice-work, which I was told serves to prevent the men on pay day totting up accounts with their masters in other than a legal manner. When several of the crew were collected, the clerk read the articles aloud, previous to our signing them, rattling them off at such a rate that we could form but a vague idea of what he was reading about. I could gather that we were to sail on the Balæna, bound for the Antarctic and the adjacent seas, and there was a something about plum duff on Sundays, and beef and split peas on some other day of the week. These were the rations the men were signing for; but they could tell no more than I could what the clerk had read.

The men received their first half-month's pay in advance wherewith to supply themselves with clothing and a *deoch an doris*. I can vouch for their having had the latter when they came on board; but a good deal of the clothing they have bought since from the master's slop chest, for which payment will be deducted out of their wages—an extravagant way of doing business, so they say. I signed articles as assistant surgeon, at a shilling a month for pay, and I felt grievously disappointed when my modest request for one half-month's pay in advance was refused. I had intended to do all sorts of things with that sixpence.

I shall never forget the excitement and bustle of that afternoon when we left the Camperdown dock.

The expedition had been much talked of, so all the Dundee citizens who could leave their factories were down at the dock gates to bid farewell to their friends. The decks were still littered with sacks of coal, ropes, and spars. And the crew, up to summer Plimsoll line with grog, were staggering on board under deck cargoes of mattresses, blankets, and provisions. Some were hauling their sea-chests along, and wives and children were picking their way about the decks, staring round them at the little barque that was to take their men to the Southern Seas. Some of the older women, when they thought they were not observed, put money into the crevices in our rudder head to bring us luck, with who knows what result.

The change from the weary monotony of shore life to the sea-going life was marvellously rapid and complete. It was as if a great stage-curtain had been rolled up before us, and all that we had heard or read of the ways of the sea since we read Marryat and *Robinson Crusoe* was acted on the deck before us: each man took up his part as if he had played it from the days of the Flying Dutchman onward.

As we warped through the dock gates the last of the
crew bade good-bye to their wives and children, hardened
their hearts, and tumbled on board, leaving many a kind
face wet with tears, but smiling hope and encouragement;
then we swung out into the stream, and the men came aft
to the taffrail and mizzen-shrouds and shouted a hoarse

farewell to the distant crowd on the pierhead, and a faint
'Hoorae, hoorae, hoorae!' came back over the calm,
silvery Tay. Then all hands bundled away forward
again, shouting and singing, dived down the focsle-hatch,
threw off their shore togs and shore cares, had one last
pull at the bottle, and were up on deck in a minute,
drunk and glorious, ready to go to the world's end or
beyond it—a jolly, motley crowd, not two dressed alike, in
dungaree suits of every shade of blue and green, in faded
jerseys and red handkerchiefs. Men and boys there were
of every sailor type: old Arctic whalers, red cheeked and
bearded; tanned South Spainers with shaven chins and

faces lined with the rough and smooth; quiet men and boys from the East Coast fishing villages, and gentle men from the Shetlands. Fifty men from all the world; strangers an hour ago, brothers now—in the one spirit of whisky, devilment, and adventure.

What a picture they made as they swung together at the topsail halyards, their eyes gleaming, with open, thirsty mouths shouting the old shantie, 'Whis—ky John — nie. Oh—whisky makes the life of man. Whis—ky for—my Johnnie,' with the shantie man's solo, 'Oh, whisky made me pawn my clothes,' and all together again, with a double haul and a shout of 'Whis—ky—John—nie,' that makes the blood tingle even to remember it.

All small sail set, most of the crew disappeared, and left the clearing up of the decks to some of the Union and other clear-headed men.

Going down the Tay a search was made for stowaways, and twelve poor young chaps were routed out and sent back to their mother country in a small boat that went ashore at Broughty Ferry. It was very touching to see the group of hungry-looking boys standing together in the waist; some of them were crying with disappointment.

The wind was light and from the south, so when we passed the buoy of Tay we turned northwards for the Pentland Firth instead of the Channel; but we did not know what sort of weather was before us. Surely the money of the spaewives never sent mariners worse winds.

Our first night at sea was quiet. The harvest moon shone over a broad track of rippling sea, and the doctor and I chatted till late with Nicholas the steward.

CHAPTER III

IT is just possible that there are persons living in London and other remote parts of the country who may not have heard anything about this whaling expedition from Dundee to the Antarctic. For their benefit I shall here give a short account of its origin and 'the gran' commurrcial aspecs o' the expedection.'

The *Balæna mysticetus*, right whale, Bowhead or Greenland whale, or whatever the reader may choose to call it, is, as he perhaps already knows, of great value on account of the bone in its mouth. You will find in the *Ladies' Pictorial* plenty of pictures of the people who keep up the price, or you can see them half alive in the streets—willowy things with their blood all squeezed into their heads. The whalebone in the jaws of one whale sometimes is worth two or three thousand pounds. Naturally, a whale with such a fortune in its mouth has been in great request, and in consequence has become so scarce, or so retiring, that of late years Arctic whalers have found their formerly profitable industry almost a failure.

To make a new start, the Nimrods of Peterhead, three brothers Gray, of Arctic fame, proposed taking their ships to the Antarctic to look for whales there. From the account given by Sir James Ross of his voyage of discovery in 1842, there was reason to believe that all that was necessary to make a 'full ship' was to sail south, haul the bone aboard, and sail home again with a fortune between decks. Glorious castles in the air were built in this prospective foundation of bone and blubber. One of these three whaling brothers, Mr. J. M. Gray, I believe, the eldest of the trio, had the enterprise to start a company with this object in view in 1891, but, fortunately or unfortunately, failed to collect sufficient capital. Next year, Mr. R. Kinnes of Dundee followed Mr. Gray's example, and succeeded in equipping four ships for the purpose—the *Balæna*, *Active*, *Diana*, and *Polar Star*, all wooden barques built for ice work, with small auxiliary screws. The Balæna, originally called *Mjolnar*, on which I write, is considerably the largest of the four, being 260 tons register, gross tonnage 417, with a 65 horse-power engine, length 141 feet, beam 31, and draught $16\frac{1}{2}$ feet. She was built in Drammen in 1872, and was then ship-rigged, I believe. She was what is called a pet ship, built to suit the ideas of her master. Her sides, with timbers and linings 32 inches thick, are supported in every direction by huge beams and natural knees. The focsle is forward, below the main deck. Aft, the deck-house roof rises about 2 feet above the poop—what is technically called a Liverpool house—leaving a narrow alley-way round the stern. Her sheer is greater than in British ships, and her lines are somewhat after those of the Viking ships. The Active is the next largest. She was built at Peterhead in 1852, and has an old-fashioned, homely look,—low in the bow and high in the stern, reminding one of the ships in the pictures of Vandervelde. Her length is 117 feet, beam 28 feet, draught 18 feet, and engines 40 horse-power. The Diana, like the Balæna, was built in Drammen, and bought from the Norwegians: length 135 feet, beam 29 feet, draught 16 feet, engine 40 horse-power.

Then comes the Polar Star, a pretty vessel to look at, but very small, and as old as the hills, I'm told. She has a most diminutive engine that just moves her. The funnel is about the size of a pipe-stem. I nearly signed before the mast on her, but from what I hear of her now, I am rather glad I did not. All four vessels are barque-rigged, with single patent reefing topsails. With their small, buff-coloured funnels, they look like old-fashioned men-of-war at a distance.

Before the expedition started, the newspapers got hold of these dry facts, and apparently found them rather too dry for general consumption, so they flavoured them highly, and then the public took them and passed them round till they became very sensational indeed. One of the accounts that was whispered from lip to ear in the shipping offices, and bandied amongst the men about the docks, was that the four ships were being sent out never to return. Only one of them, it was said, would possibly come back, and it was comforting to hear that probably this would be the Balæna. The others were heavily insured, and their fate was expressed by a shrug and a wink.

The report that there was a berth on one of the ships for a passenger, though hardly of public interest, gave me a lot of trouble, and caused much disappointment to several people who applied.[1]

Another unfounded report was that the Royal Geographical and Meteorological Societies intended to pay £25,000 of the expenses—an extremely liberal intention, which would have left the Company to supply only about £3000 more. Then Government was said to have offered help. So thoroughly were the papers and people convinced that no such expedition would be started by private enterprise, that some of our crew signed for a less proportion of bone and oil money and larger weekly wages than they would have done if they had believed in the merely commercial basis of the undertaking.

It is true that these Societies did take a keen interest in the scientific prospects of the voyage; and both the Royal and the Meteorological subscribed instruments. Some private individuals, also, who arranged that the ships' doctors should be men of scientific tastes and acquirements, supplied them with necessary material for their observations.

These are all the facts and fictions about the expedition that I have heard, and I hope the reader will fully appreciate them, as it has been very dry work writing them down. Further on in my log I may happen on more information that may interest those interested in

---

[1] One of the applicants, an enthusiastic naturalist, when he heard the ships had sailed, even went the length of steaming to the Falklands to secure the berth there, when we called on our way south.

the commercial aspects of whaling and sealing. I hope so for their sake; but my present intention is simply to give rough sketches and notes of what interests me on the voyage, trusting that they will not be so horribly disjointed as to be quite unreadable.

The morning of the 7th was wet and foggy. At 8 A.M. Peterhead bore W.S.W. ten miles—so a fisherman shouted to us as his brown lug-sailed boat crossed our bows and disappeared in the mist, hurrying home with their night's catch to get the first of the market. Later in the day the fog cleared, and we set all sail with a fair wind. The crew were very busy all day setting up rigging, but rather sad and quiet as they worked. No doubt their heads and hearts were sore. In the afternoon came a change; the S.E. wind had fallen, and scarcely filled our sails, when a patch of black clouds formed over the land in the N.W. in clear grey sky. Slowly it came out towards us, hanging low, growing gradually larger, and throwing a dark shadow on the leaden sea. Round us the sea fell glassy calm, and the black monster came down twisting, twirling, forming out of nothing below, vanishing raggedly above in the chilly air. The men stood by the sheets and halyards silently waiting the orders to shorten sail; their faces looked pale and ghastly against the dull, lead-coloured sea. Then it came down on us with a sudden rush, lightning flashing and thunder rolling in the black cave over our heads. The sea was ripped into short angry waves, and we lay suddenly over till our lee scuppers creamed with seething foam, wind and rain struck us at the same time, and the sails that had been hanging in white soft folds filled out hard and dark, and streams of water poured down their hollow sides, and splashed on the glistening decks. The air was filled with the sound of the rushing wind and the hissing of the sea as we tore along before the squall. Hoarse orders were shouted along the deck :—' Let go flying jib there! Clew up fore-to'gallant! Main-to'gallant! In spanker!' the men repeating the orders, and yeo-hoing in all different high keys as they hauled on the down hauls. We were pulling on the topsail reefing halyards when the squall passed, rumbling and growling, into the distance.

And so began our troubles in the Northern Seas. Was there no weather-clerk or spaewife wise enough to tell us that gales and head-winds waited us in the north, when we would have sailed south down Channel with a fair wind on our quarter. The weather cleared with the squall. It had besides a vivifying effect on our men. They went about a little jollier than before; but the wind had gone round to the N.W., and there it stopped. In the evening we steamed past Duncansby Head, past the Paps of Caithness, bathed in a yellow sunset, past Stroma, the island of many streams, through the Firth with a nine-mile tide helping us through to the Atlantic. It is an interesting country that Pentland Firth, with its islands, with its mixed people, and its stories and legends, Celtic, Spanish, Norwegian, and Dutch—plenty store there for a New Argonautica. On the 8th, with fresh westerly wind and clear weather, we steamed past Cape Wrath. In the afternoon we took in the two whale-boats that were hanging on the davits, and lashed them down to the ringbolts aft the foremast, on the part of the deck between the fore- and the main-mast called 'no man's land.' The two quarter-boats were left on the davits, whilst the main-chain and fore-chain boats were turned keel up on the skids or beams that cross in front of and behind the main-mast and foremast. They make a welcome shelter in bad weather, particularly so in these hot days when the hammocks are slung beneath them, and the watch off duty hang sleeping there like bats from rafters. Then the anchors were brought inboard, and made fast on the focsle-head. The cables were stowed, and we stopped steaming, and set all sail, heading N.W.; but the wind increasing, we soon had to take in all small sail.

From the 9th to about the 29th it blew every sort of squall and gale known to meteorologists or seamen. My diary, I find, is one long wail at the wretched weather. So, instead of it, I shall give an extract from Mr. Adams' (our first mate) log for a few days. His log gets over the ground far quicker than mine, and besides has a certain stoical pithiness of expression that I feel mine lacks.

September 9th.—Wind westerly; making an offing from Irish coast.

From 58.46 N. stopped steaming; set all sail 8 P.M., burst foretopsail and topgallant; bent another topsail. 12 P.M., wind increasing; reefed topsail.

10*th.*—Noon, 58.35 N. 4. Furled jib and mainsail; carried away flying jibboom; strong wind; heavy showers. Noon, 2, strong wind; very heavy sea. 4. Wore ship;

vessel labouring heavily and shipping quantities of water.
12, fresh gale with heavy sea.

September 11*th*.—Very heavy squalls, with much rain.
Close-reefed topsail; strong gale and heavy sea. Lat.
59.13; long.——. Strong wind S.W.; very heavy sea; out
first reef topsail; wore ship. Strong wind and squally
weather.

12*th*.—6 A.M., very heavy squalls; close-reefed topsail.
10, strong gale; high sea. 12, no alteration wind or
weather.

So the log continues. We lay in the hollow of the
grey valleys day after day, night after night, pitching,
tossing, rolling, down to our chain-plates with our deck
load of coal,—there is no Plimsoll line on a whaler—the
deck all awash with foam, every second wave thundering
on board. The black and yellow oilskins of the men at
the pumps now glistening in a gleam of sunlight, and
again sombre and pouring wet as they plunged knee-deep
through the sea in our waist, and hauled on the braces
and halyards. But thanks to the immensely strong
timbers and bulwarks, the heavy seas have done us no
great harm, though a vessel of ordinary build would
have left her bulwarks scattered over the ocean.

One gleam of hope we had on the 11th—the barometer
went up a little and the wind moderated. The monotonous insistent humming in the rigging ceased, the splashing
and the thumping and the noise of the storm stopped for
a while. Then we breathed again, and stretched our limbs,

took off oilskins and sea-boots, and hope grew strong within us.

Nicholas, our steward, ventured to hold a 'shoppie' on the strength of the lull; and the 'shoppie' is a great function on board a sailing ship. The lamp is lit in the cabin, and Nick unpacks bundles of sea-boots, dungarees, jerseys, socks, caps, red handkerchiefs, and all things of a seaman's wardrobe.

Then the men come aft out of the darkness and wet, and stand in the passage and cabin, and the first man buys what he needs—boots or jerseys, or what things else he has not been able to buy out of the pay he received in advance when he signed articles. Probably he has brought but little with him beyond his mattress of chaff and the clothes he stood in, not having great capital to invest in these things. If an able-bodied seaman, he probably received some four pounds when he signed. Two or three he would leave with his wife or children to tide them over the first four weeks till they could call at the agents for the next half-month's pay ; of the remainder, a few shillings would go on clothes, a few shillings for preserved milk for the voyage ; and if he stood his chums and wife a grog or two before leaving for nine months' abstinence, he can scarcely be blamed, can he?

In the sketch I see I have made the men look rather melancholy. Starting an account against their future pay possibly is the reason for this expression. Nicholas is writing down the name of one of the purchasers. He, behind, examining his new sea-boots is not like the Hebrew purchaser who said it was naught, and went away boasting ; he describes the purchase as something or other bad before he buys, and worse afterwards ; but sailors all growl. Fifty per cent. the skipper makes on his purchase, so Jack says ; which of course is a lie, as skippers are just as honest as other shopmen, and make a dead loss on such transactions.

Bruce had his first surgical operation to-day. An iron-bound block carried away somewhere aloft and came down on a man Bonnar's head. He was a stout, elderly A.B., and made no moan, but clapped his cap on the hole in his skull and was helped along to the cabin. As assistant surgeon I did my duty on this occasion by holding the doctor's legs—there was a heavy sea on—whilst he tinkered up the head, and Nick held the carbolic and plaster.

On the 13th, lat. 58.20, long. 9.47, the weather still held

fine, though the wind was ahead, and with the engines kept going and our fore and aft sails, we managed to make a few knots in nearly the right direction. Every one made the most of the gleam of fine weather. We have turned out all our wet books on deck, and got our bunks dry, and have our clothes hanging out to dry on the rigging. Aft on the quarter-deck the sailmaker is busy patching up our torn sails, of which we have quite a collection now;

the flying jibboom carried away in one of the squalls, so we shall have to have a new one made. The whale lines were hauled out from below the cabin on to the quarter-deck and dried in the sun, everything in the after-hold, sails and lines, being more or less wet with the water that had come on board and made its way through the cabin-flooring and hatches to the sail-room. The Balæna was plodding along steadily when we turned in, with a light wind on our fore-quarter, making five knots an hour,—no great speed, but enough to keep our hearts up in the fond belief that we would get out of the Western Ocean some day. But, alas! at 7.30 the engines stopped, the wind began to rise again, and in my bunk I could hear the orders shouted to shorten sail, and in a few moments we began the old motion again: a slow climbing up watery hills, with a throw on the crest enough to twist our masts out; a nightmare-sinking as the billow passed beneath us with a thump and a crash and we reached the bottom of the valley and plunged into the next hillside, to rise slowly again, with the white sea surging, tumbling madly on our decks, swishing from bulwark to bulwark, surging against the cabin door, till it escaped at the scupper or over the

bulwarks as if thrown from a full cup—just to come thundering on deck again.

Oh, the weariness of that wind's song in the rigging, that persistent humming as we sink into the trough, rising and howling as we mount the angry grey ridge. What does it mean, that dreary booming everlastingly passing us under the hard grey sky, driving the Lord knows where? Is it a great tune with great words that human ears cannot distinguish, or moaning of lost, hopeless spirits?

All the crew are in oilskin again—dripping oilskin on the top of damp clothes. We have oil-bags towing to windward, and the oil helps greatly to keep the sea from breaking. Now and then a wild sea burst on our bow, making glorious painter's effects; but, oh! the weariness to have to face another gale and again run off our course. About mid-day, as we were trying to forget our misery, one of these white demons caught us full and fair on the bow just as we began to rise to a wave. With what a staggering crash it struck us! We felt as if our ship had gone full tilt on a rock, and thought to hear the deep sea singing in our ears. The mass of water on deck seemed fairly to take the Balæna's breath away, and she sat down deep and almost still, rolled gently from side to side, her rail almost flush with the sea outside, and seemed to debate whether it was best to slip under quietly or rise and fight it out. She made another effort, fortunately, lifted one dark bulwark a little, heaved over half the sea to windward, gave a lurch to leeward, and got rid of the fifty tons or so, spouted the rest through the scuppers, and slowly rose and took time with the rollers as pluckily as ever. It was a cheerful feeling, that rising again, and very sad that slow movement when we were almost under. A hole, two feet square, was left in our bows, under the anchor-deck, to mark the kiss of the Atlantic, and for months afterwards the sea and the sunlight came pouring through it alternately. Of course everything on deck went adrift, buckets, harness-casks, tubs, and spars went

pitching about in the seething foam like the stocks in
Fiskum Foss. I wish I could have done these subjects
justice in paint. Perhaps in the future, in the quiet of a
studio at home, I may try to recall some of the dreary
turmoil and the cold feelingless glitter of sea and sky,
and frame it with a gold frame, and have it hung in
some man's dining-room; it would make the room feel
calm and comfortable by contrast. But all one could do
at the time was to make small jottings, and then hold on
when the seas came over. Water colours were out of the
question; even pochades in oil, with salt water pouring
over, were difficult.

CHAPTER IV

SATURDAY, 17*th September.*—Lat. 54.40 ; long. 11.1.
All night we have sailed with a fair wind, and have slept the most refreshing sleep. A contrast to last night, when the seas were going over us, and we expected every moment to go under. But our comfort has been of short duration. The wind has gone round to the old quarter, the S.W., and blows big guns. None of our crew, old Arctic men, have had such a buffeting as this in the North Atlantic : this fortnight has been a revelation to most of them. This afternoon we hung on to the rails on the poop, occasionally plunged in foam, whilst the first mate spun us yarns of the sport the whalers have in Davis Strait. Tales of bear shooting, reindeer stalking, and long excursions in the boats for days and weeks together, in the Arctic summer, up silent, sunny fiords, unknown, unnamed, where the splash of oars is never heard, where the rivers are filled with salmon and never a one to catch them. The whale-ships leave Dundee in the spring of the year and are in the Straits in about two or three weeks. Sometimes a passenger goes with one of these ships, and if by good luck he happens on a decent skipper, such a trip is most enjoyable.

By far the best plan—a plan that I am surprised has not been carried out yet—would be for some five or six sportsmen to charter a whaler for the summer, take just enough men and boats to kill a whale if they were fortunate enough to fall in with one, and spend the spring and summer hunting reindeer, bears, walrus, white whales, white hares, netting salmon, exploring, etc. The drawback to such sport is apparently the tameness of the reins and the meekness of the bears. But as against that there is the enormous improvement on home sport, that there you shoot and fish for your dinner, which, after all the talk of Sport for Sport's sake, is what gives fishing and shooting their real zest. A whaling barque could easily be bought now for an old song, especially if this Antarctic whaling proves a failure. The owners would then part with them at any price. There are any number of splendid Arctic seamen, old whalers and hunters, ready to be engaged, and I know of the very man for master. Then, if the ship was lucky and fell in with a whale, all the expenses would be paid, and the walruses and seals would realise a profit. Five months' sport, free-gratis-and-for-nothing!

Is it not wonderful that people invest in forests and chivvy red deer from fence to fence, and pot partridges over endless miles of turnips, when up north they could kill big game on unnamed mountains, sail up under covered fiords, and run great whales on miles of line!

To me, a Scot of the proverbial lack-penny type, whose natural inheritance of sport was long since advertised by Scott and sold to English tradesmen, such a prospect appears most powerfully attractive. I am now afraid, from all that I have heard, there will be little sport in the Antarctic; but the uncertainty, the possibilities of falling in with unknown animals, has a great fascination. At present we are surrounded with bird-life. Mollies are in hundreds wheeling and dipping round our stern—perhaps the oil-bags we have had hanging over to windward to break the seas has attracted them, or possibly it is the relationship that exists between them and our sailors. Mollies were once sailors: this is not generally known. Our men know them, and can tell you who they once were. Here is a very tame one that comes so close that we could almost touch it as it passes. We know it quite well now by the expression in its dark eye and by certain marks on the feathers. In the body, the men say, he was John Jack, an old Arctic sailor lost in the West Ice.

There are, besides, Mother Carey's chickens, or stormy petrels; they keep by themselves, a little aloof, following in our wake behind the Mollies, dipping the points of their dainty black beaks into the seething water, patting the surface of the waves with their delicate black feet, picking up invisible food. They are very gentle little birds, rather like swifts, black, with a white patch just above their tail, and have a peculiar moth-like flight. They look like flakes of soot driven about in a windy sky.

The Dutchman's troubles were a jest to ours. On the strength of the comparatively quiet weather we had a clean table-cloth to-night; but just as the stew was put down a heavy sea caught the *Balæna* and sent us and the stew all over the cabin. Poor Nicholas! I did feel sorry for him. He has felt the parting with his family very much, and the continued storm has been trying to us all; but this last accident, which he has so wonderfully succeeded in averting for such a long time, has almost broken him up.

Sunday has passed soft and grey, a long day of perfect rest and contentment. The sea has gone down, and we are slipping quietly along before a light N.E. wind. All day we have been lying about the deck enjoying absolute idleness and dry clothes, and the soreness is going out of our limbs. We are too tired to read, just alive enough to enjoy the gentle roll, and to watch the sea-birds and listen to the man at the wheel yarning to us. He ought not to speak; but the ways of a whaler are not those of other ships. This man was well worth listening to; he was one of the *Eira* men who spent the winter with Mr. Leigh Smith in Franz-Joseph Land, so his experiences were somewhat out of the common. Most people interested in matters Arctic have heard how the Eira went down off Franz-Joseph Land, and how the crew lived on walrus' and bears' flesh all winter, and sailed in their boats in the spring for forty-one days through the ice-floes, and arrived in Scotland none the worse. Such tales are interesting, even to read of; but when told by one of the actors, they are doubly so. Mason looked back to that long dark winter with feelings of nothing but regret and longing, for the fastings and great feeds of walrus flesh. He recalled the handful of broken biscuits they had served out to them on Christmas evening as one of the most pleasant recollections of his life.

A blue shark paid us a call this morning. Being Sunday, however, we did not introduce the subject of sport; but we have prepared the line and chain, and baited the great hook with a hunch of salt pork. We are still too near Scotland to show our true colours; nearer the line, or in the ice, we will put on the whaler and kill and spare not, Sunday and week-day alike.

The end of our first chapter of troubles.

In the fo'c's'le.

CHAPTER V

MONDAY, *19th September.*—Lat. 53.9; long. 13.51. Fine weather at sea. Two days ago our thoughts

went ever roaming northward and homeward; to-day they follow the track of the wind to the south. We think of the voyage before us, and picture the ice world away in the Southern Seas. Yesterday's rest has done us all good, and to-day the crew, instead of stamping about the foaming decks in streaming oilskins, are all busy at different works on deck in the sunlight, with coats off and bare arms.

In the galley Peter and his mate are making great preparations for a regular fine-weather dinner; they run no risk of scalds and broken dishes to-day. Forward, the boys are spinning foxes and marline out of old junk, dipping their fingers into tar pots and rubbing the twisted strands with it. Our two 'stowaways' are busy with the rest. Poor fellows, they did not bring a very extensive wardrobe with them! It was difficult enough to hide away their bodies in the harpoon chest, without bringing any baggage on board; but they look cheerful and hopeful now, seemingly well satisfied with the berth fortune has given them.

Another group is at work tautening the main-shrouds and backstays, hauling on them with block and tackle. We have old-fashioned shrouds, with dead-eyes and lanyards, much more elastic and picturesque than the modern screw-till-you-break style of thing. The backstays are quite a feature in a whaler; we have three for the topmast, two to'gallant, and a royal—more than the usual number, to make the masts stand the violent jerks forward when the vessel collides with the ice. Aft on the quarter-deck or poop the group of figures at work suggest the great London painter's picture of the 'Arts of Peace,' with the ladies and the elegance left out. 'Sails' is working for dear life, making his needle fly through the tough canvas. The second mate and some of his watch are hauling long rolls of sail from below the cabin for repairs, all wet and torn, and promising 'Sails' many a day's work before they are fit to hold wind again. I am busy, too, lettering the flag-signal bags, and making pictures—quite in my element, I confess, for I believe in the usefulness of art. It appears to me that what is called Art for Art is dilettantism, just as Sport for Sport is butchery.

The sea is deep blue this evening, tinged with red from a fine-weather sunset. A pleasant warm wind from the north sends us steadily on our course. Our square sails are sleeping—round, and taut, and motionless. Porpoises play round our stern, leaping out of the deep blue with a sigh and a shower of sparkling drops; for a second they hang with a glint of the setting sun on their black polished shoulders, then plunge like a cannon shot into the darkening waves, leaving a phosphorescent trail as they dart in a zig-zag course beneath and round our hull. How often I have read of these sea effects and heard them described, and yet how poor, thin, and feeble was the

colouring of the mental pictures I drew! Clark Russell had painted the sea for me with the strong colours of Rubens, Pierre Loti had described its pearly tints with the grace of Corot; but they had only turned the first pages of an endless, enthralling picture-book.

Tuesday, 20th September.—Lat. 53.9 : long. 13.5. Three sparrow-hawks visited us to-day [1] at different times,

---

[1] About 130 miles west of the Irish coast.

bringing thoughts of land into this horizon-bound prison. They had but an unkind reception. Our mate dropped the first arrival on deck with my gun: I supplied the gun, and he took the risk of the evil consequences that might follow so inhospitable a deed. At mid-day there was another cry: 'a hak, a hak!' and all hands stopped work and looked aloft at the little traveller, which lighted finally on the mizzen gaff, and another shot dropped him on the poop as we rolled to windward. I wonder where they were bound for?

A few more days of this perfect weather, with the sails looking after themselves, and the mate will find it hard to get work enough to keep the crew busy. We have over forty men forward, but as yet there seems to be work for all hands. We have hardly any modern wire-rigging, so our ship's toilet, being all of rope, requires constant looking to, serving, tarring, and a hundred little attentions.

The air is full of golden light this evening. Rosy reflections touch the sides of the deep purple swell. Our masts and rigging and broad sails show dark against the sunset. Vague groups of men sit about the deck, some playing and some dancing, their outlines so blended and softened as to be almost indistinguishable. Amber light pours over the bulwarks; it falls white on the neck of a man reading, burns red on the turn of a brown cheek, and sparkles on the wet skin of another washing—detached spots of colour that give transparency to the low tones of the shadowed deck.

On such an evening, when every atom seems trembling

with harmonious colouring, sounds soften and tune themselves; even the wheezy spasmodic notes that the mate draws from his melodeon are sweet and beautiful to-night.

Nicholas is having another shoppie aft in the cabin. He has brought out a miscellaneous collection of articles for sale—Arctic mits, whalers' caps, broad-brimmed straw hats for the tropics, snow spectacles, red handkerchiefs, tobacco, pipes, sea-boots, and carpet-slippers. If any one wants straw hats or light dungarees, now is the time to get them, for there is quite a rush upon thin clothing for the tropics; our Arctic men look forward with dread to the heat on the line. The South Spainers amongst us who have crossed the line as often as the Arctic circle, have brought old topies and karkee jackets, so they do no trade, but look on and throw in advice to the youngsters and old men who have not been south, but have served their time in the seventies and eighties North latitude.

Wednesday, 21st Sept.—Lat. 50.15; long. 15.49. The doctor has got the scientific interest of the expedition well in hand now. Lately science and art have scarcely had the attention from us that we believe to be their due.

When a man neglects his pipe these high interests must suffer. The last two days of fine weather and sunshine have worked a great change, and now the pipes are smoking gaily, and the scientific instruments are being polished up and attended to with great regularity and solemnity. The possible results from the notes of the men of science of this expedition may, and probably will be, of the greatest interest to all peoples, and may materially affect the progress of man, therefore the subject should be approached with decent calm and solemnity.

Imbued with such a spirit of reverence, I offered to assist the doctor with the preparation of his tow-net and line. The tow-net, I must explain to the uninitiated, is a conical bag of silk gauze slung on a metal ring, much resembling a jelly-bag in shape,—but perhaps there are those who know not the homely jelly-bag! For those, I would liken it to a landing-net, and continue. The tow-net was large, and the line attached was long, thin, and hard. Having uncoiled this line on deck, upset the coil, made all ready in a proper and seamanlike manner, the net was dropped over the stern and the ship continued its course without a pause. We were doing our best speed —a modest five knots—at the time, and naturally the line went at the same rate through the four hands of the doctor and myself. A salmon line, with a forty-pounder's first rush, *can* touch up your fingers, but I warrant this new whip cord, burning through our hands, was a higher style of experience; and, if it had not been for a timely hitch round the taffrail, the doctor and I might now be studying science with mermaids.

The doctor used a net afterwards about the size of a small butterfly-net. We made a splendid haul. In the few hundred yards the net was dragged we caught some millions of animalculæ that would scarcely have felt crowded in a wine glass. We diluted a teaspoonful of the mixture in a tumbler of water and gloated for hours over its marvellous beauty. There were minute crustaceans, clad in glittering coats of mediæval armour, transparent bells, visible by the fairy iridescence of their palpitating outlines, microscopic cuttle-fish and minute jellies, each with its own costume and colouring, varied and harmonious, schemes from which a lady could choose a dress or an artist the colours for his picture. All were struggling, powerfully and blindly, to find their way through the dim glass that divided them from the sunlight that came pouring into the cabin through the open hatch, struggling as if the fate of worlds depended on their individual efforts. And this little world of ours does depend on their existence; for, as each dies, his tiny shell and spiny armour sink slowly down through the ocean depths —far deeper than the depths to which the bones of the great whales go—there they rest and form the deposits that will form the beds of the peoples of the time to come.

Friday we keep according to the rules of the Mother Church, and eat fish—the dried stock-fish one sees in grocers' shops, but rarely sees on the table; and most excellent food it is when served with sea hunger for sauce.

We had hopes of porpoise steak this morning—a succulent dish—but you have to catch your porpoise first, and we find they always disappear when the harpoon is brought out. The way to spear them is as follows:—The most venturesome of the crew—one who can swim and doesn't mind a ducking, preferred—takes a hand harpoon and gets out on the martingale. (The martingale is a short spar projecting downwards from the end of the bowsprit, and the bowsprit is what sticks out in front of a vessel, on which the jibboom rests.) He clings to this with one hand, with his feet on the stays and the harpoon in his free hand, and the line attached to the harpoon is passed to the men on the focsle-head. Whilst he hangs on, occasionally getting a dip into the waves, the crew lean over the bow and give advice and hold on to the line. The porpoise comes dashing round the vessel right under her bow. Down goes the harpoon, fair and true into its back, the crew haul away on the line, which is rove through a block, and up comes the sea-pig, kicking and spluttering in mid-air. A running bowline is then chucked round his tail, and he is hauled on deck amidst great applause, and handed over to our gallant cook.

We executed all the above manœuvres, except that of bringing the pig on board. Either the porpoises disappeared just when we were ready for them, or the harpoon drew out of their backs.

. . . The air is warm, the sky grey, and the wind in the S.W. We are only getting very slowly ahead. If we could just continue this course for a couple of days we would make the south coast of Portugal. One of the vexations of a long ocean voyage is that one passes within a few hundred miles of so many interesting places which one would give anything to see, and yet may not land. What would I not give just now to see our helm put up and a course made for shore, to land and stretch one's legs on solid ground, to see Velasquez and eat oranges?

We brought forth Kipling's *Ballads* to-day for the general diversion. The writer is wrong to suggest, in one

of his poems, that a thirst can only be raised somewhere
'East of Suez.' We are considerably west of that, and
the thirst raised by this warm weather and salt sea air is
remarkable! The mere mention of oranges makes us feel
parched. The worst of it is, that outside the medicine-
chest, there is absolutely nothing to quench our thirst but
lime-juice and tepid water of many flavours. It is reported that some bottles of Talisker were put on board by
some unknown friends for the crew on New Year's Day,
or other great occasions. But these have not appeared
yet, and it is a weary time to wait till the New Year.

The men did not rise to Kipling's Tommy Atkins
rhymes at all; but it was a treat to see how 'The Bolivar'
went down. How they cussed when they read it! Not
one of our old hands but had sailed on just such a coffin-
ship,—old, over-insured, undermanned, meant to founder.
Such vessels are getting scarce, thanks to Plimsoll and his
white mark, though it unfortunately is a moveable object.
How the men bless his name! Their own united efforts
have done much to do away with the evils of a sailor's life,
and at present the leader of the S. F. Union is fighting
for a scale of provisions to be regulated by Government.
At present men are far too dependent on the generosity
of owners and masters in this respect. In two ships
they have enough properly cooked food, whilst in the
third—a dog's food is more plentiful and better served.

Saturday, 24th September.—Lat. 46.53; long. 13.49.
Calm as calm can be. Last night we were bowling along
at seven knots, a tremendous speed for us, and this

morning we lie rolling on a leaden grey sea, with the sails flapping, and all the blocks creaking and complaining. George, the second mate, is walking up and down the poop whistling quietly and looking hopelessly round the horizon for the least air. We may not boil the kettle (steam), for the coals must be economised, so we resort to the bagpipes and play half-a-dozen pibrochs and a lament or two, to bring up a fresh breeze. If you play the right tune, and play it long enough, you can always work up a breeze, even a gale, possibly. The pipes brought the breeze, but unfortunately it was dead ahead; still it was better to move, even in the wrong direction, than to lie bucketing our masts out on a glassy swell. And it was also satisfactory, to prove finally that piping has an effect on the wind. I have long known this from personal experience, but it has other effects that are perhaps not so generally recognised. For instance, a pipe-tune will make salmon take and pike revive on the hottest day in summer and feed voraciously. They make wakeful children sleep, enchant red deer, and seals come out of the sea and listen in such rapt attention, that you can shoot them—if you so please.

Mais à nos moutons, the various impressions of an artist at sea. Impressions innumerable, so many varied and new, that, seeing them, I can do no serious work—an ideal state of affairs. The broad daylight and the flood of sunlight is so bright and dazzling that the colours and forms of the groups of workers on deck are blurred together, and each figure is blotted into the patch of intense shadow which it throws on the hot, yellow decks. Up aloft the men on the yards and rigging are seen,—dusky, foreshortened figures against the broad shadowy sails. Forward, the smith is thumping soft red iron on his ringing anvil, whilst his mate works the bellows, sending the smoke curling aloft, faint blue against the shadows in the hollows of the sails, and rusty red as it swirls across the patches of blue sky. In the shadow thrown on deck by the foresail, men are tarring spun yarn and weaving mats for

chaffing-gear, and the carpenter sweats in the heat as he chops with his adze at the yellow pitch-pine spar for our new jibboom, making great chips fly into the sunlight like lumps of gold.

No two days are quite alike; but always when the sun sets there is the same rich light filling our decks, lighting brown faces under broad white hats with a ruddy glow, blending and softening the various groups on deck with a rich golden light that makes one think of the yellow depths of a Titian.

I would hardly have believed that a Sunday at sea could be so different from the other days of the week. To-day, on the Balæna, this is the case. The men have the whole Sunday given to them for rest to their bodies, —when there is no work to be done. And they do appreciate it. It is warm to-day, and sunny, and there is a peace and quietness that quite passes anything we know on shore. No hideous bells clash and bang, advertising with vulgar discordancy God knows what sort of churches. No heated preachers are for ever telling the way to be good, labouring to save sinners. But great Nature sits on our stem and soothes our souls, and shows how good is The Beautiful, and how beautiful is The Good. And the sea and the breeze whisper to us sweet secrets of the glorious day to come, when we shall resolve into universal life and begin to live again, in the wind and the sea and the sunlight. A Sunday at sea, under God's sky, is a day from Eternity; a Sunday in town a day from Hell. The crew lie in luxurious repose on the focsle-head, curled up in the anchor flukes and chains, smoking, or stretched flat on their backs reading novels, or old letters. Some are sewing. One of them is sitting on the foot of the bowsprit sewing at a pair of canvas trousers, and a boy on the capstan-head watches him with lazy interest. Below, on the foredeck, one or two are washing themselves, getting at least the rough of the tar off before they put on clean clothes. Here is a jotting of one of our many barbers at work.

It is a pity we have so few books on board. Our men are fond of reading, but unfortunately all the literature supplied for them consists of a very juvenile style of literature, mostly pamphlets and tracts.

Philanthropic persons might lend a few good books to such a large ship's company when going on so long a cruise; Scott, Shakespeare, or the like, how they would be appreciated! The men have the utmost reverence for books. The few I was able to lend forward, came back, after being read by the crew, carefully covered, and as unthumbed as if they had come from the printer's.

I had a look at some of the above-mentioned literature, which is served out to the crew in weekly instalments. The bound volumes are sent on board for cabin use, and the pamphlets for the crew. The first piece was called *Discontented Fanny*, a simple tale with a moral, about a little girl who coveted another little girl's frock, or whose own frock did not fit—I forget which; but it seemed to me hardly the sort of thing to give a man to read on a nine months' cruise. *Sermons in Candles* was a book with a binding, sent for the cabin. It dealt, in extremely subtle allegories, of candles and ethics. One hundred and sixty-nine pages of similes there were, between candles (wax and tallow) and religious principles: *e.g.*, 'If you have no candle-stick, a ginger-beer bottle does mightily well. How

In the dog-watch.

often our Lord has used men of scanty education!' This may be true, but is it not a pity that such similes should have to rough it on a whaler? All thanks, though, to those who gave the books: their intentions were kindly.

Last night our engine stopped grinding: what a relief it was! It is a tiny machine, but the doctor and I sleep right above it, so we have the full benefit of the vibrations. The change from the throbbing and the 'in-and-out' steamer's motion to the quiet gliding of the sailing ship is very pleasant. The sound of the lip-lapping of the sea against the ship's side just reaches us in our bunks through the thick wooden sides.

Tuesday, 27th.—Lat. 42.24 ; long. 14.25. A Danish ship passed us to-day ; she came up from leeward, passed under our stern, and faded out of sight in a veil of mist ahead of us and to windward. She was sailing quite two points closer than we could. She had a windmill working her pump, an arrangement much despised by our sailors—without reason, I think, as it saves an immense amount of work. We have to pump ship every four hours, and it takes about ten minutes each time. After heavy weather and the ship has been straining we have to pump her for about half an hour out of each watch. The pump stands at the foot of the mainmast inside the fife-rail, and has a handle on either side ; some of the watch turn the hands and the rest stand in a line along the deck and haul on a rope attached to the pump handle each time it comes up. As we pump, the chantie (pronounced shanty) man trolls out some old sea song, and after each line all hands join in the refrain. Some of our men have a large stock of these songs. Most of them are sung to sad, minor tunes, with sometimes almost meaningless, but time-honoured words. The airs have much of the dignity of early Norse and Gaelic tunes, quite unlike any modern music ; when and where they originated I should like well to know. Here is one of them that the men sung frequently. It refers to some ideal skipper, beloved by his crew, who had died and gone to his rest a long time ago.

Chantie man sings: Oh, Storm-ie's gone, the good old man.
All sing: Aye, aye, aye, Mis-ter Storm-a-long. Oh,
Chantie man: Storm-ie's gone, that
All: good old man, To be with you Storm-a-long.

Chantie man :   We dug his grave with a golden spade,
All :   Aye, aye, aye, Mister Storm-along ;
Chantie man :   His shroud of finest silk was made,
All :   To be with you, Storm-along.

We lowered him with a silver chain,
   Aye, aye, aye, Mister Storm-along ;
Our eyes were dim with more than rain,
   To be with you, Storm-along.
         *   *   *   *
And now he lies in an earthen bed,
   Aye, aye, aye, Mister Storm-along ;
Our hearts are sore, our eyes are red,
   To be with you, Storm-along.
         *   *   *   *
Old Stormie heard the Angel call,
   Aye, aye, aye, Mister Storm-along ;
So sing his dirge now one and all,
   To be with you, Storm-along.

Think of this very slowly chanted, in time to the clank of the pump, the waves surging over the decks, sky and sea grey, and the wind booming through the shrouds overhead, and you have as dreary a scene as can well be pictured.

In some ways this sea life is much against painting or drawing. The fresh air and the full light and the simple life are all favourable, but the want of exercise is a great drawback. If it was not for the pumping, which slightly resembles bar-bell exercise, I should get into a too enfeebled condition to draw a line. The doctor endeavours to keep in good form by systematically promenading up and down the poop; but that is most awfully monotonous, and walking has such a bad effect in unsteadying the hand for drawing. Fencing or boxing are the exercises for a man who does fine work with his hands and head. They keep the nerves steady and the eye clear; but of all exercises they are least suited for a ship's deck.

One of the results of this lazy life is that my journal notes become reduced to the shortest, as :—' Jotting before breakfast, hands washing deck ; no go. Made pochade ; sky, calm sea ; cumuli ; inferior oleograph. Slept ; read ; tried walking poop—poor sport. Attempted drawing 'stowaways'—no go. Made jotting sunset—one of Scientific Series (the third)—won't continue them. Played pipes.'—What a day of fruitless attempts and consequent misery! No wonder the pipes were resorted to, and no doubt wailed out the most melancholy dirges.

The moon rose in its utmost glory to-night right ahead of the ship : how grand our sails look, like great bat's wings! Between the bend of the foot of the sails and the yards the dusky blue light shows. Some dark figures lie out noiselessly on the lower yard and clew up the mainsail, for the wind is right aft, and the foresail is shaking; then they come down the shrouds, stepping noiselessly with bare feet on the bending ratlins, blots of dark-blue shadow against the moonlit sky. Nick and I lean with our elbows on the bulwarks and watch the shifting path of moonlight on the waves. He tells me long stories of

Nicholas

all the world in a quiet, subdued voice, that goes well with the stillness and the moonlight. It was many years ago when he left Innisphail. Now the world is his country and Dundee his home. He has served in every berth on board all kind of crafts in many trades—in racing schooners, in the Channel fruit trade, in clipper ships to China, in ocean tramps, liners, trawlers, yachts, and whalers in the Arctic. He went up to Franz-Joseph Land with Mr. Leigh Smith when they relieved Nordenskeold in Spitzbergen in '73. What interested me most in his description of that land was the picture he drew of the lonely graveyards on the shores there, where the whaling men were buried centuries ago. One hundred and fifty whaling vessels used to sail from the port of Hull alone. Fleets sailed from London, Poole, and Liverpool, so the graves were not then unvisited; now it is but rarely a voyager looks at the rough wooden crosses and the grey stones. . . .

We have made up on our Danish friend, for we have been steaming, and the wind is light and southerly. So far as I am concerned, the greatest event on board or in this round world was the painting of my bunk. I did it myself. Unfortunately, I allowed myself to follow gratuitous advice, and first coated it with carbolic; and the smell of the paint and carbolic mixture afterwards was bad— bad even on a whaler. The moral is scarcely new; but it is intensely true: Never follow gratuitous advice, and in art matters go your own way if you have any; most people have none.

The only other event—quite a trifling one by Jock Harvey's account, was his driving a marline-spike into his arm while he was working at something on the mizzen-top. He merely clapped a quid of tobacco on the hole and went on with his work; then when he came on deck, seeing that there was a doctor on board, he came aft and had it bandaged. There is no mistake, a sea life makes men hardy.

Finished my drawing of Nick bringing aft the soup. It is of the kind called 'popular pictures.' Here is what the engraver calls a reproduction. God forgive him, and may we artists be forgiven our too great obligingness in painting too much of what is asked, and not enough of what we please. It is difficult to avoid aiming at momentary popularity on board; the men are so flattering in their criticisms, and so good-natured and interested in my drawings, that it is difficult not to paint only what they most readily understand.

Sometimes for the good of my soul I indulge in fan-

Bringing aft the soup.

tasies, paint colour pictures—attempts to express thought rather than form. How they puzzle these critics! Unlike the artistic middle classes, they look at pictures with no narrow preconceived notions, and at once recognise there is an idea that they cannot quite grasp. Their puzzled looks remind me of the expression of a staghound I once saw with its fore-feet on a wainscot studying the figures in a *Fête Champêtre* by Watteau. Our second mate, a big, energetic, bustling, blue-eyed, light-haired fellow, who delights in seeing ropes, spars, and portraits set up in a picture, gets quite wild when he sets his eye on these things that he feels he can't quite grip.

(*Saturday*) '*Plum-duff day.*'—I wish I could relate some of the stories we hear at table at meal-times ; all our party have seen something of the world abroad, so there is no end to them. We have Arctic tales of sport and adventure, whaling stories naturally being the most popular. We had some of the experiences of one of our party this morning—a short, obese little man, not a good story-teller, but familiar with that strange life up in the north. He described the days not long past when the Shetlands provided the Dundee and Peterhead ships with their crews. The ships put into Lerwick on their way north, where agents supplied the men, much as they now supply men to the Scotch whalers for the seal-fishing in Newfoundland in the spring of the year.

The men's shore debts to these agents, who were store-keepers as well, were paid in advance by the shipping companies out of the men's wages, and their kit and private stores for the voyage were covered in the same way, so the men were pretty well bound to resort to the agents soon after their return. The companies, with the humanity characteristic of companies in general, and for the men's benefit, no doubt, forbade the agents to send men on board with supplies of drink. As there were no objections made to their being supplied with soap, the agents got over the restriction by giving the men whisky and iteming it in their accounts as bar soap, so the amount of bar soap taken on board these ships by the men was alarming. When the men were well over summer Plimsoll line with the equivalent for bar soap, they naturally found some difficulty in getting on board, especially as it was the custom to take with them anything of value that came in their way that was neither too hot nor too heavy. Our narrator described his bringing on board one of the men who is with us here,—who, in this happy condition, had gone astray and wandered into the country and looted a farm-house of all the ducks. It must have been a strange picture, this stuffy little black-haired, red-faced sailor staggering along the shore with our sixteen-stone blond pirate on his shoulders, quite unconscious, but grimly hanging on to the ducks.

Plum-duff day is a conspicuous day in the week, distinguished from the other six by this very delightful pudding being served to all the ship's company. The name is slightly misleading, as it is at least suggestive of plums. But sea plum-duff, though it is very good, especially with treacle on the top of it, is in no way connected with plums. We have, however, more modern dishes on our *menu* than this last. 'Electric Soup,' as its name suggests, is quite a new sea-dish. It is like the Argonaut soup mentioned by one of the 'Three in Norway,' and is not considered nutritive. The richest sea-dishes have the simplest names and the simplest dishes the most sensational. 'Dandy Funk,' and 'Strike me Blind,' suggest rich, spicy dishes, whereas the first is simply ship-biscuit broken into powder and mixed up with molasses. 'Strike me Blind' has its sensational name from its absolute innocuousness; it consists of boiled rice and molasses. We have it on Fridays, and the crew say it is not a good thing to work on. 'Dead Dog' is rather a horrid name given to pounded biscuit, mixed with salt beef and margarine (butter preferred), and roasted in the oven. The pleasant quality of this dish is its elasticity: after loosening one's teeth with months of hard biscuit the elastic feeling is a welcome sensation. 'Harriet Lane' is one of the simple dishes,— a sort of brawn.

The men like it, but don't often get it.

... A day of heat and rest and disappointment. We saw a turtle asleep, and we thought we would catch it. If we had not been steaming we should probably

have done so, but the beating of the screw wakened him, and he went below. The crew are turning out in regular tropical kit now. A dungaree jacket, trousers, a belt, and broad straw hat is about all.

Tuesday.—The wind has freshened, and is blowing from the N.W., and we are bowling along merrily. But it ought to be blowing from the N.E., for we are in the track of the trades for this time of the year, so the Books say. Yesterday was very hot, with towering white cumuli rolling up from the horizon almost to the zenith, perfectly reflected in the calm, steely-blue sea. On such hot, still days we feel very lazy, and this northerly breeze is welcomed by all.

We signalled a steamer this morning, the first we have spoken to. The flags, as they lay strewn about the poop, looked splendid in the bright sunlight. How crude they look at home in our delicate grey light! Here, the reflected complementary tints are so vivid that the crudity of the primary red, yellow, and blue colours disappears. I spent the afternoon splicing loops to the flags, and then had a spell at the wheel, and poor sport it was. I would as soon drive a dray horse. The pleasure of steering seems to be in inverse proportion to the size of the vessel. When a craft is over five tons, then the subtlety and pleasure of steering begins to go. When the wind, the sail, the tiller and the hand are one, joined by the same delicate thread of sensation, then there is perfect pleasure. But to steer our good ship Balæna with a wind on the quarter is rough-and-tumble work.

These light winds, head winds, and calms are beginning to make us all suspect there is something wrong about our ship. What is wrong, we scarcely know! Some say there is a man on board who has left his tailor's bill unpaid, and there is a talk of burning somebody's effigy to see what effect that would have on the wind; but the difficulty is, whose effigy is to be burned? Suspicion has fallen on a black cat that leads a dog's life on board. It goes wandering about the deck, and belongs to no one in particular. This morning it got itself into trouble by coming aft the mainmast from the focsle, where it is supposed to have its quarters. For a focsle hand to do this without orders is a heinous offence. It then stole into the first mate's bunk, where he was enjoying his well-earned four hours below. When the mate felt it stealing over his legs his actions were prompt and his language explicit, and so were the cat's. Then it made its way into the cabin, that Holy of Holies, and in its expulsion endangered our curry, which we were doing our best to balance on the table; thence it got down into the sailroom, and in the dark, amongst the wet sails, sorrowed for itself.

George, the second mate, found it there, and though he has a sailor's reverence for cats, and is generally fond of animals, he felt it was his duty to do away with it.

... At 2 P.M. this Tuesday the cat was dropped over board with a piece of furnace-bar tied to its neck.

Since we made a Jonah of the cat, we have had two perfect sailing days, with a clear sky and warm sun, and blue white-crested waves tumbling under our counter.

Poor beast! how it would have enjoyed some warm corner on deck now! ...

I have not yet introduced Willie Watson in my log. I must do so here. He is one of the jolliest characters on board. Some call him Willie Watson, others 'Dee Dong,' from his generally Frenchie appearance and lively wit. But Willie Watson, The Hayne, Carnoustie, would find him any day. I was talking to him to-night for a long time under the break of the poop. It was just the sort of night for story-telling: everything was quiet, the sails aloft were all asleep in each other's shadows, and the Balæna rolled gently before the north wind, and at every roll the dark warm sea came flopping in at the scuppers, filling the waist with glittering liquid moonlight.

Willie is of the sea, as his parents were before him, and has lived in every corner of the world, and has served in many trades. Like five sailors out of every ten, he ran away to sea when he was a boy. Then he took to line and herring fishing, travelled with Wombwell's menagerie, sailed in the nitre trade till he grew tired of the Horn, went whaling to the Arctic, tired of that, carried golf clubs at Carnoustie links, netted salmon in the Tay, with every now and then a spell at the deep sea. He came on this trip almost by accident,—one of these chances that give a sailor's life its zest. Having scraped together a few pounds, he left his quiet fishing village and went to Glasgow to take ship to any part of the world on any ship that might be going. Fortunately his friend, the stationmaster at Carnoustie, persuaded him to buy a return ticket, and when he had spent the last of his cash with some old sea-cronies that he fell in with in Glasgow, he was still able to get back to Dundee instead of being Shanghaied from some boarding-house. At Dundee he found the Balæna in the dry dock fitting out for the Antarctic, and gaily danced across the gangway plank at the risk of his neck, and promised to sign articles; and right glad we all are he did so, for we need such jovial spirits on board to keep things going cheerily. Whilst yarning away to each other, he used a number of expressions that had a slightly French sound about them, so I asked him where he picked them up, and to my surprise he told me that, in addition to his other adventures, he had served in the French army. He had put into Rochefort or Charente, I forget which, in a trading schooner in '71, and the bounty money of forty francs offered for recruits was not to be resisted. So he just left his ship, without any formalities, and 'listed' with some two hundred volunteers, mostly Scotch and Irish. 'No vary likely callants,' he explained, 'a sort of pick-me-up lot, ne'er-do-weel lads, like mysel', ye ken.' The forty francs were spent in a couple of days, but the spree Willie remembers to this day. 'Eh, sir, they blithe French lassies, let alane the reid wine,—there's jist nae abstainin' frae them. They countrie folk, tae, they're a' dacent bodies—mony's the guid meal I've had frae them, sittin' by the roadside, or ben the farm-hoose,—gin there's mair war in France, it'll no' be lang afore they see Willie Watson back til them. They gied us a' braw new uniform, tae, a' blue an' yellie an' reid. Save us, but the auld folk at hame wouldna hae kent me! Syne they took us a' to a grand muckle hoose, a' windies and guns, an' gied me a gun an' a bagonette—nae drilling ava, jist pit us intil a yaird an' telt us, "Ye're gendarms noo, gang and fecht the Proosians," deil the Proosian was to be seen in a' the country-side, an' a' we had to dae was to gang aye tramping up and doon they boulivards in the sun and the stour wi' a musket at oor shouthers, —gey drouthy wark it was, tae, an' gin it hadna been for they bonnie black-eyed wenches an' they wine-shops, we wouldna hae tholed the sodgerin' muckle langer. ... Eh, sir, but I was skeered ae day coming oot o' ane o' they wine-shanties after slockin' the drouth wi' some freen's; wha should I see but the auld man, the skipper, ye ken, coming doon the road fou, and by wi' his weather e'e glowering frae under his bannet. Ma certie, an' I was skeered. The auld man was coming up ahint me, and stracht aheid there were twa gendarms steering richt athwart ma coorse, sae what to dae I didna ken. A daurdna gang ben the public-hoose, and daurdna meet the auld man. Weel, I jist had to gae stracht forrart, and brocht ma hand up to ma bannet, sodger-like, when the twa officeers gaed by. Thinks I, that will stooner ye, Mr. ——, but na, na, the auld man wasna to be daffed that gait, but up he comes astarn, aye keeking ower his shouther as he gaed by; but I keepit ma heid i' the air, an' ye ken I had they French whiskers, so it wasna jist sae easy for him to ken me. At last he slewed round and looks me stracht i' the face and says he, 'Wullie Watson, is that you?' 'Voolzey voo, Mongsieur!' says I. 'Mi no savez.' That's the French, ye ken, for——. But I'm no jist mindin' the richt translation the noo. Ony way, it gar'd the auld man look sae blate that it was maist a' I could dae no' to lauch outricht. Weel, awa' gaed the auld man, and I sees him gang intill the hottle where he aye bided when the *Tay* was in port, and, thinks I, I'll no' be fashed wi' ye ony mair; but wha should come oot twa meenits efter but Tam Robson, oor first mate! I didna see him, ye understan', for I was trampin' doon the road tither gait whustling the 'Piper o' Dundee,' an' whiles havering to mysel' aboot that fusionless carlin wha didna ken his ain man wha had sailed wi' him they twa years forbye, when, save us, I got a clout i' the braid o' my back that brocht me up a' stannin', an' wha wad it be but Robson, whustling the Piper, an' lauching whiles. 'Guid-day to you, an' hoo's a' wi' ye, matie,' quo' he, 'an' whaur did ye get the braw duds an' the gun? Man, but ye're braw! I'm thinkin' the folks in Carnoustie would weel like to see ye noo, ma bonnie laddie.' Eh, but I was fair dang dyght, and thocht there would be a grand splore; but Tam was ane of the richt sort, an' said he would put a' richt wi' the auld man. Sae we gaed ben an' had anither stoup o' the reid wine. Ay, certie, we did a' that.' . . .

Next day Willie was taken off the patrol duty, as being more suited to live on water, and was sent up the Seine in a flat, to send provisions into Paris in balloons. And at last he saw the Proosians, and plenty of them. He and his mates were lying in the flat fast to the bank amongst the rushes, when the 'Proosian came doon like cushats on the neips' (pigeons on the turnips). They pulled bushes and reeds over the craft, and lay trembling till the enemy disappeared, when they went hastily down the river again.

The most dramatic of the many incidents he had to relate of the war time was the fate of two German sailors. He told it simply, and with the light dramatic touch that only comes to men who have lived amongst events and scenes. A *raconteur* would become fashionable had he Willie's skill.

A German barque had managed to get into Rochefort with provisions and ammunition. Having discharged the cargo, the men got loose about the town, contrary to orders, and two brothers in particular became riotous, and hectored it over the townsmen in the cafés. Finally, one cast his eye on a Frenchman's girl; Frenchie objected, and in the row that followed Frenchie was killed by a stab from one of the brothers' knives—*whose* knife, neither would confess. To settle the matter quite fairly, the brothers were taken down to the river and posted on either side, and bade to shoot at each other. Willie stood in the neighbourhood of one of them as a sort of second, and his man was the quickest and nailed the brother on the opposite side.

So we yarn away in subdued voices till some one wakes and shouts: 'Heave the log,' and the deck becomes alive with dusky figures. Forward, eight bells is struck; the watch below come on deck into the blue moonlight, rubbing their eyes. Willie and I say good-night, light our pipes, and turn in.

This is a pencil jotting of chequers on the main hatch. Bonnar is playing the bo'sun for the championship, the first mate on the right, the engineer and the cook's mate on the left giving advice.

CHAPTER VI

*O*CTOBER 6th.—Lat. 30.30; long. 20.4. Old Horse day.
The cat's wind has held fair, and the Balæna, with a white feather in her teeth, bowls merrily southward.

The Old Horse came out in great style. The sailors consider that they do their first month's work at sea for nothing, having received the month's pay in advance when they signed articles, and the old horse is made an emblem of this month, and is hanged. I fail to see the analogy between an old horse and an unpaid month's work, but I am told that it is quite evident. However, I relate the incident as I saw it. It may be a custom of the past in a few years, for the reason that men are now trying to have their wages paid weekly. They would like to have a portion of their first pay handed them in advance, and would like their wives to receive their half pay in weekly, instead of in monthly, instalments. There are several other regulations they wish to have formed as to their pay; for instance, that in case of shipwreck, they should receive pay up to date of reaching home, or at least till they make land, or a port. If we were to lose this ship in the Antarctic and lived in the boats or on the ice for a month or so, and then had the good fortune to be picked up by one of our companion vessels and brought home alive, the men would only be entitled to claim pay up to the moment the ship went down, and instead of returning with their pockets full of money, they would arrive in debt to their employers for the cost of their board on the vessel that took them home, whilst the owners by insurance might lose nothing, and might even profit by the wreck. This seems hardly a considerate arrangement in regard to the men; and if employers would still be employers, they ought to be very considerate in this respect, or the time will come for sailors to work for their united interest, and the consideration of the employers will be of no account.

For some days reports have come aft from the focsle that the horse was being constructed. When I heard an unfamiliar song being chanted this afternoon, I went forward and found the men hauling on two lines that led down to the focsle-hatch. At the end of the lines came the dummy horse, made of wood and canvas, bestrode by Braidy, arrayed in a scarlet flannel jacket and a black jockey's cap. The horse was supported on either side and at its latter end by some of the old hands. As the hatch is very steep, they had some difficulty in hauling up the horse and its rider properly and in time to the chant. At last they got him on deck and then began a slow march round the ship, going aft on the starboard side, round the poop, and forward again by the port side. The procession really made a splendid picture-subject, the colouring of the men's clothes in the sunlight was so varied and so harmonious; there was faded blue, and purple, and pale green, and a sky-blue Tam-o'-Shanter, and all the faces and arms were dyed nut-brown by the sun. In the middle of the group sat Braidy in his scarlet coat, with

the brown unpainted wood of the bulwarks and the blue
sea above forming a back-ground. Round the deck they
went singing 'The Old Horse,' chanting the time-honoured
song with all solemnity, making the old horse plunge at
times, for they had to pull it along the deck in short jerks
to keep time to the tune. In the lee channels the sea was
frothing white, and I thought Braidy would come off, for
the horse grew very restive there; but he held to its neck.

Under the foreyard the procession halted, and a running
bowline was dropped over the horse's head, and Braidy
got off, and to a second mournful chant it was hauled up
to the yard's-arm. It was a curious, quaint, and pretty
performance; the solemn seriousness of the whole affair
and the suppressed childish fun were in extreme contrast.
For a minute the horse hung swinging against the bright
sky, then a man lay out along the yard and drew his

knife across the line, and the 'Poor Old Horse' dropped with a splash into the blue waves and floated sadly astern. These are some of the words of the song, and the air as nearly as I can remember it.

THE OLD HORSE

Chantie Man:	For one long month I rode him hard,
All together:	And they say so, and they hope so!
Chantie Man:	For one long month I rode him hard;
All:	Oh, poor old man!

* * * * *

But if he's dead I'll bury him low,
And they say so, and they hope so!
But if he's dead I'll bury him low;
Oh, poor old man!

* * * * *

Then drop him to the depths of the sea,
And they say so, and they hope so!
Then drop him to the depths of the sea;
Oh, poor old man!

After the tragedy came a reaction. The bo'sun chaffed Peter,—Peter White, cook of the Balæna, in full. Peter replied with a bucket of water, and before you could say 'knife,' water was flying in every direction. Peter bolted himself into his galley, but was washed out from the hatch in the roof. What a battle that was! It began in the afternoon and raged till night with unabated fury.

Swish—swish—went the buckets, filled in the ship's waist, till there wasn't a dry spot from stem to stern. The moon rose and poured down its soft light on a fantastic scene, on black, soaking figures with glittering, clinging clothes, wildly struggling in the foaming channels and slinging water right and left. Such a scene of devilment and fun, to be remembered in the quiet days of propriety at home.

CHAPTER VII

WOULD the reader like to have the full and true account of how it came about that William Brannan and his chum Terrence M'Machon came to stowaway on the Balæna? I have already told how we sent twelve of these poor lads home as we went down the Tay. This William Brannan is one of the two who escaped the search and came with us. He is about sixteen, pale and dreamy-looking, but strong, and has an exquisite voice. Stowaways do not often publish their personal impressions, so, with his permission, I give them here word for word. The doctor has taken in hand to improve the education of some of the lads of the crew, and I suggested this subject for one of Brannan's exercises. He first wrote the account with the assistance of an English public-school man, who is serving before the mast, with the stereotyped result that might be expected; then he wrote the yarn himself, as follows :—

3rd Sep. 1892.

As i was walking down the overgate is met one of my chums who was going to a football match but he was over late so we went round the docks for we heard that the whalers was going to sail on Tueasday 6^{inst} so we made up were mind to stowaway so we came on the day fixed. First we went to diane but we didn't like her so we went aboard the balenea we went down in foxel to stow ourselves away; but we got seperated an as i was looking about me i seen a lot of boys younger than myself into a keg

of meal, but i didn't look long for the time was drawing near to
sail i espied a place where a lot of cans full paint and ile, i well
get in here, so ,in i went i wasnt long in when another fellow
came looking for place then he came where i was he knocked all
the paint and ile on the top of me so i came out for i was in
afful mess an then i went to look for another place an then ise
seen my chum and i asd if he got a place yet he said no but i
espied another place on the top of a lot of barrells i then tried to
get in but it was over stiff so i got a shovel for a batering ram an
then we got it open so in i went and then i made room for my
chum so he got in—an then a lot more made rush for to get in
but we said their was no more room an then we shut the door
and then we got steel rod wat they called harpones. but we
didnt now what they were antil we came out and then the men
told us we wasnt long in when their was afful uproar which was
the men coming aboard an then we seen them drinking and
singing an dancing geting their beds in their bunks an then
felt the ship moving along but it was not long out of the docks
when we heard a man roarin out some of yous come and clear
the decks up which we learned after that he was the bosun, an
then about five minutes after that we heard him say some of
yous get an deck but one of them did not seem to care. but the
bosun ordered him on deck but he wouldnt go and then their
was a fight we seen them throwing each other about an then
we seen the mate an some looking for stowaways they were
looking among the barrals an then they came to where we was
then the mate he came to where we were stowed we seen them
coming through a hole in door the light shone through i thought
they seen my breeks but they went away then we slept then in
morning tow of the men who seen us going in gave us a scouse
(soup) an some ship biscuits then at night time we came out,

for tow hours then we went in again then the men tolds us to come out then their was a squall then in the afternoon we went on deck we met the mate at the top of the hatch he says to us hullo where did you come from but we did not speak he says O well we will have to get a job for you then he gave us some tar to put on twine and then ball it up.

This is since we came on board

William Brannan
&
Terence M^cmachon.[1]

This 'process reproduction,' from a water-colour, represents one of the old hands in the foc'sle tatooing a boy's arm. When tatooing became the craze on board, the artist had his work cut out for him. Crucifixions and S. F. Union badges were the favourite designs. The men believe that the cross ensures them burial if they are wrecked and washed up on some Roman Catholic coast.

---

[1] At Port Stanley Brannan and his chum signed on the articles as members of the crew in place of two deserters, and now have made themselves a niche in the world's progress.

7th October.—Lat. 29.31 ; long. 20.35. It was a great idea drowning that cat; the result has been a whole week of perfect sailing winds. Just enough wind to keep us cool, excepting at mid-day, when it becomes a little too warm for perfect comfort. Wish we had more cats now.

We had '*the awning*' up this afternoon—the awning that the newspapers wrote so much about before we left Dundee, which was to shelter our northern sailors from the vertical rays of the tropical sun, to create cool draughts in the sweltering heat of the Doldrums. The awning was a torn sail, the size of a blanket, and all holes and dirty ; it was dangled in the middle of the poop, and shaded about a couple of square yards of deck at a time. If you kept dodging about you could keep in the patch of shadow, but it was scarcely worth the trouble. Our sails give us all the shelter we require, and our Arctic sailors, instead of objecting to the heat, seem to take to it very kindly.

Blue—blue—blue, and hot, so hot that it is undiluted pleasure to do nothing, and our bare feet burn with the heat of the deck, and hold to the melting tar in the seams. The men go about their work very quietly, and scarcely speak ; the only sound is the click-click of the carpenter's caulking mallet as he hammers oakum into the seams of the deck. He comes from Peterhead, but he doesn't care about the heat ; he is squatting there on deck, with the full blaze of the sun on his flat, brown neck, hammering away as contentedly as if there were some 50 degrees of frost.

It is in the dog watch, when the sun goes down, that we waken up, I draw, and the men stroll about the decks and play and sing for a while. Then the moon comes up a round shield of red gold, and the decks become still. Northern moonlight nights are beautiful but cold, and ghostly compared with a night like this, when the hot air feels thick with the richness of half-hidden colouring. I have thought that no scene could be more beautiful than the full moon as it rises at home from behind some dark hill, when it pours its pale beams down the rocky glen, touching the white birch stems with a fairy light, throwing chequered shadows where the roebuck crops the short grass. Such a scene, with the gun's barrel lying cold in my hand, has given me more pleasure than the words of poets; but it is a cold and colourless picture, in dull green and silver, compared to the depth and beauty of such a tropical night as this. The darkness seems to throb with poetry and passion, and the warm damp air is soft as a breath of romance from the tales of Arabian Nights. The sky is dark, mat blue,—the blue you see in a Turkey carpet,—and the stars seem hung out against it like silken lanterns,—green, yellow, and ruby red.

It is so quiet to-night that the ship feels almost deserted. The mate stands on the bridge leaning his elbows on the white rails, gazing dreamily over the dark sea into the vague horizon, motionless, a dusky silhouette with one spot of moonlight burning on the glazed peak of his cap. At the stern there is another spark of greenish light, where the moon glitters on the brass of the binnacle; behind it stands the steersman bathed in full light; his soft straw hat gleams white as a ghost-moth's wing, and his face is in deep shadow. He, too, stands almost motionless; for the Balæna needs scarcely any steering with this light air. ... Slowly to and fro the dusty-white sails swing across the sky, showing and hiding alternately a glowing star. The mainsail, half clewed up, hangs like a grand stage curtain in splendid folds, and beneath it the deserted main-deck and the galley are lit by the full flood of light which stops suddenly at the impenetrable shadow which the foresail throws across the deck. The men are sitting in the shadow, to avoid the baneful light, and I hear them talking slowly in subdued voices. ... Now a boy's voice rises on the night,—exquisitely clear and tuneful. The notes seem to rise and linger in the sails and lose themselves in the velvet darkness beyond. It is the 'stowaway' singing, and I go forward to listen, enchanted by the sound.

... Men and boys sit round him on the deck and on the spare spars listening enthralled. The reflected moonlight from the deck touches a bare arm or foot here and there, and gleams with a half light on the singer's pale face.

Sunday, 9th October.—Another day of perfect rest, sunshine, and cool breeze. The old Spanish sailors called this eastern ocean the Ladies' Gulf or Bay, and truly they named it well. One could fancy a ladies' ship on such a sunny sea, sailed by a lady crew: parasols and veils would look beautiful against the rippling blue waves, and the crew might read Tennyson and wear pretty dresses for weeks together in such a pleasant summer sea without fear of storm or gale. But the gales do come at times, with such a vengeance, and with so little warning, that the name bears out the gallant Spaniard's simile but too well.

I have heard people say the enforced idleness on board ship is unbearable; these people who cannot appreciate their mercies are much to be pitied. To my mind idleness, enforced or otherwise, is infinitely preferable to enforced labour. One has only too little time to have the 'butter and honey' of existence. For an artist

there can be nothing better than many months spent on a sailing ship, by reason of the absence of all necessity for working. It gives him time to rest and think out his artistic creeds. The leisurely progress, the quietness, and the endless effects of sea and air ought to lift him into that world of thought and fancy that we all forget in the noise and hurry of the life at home on shore. If he is realistically inclined, there is wealth of subject, and models are constantly grouping and posing in endless effects of light and shade. A quid of black tobacco well repays your model for a sitting. If an idealist, what life can be more suitable? The sea and sky allow of ideal flights. There are no engagements to-night or to-morrow, no letters to write or to answer, no new books, no newspapers, and no duns. 'To be honest, an artist must be frugal;' at sea you cannot be otherwise.

On Monday, a barque made up on us and passed us. The few vessels we have fallen in with on our course seem to do this with the greatest ease, and we do not quite like it. This barque hailed from Bristol, loaded with coal. We talked to her very politely for some time with our flags, wished her a prosperous voyage, and let her go by as if time to us was a matter of no consequence. Our heavy wooden sides make us stiff and slow; but they will feel none too thick when we reach the 'country' in the south where

'There's ice and there's snow,
And the stormy winds do blow,
And the daylight's never done, brave boys!'

as the whalers sing of the 'country' in the far north.

The accompanying sketch which I find in my journal to-day is a modest attempt to represent our worthy doctor pursuing science. I have chosen happily, I think, the moment of suspended action usually so fraught with expression. Another artist with a less delicate taste might have represented the doctor in full pursuit; but such a rendering, considering the costume, would, I think, have lacked dignity. I give this explanation, as the reader of artistic, rather than scientific, tastes might take it for a study by Fra Angelico, to whose work, especially in the simplicity of the arrangement of the drapery, I confess it bears a certain resemblance.

In the still hours of the night watches and the grey of the dawn this strange figure is seen flitting around with lamp and book, reading temperatures, noting barometrical readings, and the flight of birds. The least flicker in Nature's pulse is carefully noted down. I made this drawing because it gave me satisfaction to treat such a weighty subject as Science in such a free and easy way, and reproduce it to prove to all and sundry that on one occasion I too was up with the Sun.

The carpenter finished the new jibboom to-day, and in the afternoon both watches turned out and hoisted it from the deck forward on to the focsle-head, and out into its place on the bowsprit. It was a mighty big lift, even for our crew of forty-three men. The spar is full thirty feet long, with girth in proportion, so there was much yeo-hoing and yeo-ho-heav-oh-ing-altogether-lads, before it was fixed in its place.

The barque is still near us to-night. We played the

pipes, and her red port light seemed to come a little nearer, till we could just distinguish a dark mass of hull and sails. Then she gradually forged ahead, and the light was hidden by her side-screen. It was pleasant to have a ship near us for a little while, and the spot of warm red light in the night made the darkness feel not quite so empty.

CHAPTER VIII

SUNDAY, 16th.—Lat. 16.18; long. 26.15. We are fairly in the trades, running down the North-Easters.

We fell in with them on Friday, and fondly hope we may keep them on our port beam or quarter till we get down to twelve degrees north latitude at least. They ought to help us down so far, if they abide by the nautical almanac.

Ships, barques, brigs, barquantines, schooners all pass us. I think our slowness is partly due to our rigging being so bound down. The shrouds and stays have been taughtened so often that there is about as much play in them as there is in a railway line. All the vessels that can signal, interview us. We must puzzle them! Our hull is distinctly Norwegian, spars and sails are British, and our buff-coloured funnel suggests a man-of-war. When the red ensign of the mercantile marine flies out at our peak they must be fairly dazed. To add to our other peculiarities, the two whale-boats hanging at our quarter-deck have their lugsails and jibs set, working their passage, as it were.

We reply to these salutations, 'Balæna of Dundee, bound for the Antarctic,' and with that, all the information we can give them, they go on their road, and leave us plodding behind.

The doctor and I have arranged our laboratory, studio, and living and sleeping quarters under one of the two waist-boats, that are turned keel-up on the skids amidships. The hammocks are swung fore and aft from the stems and sterns and within arm's-length of the thwarts of the boats,—these make shelves for our sketch-books, pipes, etc. What ideal swinging studios they are; no matter how the ship rolls, they keep so steady that we could draw hair strokes with a camel's hair brush; and what studio could have a better light than the space of blue waves and sky that we see between the edge of the hammock and the boat above us? When the wind is on our starboard beam, and the Balæna lies over to port, our hammocks hang almost above the creaming surge that rushes past us. We look over and watch the frightened flying-fish springing from the blue waves, making but short flights to leeward; for they must go against the wind to fly far. In colouring and shape they remind me of our blue dragon-flies: their bodies are deep blue with silver sides, and their gossamer wings shine with the colours of Venetian glass; some are as large as herrings, and others we see taking very short flights are the size of minnows. The bonita are after them in eager pursuit. How frightened they are! I think that it is when they are hard pressed that they take to their wings. After the bonita and flying-fish come the dolphins, pursuing the pursuers. We have tried to catch these bonita frequently, but with little success. We fish for them from the jibboom end, dragging a hook with white rag dressing; but they are as coy as carp, and take care not to hook themselves. I disinterred my fishing-book from the depths of my chest, and tempted them with various flies. A Mrs. D——'s invention, a deadly salmon fly on Namsen, fetched them at once; but they were so strong that they snapped treble gut like thread. I tried a spoon then, and they moved to it but did not hook. I believe a blue Tay phantom would have taken them, from its resemblance to a flying-fish. The bonita is one of the mackerel tribe, but without stripes on its sides, and much resembles those we catch on the British coasts, only it is larger, deeper, and broader in proportion to its length, and tremendously strong. I should think eight lbs. was about the weight of those we saw. I drove my skate-spear into one and it was snapped off at the neck. They rush along in a zig-zag course under our bows, travelling at a tremendous rate. Their prismatic colouring is superb, as if they had dived through a rainbow and carried away the colours on their shoulders. Why does Nature insist on everything here becoming brilliantly coloured, in harmony with the brilliant sky, sea, and sunlight, and in the grey north insist on quiet schemes, subdued tints, in keeping with the grey sky? That she does insist, and that most peremptorily, is evident. Here is our crew, three weeks ago there was no bright colour amongst them, now they are blossoming out in the very brightest. One man has put on a blazing scarlet handkerchief, another wears a faded purple cowl, a third wears a scarlet jacket and a sky-blue tie. Even their skin Nature has painted with a glowing copper

Polishing the brass-work.

colour. They are quite unconscious of the change themselves, I believe. Why this universal insistence on harmony of colour, sound, force, and morals; will this 'embodied music' play on for ever, or stop with one grand, final chord?

Tuesday, 18th Oct.—Six weeks out to-day, and it feels as if it were years since we left the Tay, and at times as if we had been but a long summer afternoon at sea. The wind is heading us again E.S.E., and *it is* hot,—something —well, very warm indeed, calculated at the least to raise a pleasing thirst; but there is nothing to quench it with. We have Rose lime-juice—an A-1 foundation for a tipple— and two mixtures we call coffee and tea; but all there is to dilute these with is warm rain-water collected off the poop. Such water! a spoon will stand up in it, and the taste is horrid. It is considered of great value, so great, that water colours are out of the question just now, and if the doctor abstracts a wine-glassful from the filter for any of the crew that require medicine, there is a racket! We have a condenser, but the coals are of value. I begin to realise what thirst really means, and find myself making mental pictures of a brawling burn far away in the north, that comes leaping down the hillside over the grey stones. What would I not give just for one plunge in that black pool, where the big golden trout lies; for one deep drink of its sparkling water, flavoured with the dew that drops in the cool cave of Ranald of the Still? Here the sea-water is so warm that all pleasure has gone from our tubbing—that, of course, is the only way we can bathe. There is no fun going over the side with a hoary old shark lying under the keel.

19th Oct.—Lat. 9.36; long. 26.13. These wretched bonita have been aggravating us again. For a whole forenoon we lay out on the jibboom and tried to make them take, offered them flies from Namsen, Tay, Shannon, and Matapedia, but they wouldn't look at them. They are more capricious than salmon! One day they fight for the fly, and the next won't look at it, though it is dangled right in front of them.

20th Oct.—Lat. 8.47 ; long. 26.29. We have had thirteen heavy squalls since yesterday at noon. Our running rigging must be nearly worn through with shortening sail. The trade-winds were long in coming, and they stopped far too accurately to please us; just as we reached their southern limit for this time of the year they left us, giving us enough way to cross the line marked Doldrums. We have lain for twenty-four hours wallowing in the hot windless sea, stewing under the grey clouds as if in an oven. Rain-clouds with heavy purple skirts sweep slowly round the horizon; sometimes they pass over us and fill our sails with a short-lived squall, and leave us with streaming scuppers and steaming decks.

How we pity these poor sailing ships here without any means of moving! They lie for weeks and weeks in these hot calms, the decks roasting hot, tar oozing from the seams, hauling their yards round and shifting tacks for the faintest air. I have known a barque lie for six weeks on a spot of calm a little to the south of where we are now, whilst more fortunate vessels went past daily and nightly. No wonder sailors believe in phantom ships and the like.

About 9 P.M. we gave up waiting for more trade-winds, lit the fires, hauled in all sails but the fore-and-afters, hoisted a white light on the fore-top, and now we are plodding along steamship-wise, at the magnificent speed of five knots an hour. As the doctor and I have returned to our bunks by reason of these late squalls, and the bunks are right on the top of the engine-room, we feel that the heat is greater than any we are likely to experience here, or hereafter. The two engineers are simply cooked alive, and gasp and drink tepid water in bucketfuls.

To-day Petrie the bo'sun was seen stropping a gigantic razor, presumably Neptune's, so half the crew are in a great flutter, hairy old Arctic veterans who have never sailed to the South Seas, and downy boys on their first long voyage, are equally anxious. We aft have grown what now may fairly be called beards; but off they must come, so Neptune says. Bribed he will not be, for where is the grog to bribe him with? We discuss the question of asking the skipper for a couple of bottles of his rum for his Majesty and crew, but decide on the whole it was wiser not to.

At breakfast to-day the subject of sailors' superstitions was brought on to the tapis, and I expected to hear much of interest; but the only result was a yarn from one of our party on the comparatively modern Calvinistic form of fire-worship and the fire demon. So I put the direct  question to one of our engineers, Did he believe in second sight? 'Oh, ay, I div that,' he said, 'and in mair than second-sicht forbye. There was ma mither's grandmither, noo, wha bided up the Carse o' Gowrie yonder, in ma faither's auld farm-hoose, ye ken,—man, I mind it weel. Her sicht was somethin' wonerfu', nae specs, ye ken, night or day was a' ane to her. I hae seen her sitting i' the ingle-neuk reading awa' at her Bible, an' it mirk enow for a moose no' to hae kent the gait til its ane mou. But as I was saying, what was mair extraordinar than her second-sicht was, twa year afore she deo'd, and that wasna mickle short o' a hunert, she had the maist wonerfu' third set o' teeth, 'maist guid as her first anes. Ou ay, I can weel believe in second sicht.' I was evidently on the wrong track for superstitions.

I now have to put before you, ladies and gentlemen, a pen drawing by an unknown artist of a very interesting subject. It is executed by that prolific artist in his very best pre-Raphaelite manner. In the centre of this composition the spectator will observe a cask. Notice *en passant* the delicacy of execution, the grace of line and the masterly knowledge of his subject which the artist displays in his conscientious rendering of this unpretentious flour-barrel. To the right of the spectator there stands a figure remarkable alike for grandeur of pose and nobility of expression, it represents the celebrated character on the Balæna, namely, Jock Harvey. Harvey put the cooper in the tub and everybody laughed but the cooper. When the cooper came out with his moist face and black, stubbly chin, covered with flour, with flour in his eyes and all over him, spluttering and cussing, he made about the funniest figure I ever set eyes on. How we laughed! for weeks after the whole ship's company chuckled when the cooper and the flour cask was mentioned. The crew particularly requested me to make a drawing of this subject, and I have done so.[1]

I spent the afternoon of this somewhat eventful day listening to the three mighty men of the Balæna, Jock Harvey, Mason, and Marshall, the men Mr. Leigh Smith had with him on the Eira. They are a wonderful trio

when they get together, and tell of their experiences. Harvey perhaps starts a story, then Mason joins in, and Marshall winds it up. Their yarns about the winter in Franz-Joseph Land and their voyage of forty days in the open boats always fetches their audience; but they vary these adventures with a run down south, with tales of China, Calcutta, and Frisco that would make some people's

---

[1] I regret extremely that this drawing has been destroyed by salt water. Alas that the engraver should be cheated of his prey by a green sea!

hair curl. They have given me the exact bearings of a *cache* they made before leaving Franz-Joseph Land in the boats. There is a musical box that plays eight tunes lying there now, under the snow, two Remingtons, a splendid camera, and a bottle of champagne. We can do without the musical box or the camera, but that champagne, cooled a long age in the deep delved snow, how we should enjoy it just now! They told another tale, rather grisly, perhaps, and we must hope slightly exaggerated. The festive three were roaming on the shores of Spitzbergen when they happened on a settlement of dead Danes, each settler lay in his long and narrow house on the top of the frozen ground, and each had a bottle of rum by his jowl to give him heart at the sound of the last trump. This is the manner of the Danes, I am told, or perhaps of the Lapps, I forget which—at any rate, Lapps or Danes, the rum was rum and strong at that, and it was long hours afterwards when my three friends opened their eyes and found themselves still in the land of the dead. Can't you

picture these Danes when they awaken?—Great Scott!—won't they be angry?

... A letter was handed on board to-night addressed to the cabin. It was delivered by a special messenger from his Royal Highness Neptune, King of the Seas, and was very friendly and nice, and the spelling was a treat. Neptune proposes to pay us a visit shortly; he understands we have some young men on board who have not crossed the line yet, these he would like to deal with as is customary in these parts.

This has been a long, hot day of trifling events, and the sun has gone down quite ashamed of its dilatoriness. Such a flush of hectic colour there was! It would have staggered a bad scene-painter. An exquisite crescent moon followed, and in consequence there was much turning of luck-pennies. Poor moon! she came very close to her lover—chased him right down to the horizon; but she must have felt quite ashamed of his angry display of crude red and saffron and chrome yellow as he went down. Objects seen in this golden evening light are very beautiful, but the sky effects are monotonous and crude to my mind; besides, the sun drops behind the horizon with such an undignified plump. Far more beautiful are the evenings at home, when he sinks grandly and slowly behind the purple islands of the west—a lingering, graceful obeisance,—trailing his golden hair through the cool weft of the northern lights.

CHAPTER IX

SUNDAY, 23rd Oct.—Lat. 3.56; long. 25.15. Steaming, almost calm—blue sea and fleecy clouds. The waves seem to rest and snore drowsily, as we rise and fall on their breasts.

Hammocks—cigars—Nature—lent Sir James Ross's *Antarctic Voyage* to Allan, Spectioneer. The boys are devouring it. The night is hot and breathless—so hot my candle is soft and droops on one side, and I try to support it with matches; but it will not stand up, so drawing must be stopped. Of all weakly things a melting candle looks the weakest.

Monday, 24*th Oct.*—Lat. 2.23; long. 25.37. Drew a dramatic group for the galley of the cook and Bonnar sparring on the main hatch. Peter is tall, thin, and Scotch, and Bonnar is short, fat, and Irish, and both are wags in their own way. The drawing was quite a success in our small autocracy. I ought to have brought a lithographic stone to supply the demand for reproductions of this style of work.

Tuesday, 25th Oct.—On the line ; long. 27.4.

We crossed the line to-day. Somebody saw it under the bow this morning, a long, thin, glittering silver wire away deep down in the blue sea, and now the fledglings are crowing at the prospect of shaving Arctic veterans. The old men object ; one does, at least—a hardy Peterhead man, of perhaps thirty Arctic summers ; but he must submit.

At twelve o'clock Neptune climbed over our bows and stood on the focsle-head, just as if he had come up from the bottom of the sea. He was followed by her Majesty ; as she had a delicate tendency to embonpoint, and was incommoded by her petticoats, it took some hauling on the part of her husband and shoving from the royal officials below to bring her on deck. After her came the officials themselves, the whole party having been sitting out of sight on the martingale-stays waiting for this auspicious moment.

I must try to describe the ceremony and the costumes of the actors. Never before has there been such a complete recognition of Neptune's rights, for we attended to both the observances of crossing the Line and the Arctic Circle. His Majesty and her Royal Highness wore their full robes of state, and their magnificence was only excelled by the royal dignity of their carriage. His Majesty (Charles Campbell, A.B., The Cockney) was clad in belt and tunic of dull brown, with a scarlet pattern on it ; on his lower extremities he wore hose of the same colour, and the costume might with safety be described as that of the early part of the thirteenth century. But the most effective part of the get-up was the head-gear. The wig was made of light-coloured rope strands, and hung all over his shoulders and round his copper-coloured face, like the stiff ringlets of a sculptured Assyrian king. His crown was made of new tin, and glittered splendidly in the blazing sunlight, and his trident was of the same

precious metal. Mrs. Neptune was also a very imposing figure, and with a slight alteration of dress would have done well in the part of Mrs. Gamp. Her towsy locks escaped from beneath a tin crown in beautiful confusion, a scarlet handkerchief with white spots fell over her ample bosom, and with the ends of this handkerchief she modestly tried to conceal a stubbly chin and ferocious moustache. The hand thus coyly displayed was not of the form that we associate with perfect womanly beauty; the largeness and strength that is too often absent was there, but the colour was much too strong, and even vied with the blush on her Majesty's nose. 'Dee-dong,' or Mr. William Watson of The Hayne, took this very important part, and acted it with wonderful grace and modesty, considering her Majesty's figure, and the shortness of her skirts, which barely covered her brawny knees.

After Neptune came his clerk (Fraser from the Shetlands): costume — bowler, blue snow-goggles, black morning-coat curtailed into an Eton jacket, broad white collar, white flannel knickerbockers, black stockings, and buckled shoes. Under his arm he carried a black portfolio, and in his hand a gigantic quill pen. Such a rig would have brought down the gallery of any house in the United Kingdom. Then there came the barber (Petrie the bo'sun). He also was most effectively rigged: he wore a broad-brimmed straw hat, flowing crimped tow wig, white shirt and trousers, and a barber's apron; in his hand he carried the razor; his arms and feet were bare, and brown as a Kaffir's. Harry Kiddy was doctor and barber's assistant. He carried the pill-box, a bucket full of soft soap and water, and a white-wash brush for the lather. After these came the bobbies and the bears, all splendidly got up, and several other characters whose names I do not remember.

When they were all arranged in the focsle in the order of their going, they started in procession round the deck, headed by the cook, who endeavoured to play a march on my bagpipes. When the procession reached the stern, the steersman was interviewed, and his Majesty took a squint at the sun through a dummy sextant, and took down the ship's name and destination, and in various ways showed his gracious interest in the good ship Balæna. At the same time, his courtiers kept their weather eyes lifting for the grog that might have been expected on such an occasion, but was not forthcoming. They then proceeded round the starboard side of the poop, down the poop-steps, and along the main-deck to the staging that had

been rigged over the main hatch. This was aft the galley and a little lower, so that the galley roof could be used as a throne. On this Neptune seated himself, underneath a barber's pole and brass shaving-plate, with her Majesty on his left hand, her hands placidly folded across her ample waist, and her mahogany-coloured legs dangling beneath the red and white checked blanket that did duty for petticoat. The officials sat on either side, the clerk on the corner of the galley, overhauling the names of the crew in his ledger, and the barber and doctor stood in front. Behind the figures, the arc of soft blue sea showing under the foot of the foresail made a perfect background, and the blaze of sunlight made the colouring of the tableau most beautifully gorgeous.

All the preparations being completed, the police officers, dressed in long black coats with medals and white straw hats and bare feet, come round the ship to summon all those in the clerk's list to the Royal presence.

When some of these unfortunates are captured they are brought to the steps at the starboard side of the staging, where they are blindfolded, and led up the steps before his Majesty, pretending not to be the least afraid, but all the same, not quite sure how to conduct themselves in the novel and trying circumstances. Then supposing it is a youth who comes up, Neptune addresses some kindly words to him so as to gain his confidence. 'Wot is the name of this fine young lad?' asks his Majesty, in tones expressing kindly interest, and the clerk reads out from his list,—'Kant—from the Ferry, age 18.'

'Hall the way from the ferry?' drawls the king; 'woi, that's a wery long voyage for such a young man. 'Ow 'ave you henjoyed it so far?—Oh yer needn't be afraid to speak, mi boy.—'Ow did yer leave 'em hall at 'ome, the old people,—was they well and 'appy w'en you left?' Still no answer. 'Well, Mr. Clerk, this boy 'ere don't seem ter care about speakin' wery much. 'Ave yer not been 'avin ernough to eat, mi boy, on this 'ere ship?' At this the wretch opens his mouth to reply, and the doctor, who has been waiting his chance, jambs the pills between the victim's teeth, and the spectators shout with laughter, those laughing most heartily who still have the taste of the pills in their mouths.

Next comes a consultation about the patient's state of health, and the doctor recommends shaving; his Majesty gives his consent, and the novice is seated on a camp-stool at the edge of the platform. Behind him a square sail is stretched, between the stage and the bulwarks; this has been filled with water, so as to form a large bath. At its corners, on the bulwarks, the bears are seated. These are boys dressed in Esquimaux seal-skins; they are characters taken from the Arctic play, and add greatly to the general effect.[1]

The doctor, as barber's assistant, plunges his great brush in the soap-and-water bucket, and smothers the poor fellow's head with suds; and the barber sticks a sheet of paper on the boy's chest and scrapes all over his head with the wooden razor. This operation is hurried over, for there are a lot of other novitiates waiting their turn. The shaving done, the doctor quickly tips up the stool with a capstan bar, and, without warning, the victim is tumbled head over heels into the bath. If he does not fall in quite to the bears' satisfaction, they jump on the top of

---

[1] Esquimaux seal-skin dresses brought by some of our crew for use in the ice.

him and souse him well till he manages to pull the bandage off his eyes and struggles out gasping, with soft soap in his mouth, eyes, and ears.

The old Peterhead whaler came before the judgment-seat like the rest. A few days ago, he 'was damned gin he wad stand ony nonsense frae a pack o' bletherin laddies.' But he kept precious quiet this day, and was lathered and ducked as thoroughly as the others. Then came Geordie, our second mate, a great, good-natured, fair-haired Hercules, well liked by the crew. Great was the uproar when he stood blindfolded on the stage. And last of all came the ship's doctor, who had thought to escape by reason of the general belief that he has been round and round the the world—a belief arising from the depth of his tan and his magnificent black beard, and general appearance of having just crossed Africa. Some one who knew told the authorities that he was more at home in Piccadilly than in the tropics, and he was straightway seized, soaped, shaved, and tubbed, amidst the greatest merriment. Coming towards the end of the function, he fared badly in regard to the tubbing, for the water in the bath after thirty bathers was anything but fresh.

All hands being initiated into the rights and privileges of the subjects of King Neptune, the ceremony was over. No one saw the fun of stopping for this reason, so to keep things going poor Bonnar was seized on and sacrificed to make a sailor's holiday. Poor Bonnar was chosen because he was so fat and good-natured and Irish. He had been doing duty as policeman; it did seem hard lines. He made a hopeless struggle, and then resigned himself, and was soaped and shaved, bald head and all, and plunged into the sail in his uniform. Then wild riots began: one policeman shoved another into the bath, and Neptune's doctor followed. The bears were in the pool already, and if her Majesty had not cut and run, she would have been upset too. All day long the play went on, till at night we were so tired with the heat and the fun and the laughing that we could scarcely move.

Bonnar, A.B. and harpooneer.

Friday, 28th.—S. Lat. 4.42; long. 30.34. Called Banyan Day in polite sea circles; amongst the men, Starvation Day, because of the dinner of scouse and rice. Scouse is Tommy Atkins' skilly.

It is hot, dark, and quiet on deck to-night; the only sound is the swishing of warm sea across our waist—a drowsy, soothing sound. . . . We have passed a big ship; she was just rather too close. She loomed up suddenly to windward out of the blackness, in the time you draw a breath, and went surging past, a tower of ghostly grey canvas. There was not much time for talk between the two ships, just an angry shout or two: 'Where the hell are you driving to?'—and 'What the blankety blank do you want to know for?' toning down into sea-chaff as we passed each other: 'Ahoy there, d'ye stop out all night in that 'ere hooker?' 'Guess no, mister; ties her up to a bloomin' tree. Where the wow-wow-wow——' and the voice was stopped off in the darkness.

> 'Ships that pass in the night
>   and speak each other in passing,
> Only a signal shown and a distant
>   voice in the darkness;
> So on the ocean of life we pass and
>   speak one another:
> Only a look and a voice, then darkness
>   again, and a silence.'

So Longfellow describes a similar incident. Which of the two is the least 'brutal assault on the feelings'?

Wednesday, 2nd Nov.—Lat. 12.42; long. 33.12. This morning a shoal of about fifty dolphins came racing up from leeward, and kept us company. They appeared to be travelling. They dashed in front of our bows for half an hour or so, leaping high out of the water and zig-zagging under it close to our sides; possibly they were in pursuit of flying fish. Then off they went to the S.E. before we had time to get out the harpoon. Evidently our pace was too leisurely for them; and no wonder. Here we are with this perfect sailing weather, a beautiful S.E. trade-wind, and a small sea, and we only make $5\frac{1}{2}$ knots; one could almost walk as fast. An ordinary merchantman, barnacles and all, would reel off 15 knots with this breeze.

The only craft that we can pass are the Portuguese men-of-war, and in a calm they can beat us! They are amongst the many things of beauty we see every day. This morning we passed through quite a fleet of them. On the water they are like a claret-glass floating without a stem, or a child's broken balloon. They are of all colours—faint green, opal, and iridescent tints.

Perhaps this life at sea is good in some ways, but undoubtedly it is monotonous. It makes us realise our just relationship to space and general unimportance in the scheme of creation. Having partially realised this, we become tired of its insistence, of the feeling of littleness and shut-in-ness, and long to look over the edge of the horizon that seems to stand round us, and shut us in like a grey dyke.

If we go to the mast-head we have a slight change of view; the wall seems higher, and the hole we are in deeper, and the prospect of getting out of it seems less. The fact is, we are getting just a little tired of sea life, a little home-sick, and a little wearied with this endless fine weather; but what a rash thing to say! Bruce has taken to Scott, which is a sign that the times are leisurely, not necessarily slow; and I listen to the songs of Ossian, and the past and the present and the future seem all to be one.

This drawing represents George (second mate) weighing out stores under the break of the poop. It is a most important event, and happens once a month. The men come aft with biscuit tins and handkerchiefs to hold their tea and sugar, etc. Most of them take two whacks or shares and sometimes three: the number of whacks depends on whether they mess with one or two chums.

I see I have made George about a foot higher than any of the crew; this is one of those accidents that so often happen with us draughtsmen, 'accidental effects' we call them and pass on.

Sunday, 6th Nov.—Lat. 21.39; long. 34.29. There

were three events of importance in this day's sailing, breakfast, dinner, and tea. As we sail south the air becomes more invigorating, and these events become daily of greater importance.

To-morrow we will be out of that interesting belt of sea marked Tropics on the map. This afternoon the wind went round from the S.E. to the N., so the men had of necessity to work, to the extent of squaring the yards and clewing up the mainsail, otherwise they have spent the day in peaceful repose. Alas, that I may not say innocent repose, for a great army of porpoises or small whales (pigmy sperm, perhaps) made up on us, and our minds, instead of being filled with angelic visions, were stuffed with material pictures of porpoise steak. Full forty steady church-goers (at home) lined the focsle head, and aided and abetted a bold harpooneer in his evil designs.

At last, one of the whales came in reach, and down went the harpoon, and up went a shout from the ungodly, for the harpoon was clean through and out on the other side. Then we all hauled away at the line, and felt the weight of the fresh meat at the other end, and felt the harpoon draw, and saw the dead whale drift astern. Now on this occasion the language was profane.

At the risk of being tedious I will here give a careful account of the way in which we put in a day at sea. By we, I mean the doctor and myself, and by day I only mean the hours of daylight, for of the night hours I can say little. But the men tell me that the doctor is often seen then in his pyjamas pursuing science.

About 6 A.M. it dawns on us that Nick is patiently asking us whether we desire fresh or salt water. If we decide to have fresh, a tumblerful is put into a tin basin on the top of a bucket on deck. This kind of fresh water is of great value, as it has been collected off the deck with much pains, and contains many matters not usually found in plain water; although of a greenish-yellow colour and an unpleasant smell, it can dissolve soap. Salt water does not do so, so our choice lies between a little cleaning and a strong smell, or buckets of salt water and an all-over feeling of stickiness for the rest of the day. We did not mind the stickiness much till Bruce brought his microscope to bear on the salt water, when we found each sparkling drop contained a community of exquisitely constructed, rainbow-coloured creatures. Then it did seem a pity to use a rough towel, when each rub meant death to millions of these presumably happy crustaceans.

Having given these, or any other matters that may occur to us, due deliberation, we arise and either dabble in the tin dish of rain-water or luxuriate in bucketsful of salt and animalculæ. This over, 'the Finisher'[1] begins his rounds. With thoughtful brow he picks his way along the deck over coils of rope, avoiding bolt-rings, and keeping as nearly a straight line with the earth's centre as possible. He is bare-footed, of course—nobody wears shoes in these latitudes—and in one hand he bears a thermometer, and holds in the other a bucket devoted to

---

[1] Whalers' term for doctor, from Dutch—physician, pronounced finisher.

science. One of his patients then drops the bucket, mouth down, into the foaming sea at our fore-foot and hauls it up; the density and temperature are recorded with the utmost exactness, and copious notes are taken of sky, air, and water, and by breakfast-time there is little to be known that we have not written down in the meteorological log. In the meantime I have been wisely preparing an appetite by assisting at the already overmanned pumps. At 8 Nick comes round the deck and murmurs something about breakfast being on the table. Breakfast does not stay there long—the porridge disappears in a twinkling. We have porridge—what is breakfast without it? Unfortunately we have neither cream nor milk, but we have molasses instead, and feel fairly contented therewith. Then coffee—and such coffee!—not freshly ground, with a rank, fresh taste, but ground ages ago, with all the tastes contracted in its many journeyings, infused in water of many flavours. We drink this with our eyes shut when oppressed with thirst. Then we trifle with ship-biscuits and margerine, but the *chef d'œuvre* is curried tin *à la maitre d'hôtel*, and when we have not this we have the stand by salt horse.

After breakfast we gather our stock in trade together and seek some sequestered nook on the poop, where the sun shines and there's no fresh paint or men at work to disturb our thoughts—I nearly wrote down slumbers—and then start our day's work. Bruce attends patients and the calls of science, and the artist paints many things that pertain to life at sea.

At seven bells there is another spell of ten minutes at

the pumps to keep the ship afloat, then the sun is shot, and Nicholas makes his appearance for the second time and announces dinner.

The dinners are all the same; that is to say, Monday's dinners are all alike, and what we have to-day, D.V., we shall have this day six months hence. There is something almost grand in this, suggestive of the recurrence of the seasons. Jack's forefather this day a hundred years ago had the same *menu* and made the same uncomplimentary remarks about the dishes, and a hundred years hence on this day Jack's children will growl over their salt horse and plumless duff, unless Wilson brings in his new scale of provisions by that time. Possibly they will growl even then.

It is told that once upon a time there lived a skipper whose wife said to him that if she went to sea the poor men would never find fault with their food, so her husband took her with him on a voyage. Now this good woman attended to the cooking in the galley herself, and the scouse was thick with fresh vegetables, the bread was white and without weevils, the meat was good, and the duff was almost half plums; but still the men growled. Then the skipper's wife thought of the hens that she had brought to lay eggs for her husband, and she took them and drew their necks with her own fair hands and plucked them and roasted them and sent them forward to the focsle on the cabin china. At last she thought the men will know how much we think of their comfort. At eight bells she stole forward to the fore-scuttle to listen to the praise of her skill, and, as she listened, she looked down the hatch, and saw a big, black fist plunge a fork in the hen, and heard a hoarse voice growl, '*I say, Bill, what d'ye think this 'ere bl—y fowl died of?*'

We do not use such expressions in the cabin, for it is not right to speak in such a way either on the quarter-deck or aft the mainmast; nor yet do we waste any time at dinner in subtle disputations. If a' man has a fact to state he planks it down, and it is accepted, or contradicted, or let be. If he has a yarn to tell, we have it, and the next man tops it if he can. Philosophy, science, and art you may discuss in a crofter's cottage, but they are too fragile beauties for the life on a Dundee whaler; and it is difficult to dilate on the relation of protoplasm to cellulæ, or expatiate on the subtleties of Monticelli, when every moment you expect the soup kettle to take charge of the cabin.

After the fleeting pleasures of plum-duff and scouse we retire to our hammocks to smoke the pipe of peace or the cheroot of contentment.

I would here take this opportunity of giving to the world my still unpatented cure for all nervous diseases; it is simplicity itself, and as assistant surgeon to the Balæna, at one shilling per month, I will guarantee its efficacy:—

Advertisement.—After meals retire to your hammock. The hammock must be hung on board a sailing ship somewhere near the line (no use on a steamer), and must be in some quiet, shady place on deck, under the boats or an awning, with a view of passing clouds and dancing sunlit waves. Take with you a pipe and a book—it is immaterial whether there is anything in either of them, I merely suggest them for those unrestful mortals who can't do nothing without pretending to do something. Spend twelve hours out of the twenty-four in this retirement, two hours after meals, and eight after bedtime, neither reading, thinking, nor smoking too hard. If after you have attended to these instructions for the space of two calendar months you still feel no better, I would advise you to give up your case.

As assistant-surgeon I have spoken, as a friend I warn you—sling your hammock high enough to be out of the way of passers-by, for of all things in the world it is the most annoying when you are half awake, only dimly conscious of the warm wind whispering, soft on your cheek as a lover's sigh, when your thoughts are in time to the short frou-frou of the silky-blue waves, to receive a ·sudden violent shock from somebody's head passing below; it is so annoying, too, when you look over your hammock edge to see some fellow going away, with his hand on the back of his neck, cussing—as if he had hurt himself as much as he had hurt you. No one ever seems to think that a hammock is full till they have bumped their head against it.

About three o'clock we have afternoon tea, Indian, of course Chargola, infused fifty-nine seconds, in Nankin china, with clotted cream. This we have in imagination. As plain matter of fact, we put some of the foliage of the birch tree, that does duty as Chargola, into a china mug, and get Peter to give us some boiling water in the galley, then we stew the mixture on the galley stove, skim it, and drink it without any lingering; Peter meanwhile entertains us with quick steps on the tin whistle, or tells us tales of the Arctic. He has been wrecked up there several times, and gives us grisly adventures and bars of strathspeys alternately.

At 5 P.M. comes the regular sit-down tea—a square meal of salt beef and birch infusion, margarine, and that godsend, Keiller's marmalade. Sometimes Peter makes us soft tack, *i.e.* white bread, and on rare occasions scones, these most skilfully made.

After tea, Bruce and I go up into a high place (one of the quarter-boats) and there read Darwin's *Voyage*, or H. R. Mill's *Realm of Nature*, and 'the seas that mourn in flowing purple for their lord forlorn' seem to rise and fall in tune with one grand purpose, and we read Arthur Thomson's *Animal Life*, that poetry book with the dry name, and we feel as we read that we need no other than these two books, for they put our hands in the palm of Nature, and the long voyage loses its monotony, the ocean veil lifts, and we grope for beautiful shells in its silent depths; above and below new worlds open to our eyes, and each wave, as it bursts against our bow a shower of gold in the evening light, or surges past, darkly, in the shadow of the bulwarks, seems to pulsate with infinite, lovely life.

As the darkness falls we get down on deck and perhaps chat with the watch. What an interesting library these warm-hearted sailors make! Old-fashioned books—with ragged bindings, perhaps, but full of the most interesting, wide-world stories. Then I light my pipe and turn into my bunk, whilst Bruce by candle-light adds the little store that he has gathered in the day from the Infinite, to the Finite of science.

Peter White, 'The Cook of our gallant Ship.'

CHAPTER X

MONDAY, *7th Nov.*—Lat. 23.45; long. 36.7. Out of the tropics. As I turned in last night, there was an ominous humming in the rigging, which, taken with the flight of a great army of small whales to the south, led us to expect a change of weather. And sure enough, we have it this morning, a glorious gale from the north bowling us along straight for Rio. Grey-backs are rushing alongside us, with glass-green hollows and tossing manes, each burst of spray is woven with a shred of rainbow colour caught from the sun that we are now leaving behind us in the north.

In the night we made two and four knots, this morning five-and-a-half, and now, at mid-day, we are waddling along as gaily as a duck in a thunder-storm, the wind right aft, reeling off eight knots an hour, a terrific speed for us. The merchant clippers one hears talked of would be doing their fifteen to twenty knots quite easily!

Tuesday, 8th Nov.—The blue sea of the tropics is changing to a greyer colour, the sun shines through a windy haze, and there is a bracing feeling in the air that we have almost forgotten in the luxurious heat of the line.

It is cheerful on a bright, exhilarating day like this, with the racing waves seeming to burst with pleasure, and the air tingling with life, to think of the happy hunting grounds to come. We feel confident on such a day that a dive and a short smother beneath the green sea would be well repaid by the bright awakening in our next place in Nature's procession, perhaps in a land where men can live as man should, and no chapmen enter. But it would have been an awful thing to go out into the unknown, cold and shivering, on a night such as last night! It was black as sin, lit into an eerie daylight with hideous quivering wild-fire, with wind enough to blow one's teeth out. In the early part of the evening the breeze had fallen away, and as it grew dark, we had light rain-showers and puffs of warm damp air, and the barometer fell half an inch.

We had lit the cabin lamp and were sitting down to a calm evening of work, Bruce at science and the artist illustrating Ossian, when a tropical storm burst on us. First a deluge of rain came pouring down, sounding on the deck like the rush of many feet. Then came the wind with a blow that nearly turned us turtle; down we went on our beam-ends, more and more over till you could walk on the sides of the cabin. For a few seconds there was nothing but the sound of the blast and the hissing of the sea. Then came orders for shortening sail, bellowed along the deck from aft, the men in the darkness shouting them over again as they passed them forward. The yeo-hoing and yeo-hi-hoing in all keys increasing as both watches caught on to the ropes—a continuous, blood-curdling discord—halyards clack, clacking against the masts, an angry, impatient sound, and the clewed-up sails away above us in the darkness, sopped with rain and hard as wood, banging monotonously, angrily, threatening to burst unless made fast immediately— thump, thump, thump, what a pandemonium of noise and blackness and quivering lightning! At each flash the black straining shrouds cut sharp against the livid clouds, and the men's wet faces looked ghastly in the cool, electric light. Then came a crash and a questioning silence, and the shouting of the men hauling on the main topsail reefing halyards stopped suddenly, and some one started up the weather shrouds to see or feel what was wrong. Jock Harvey's voice came down from aloft shouting against the wind, 'topsail sheet carried away!' Then the main topsail burst with a grand report, and the main topgallant stopped thumping, blown clean out of the bolt ropes. Lights were brought aft, and by the time some of the sails were stowed and the sheet made fast, we were lifting along with a light breeze. It was a powerful picture while it lasted. The darkness and lightning, the wind and hissing sea, with the jolly reckless shouting of the men, made it intensely dramatic. But to have nothing to do on such an occasion but sit tight in a stuffy little cabin, with a smoking lamp, chewing your pipe stem, is trying to say the least.

Wednesday, 9th November.—Lat. 25.7; long. 37.10. This morning there is a crispness in the air that we have not felt since we left the North Temperate zone, a dry, crackling heat that makes us feel brimful of superfluous energy and fit for more active employment than feeding petrels from the taffrail.

We were anxious to catch some of these birds to examine them closely. So I took a fine Tweed cast and baited the flies with small pieces of pork skin and trolled with it. The oily spots the fat made on the water created great excitement amongst our little black followers, and they dabbled their delicate black kid legs about the hooks and picked at the bait, till one of them lifted the cast out of the water and foul-hooked a neighbour by the leg, another was caught by a wing-feather, and we pulled them on deck as if we were pulling butterflies, the resistance they offered was so slight. A single drop of chloroform gave their little nerves eternal rest. The presence of these birds is generally supposed to be a sign of storm. We find that during a gale there are always numbers round our stern, apparently feeding on the minute crustaceans and sea bells that we turn up in our course. In fine, calm weather they seemed to spread out over the sea and hunt in wider beats; but rough or smooth, from St. Kilda in the north, we have had them always with us. The men think they have some other than earthly relations. Is it not wonderful how these delicate, fragile birds, only about a third of the size of a blackbird, can keep the sea thousands of miles from land, flickering up the side of the steep grey waves, dipping their dainty black beaks and paddling with their delicate feet in the carded foam as if the howling gale that is tearing our canvas is a mere breath to them. I think they enjoy the cold, rough days. Their movements then are brisker, and there seems to be more food about for them. In the hot, calm days they seem tired, and wheel about languidly, close to the surface.

St. Petrous is the name the Germans give them; but they paddle along the surface of the water so neatly, and they are so gentle and such faithful followers, that the name does not suit them; and though they are fishermen, they are most gentlemanly little fellows, and are always neatly dressed; their manners are polished, and they never quarrel, and speak to each other with gentle voices, a soft twitter like the tweet of sand-martins.

... For several mornings past the doctor has been reading on the port quarter-boat after breakfast. It annoyed me to see him getting through so much work whilst I did nothing but feed petrels. Sir Joshua Reynolds' favourite quotation, '*Nulla dies sine linea*,' came back to my mind, motto for a mere craftsman, I know; still I acted on it and drew the doctor working. I could only see the top of his straw hat, his knees on either side and the book between, but they gave the effect of intense mental action and physical repose which is characteristic of so many really great works of art. When the line was drawn I took it round for scientific criticism, and lo! the doctor was sleeping.— (This drawing has not survived the voyage.) A most mistaken idea this that we artists have, never to let a day go by without destroying a plain surface. I know this, that our greatest poet-painter, all the time he was sailing amongst the islands in the blue seas of Greece, never touched pencil but once, and his artist companion scribbled all the time, and is only known to the General

Public. Why! any one with a school-board education can draw lines, but it is the thought we wish. A line is an unfortunate restriction which I trust we shall do without in kingdom-come. . . .

A wandering albatross put in an appearance this evening. We expected to see a good big bird, and were not disappointed. He beat up from leeward over the wind waves with his huge wings outstretched and motionless, just as described in books. He sailed round our stern with grand sweeping circles, and then came and hung over our wake, following us without an apparent effort; and we were greatly impressed. Then he slewed his head to one side and brought his left foot forward—a great pink, fleshy, webbed affair—and scratched his eye. It was very clever to do this on the wing, without changing his course, and I am not sure that every albatross could do it; but the poor beast lost all its little dignity and our respect, and we jeered at it.

No doubt they are foolish birds, by reason of their eyes being small and in the back top corner of their heads. I wonder why the ancient mariner shot his specimen; was it to eat or to make a muff for his girl? Why did he not catch it on a hook? A Norwegian sailor told me they are good to eat after they have been fed for eight days on ship food, biscuits, and the like. We have many birds following us now, several kinds of petrels and skuas.

We have more names for these birds than there are varieties; each man has a fancy name that he gives to the lot. One puts them all down as Cape hens, another Cape pigeons, and one old sailor who has lived on shore for a few months is convinced that one of them is a cuckoo; he is quite sure of this.

Friday, 11th.—Lat. 27.54; long. 38.13. The wind in the south-west and the barometer rising in these latitudes means more wind from the south,—a fine wild sunset, the sun going down in a bank of clouds lighting the crests of a stormy sea. With the albatross has come the weather associated with it. He has been sailing after us all day with a queer, fearful, 'Alice in Wonderland' look in his little eye, as if he had seen the snark but couldn't tell where. In reality he has been thinking about taking a bait that we have been trailing astern. Two or three times he sat down beside it in a leisurely way with his wings bundled up on his back, and looked so surprised when the pork went past; then he would wait for some time after that, paddling about as if it was of no consequence, stretch out his neck and his wings and run along the surface of the water till he got the wind under his wings, and come sailing round us again. Once he gets his wings straight out he keeps them so as if they were stretched on wire. Then he comes sweeping over the line and looks it up and down very carefully, 'with outstretched neck and ever-watchful eye,' and sits down beside the bait again; this time we have spare line and let out as fast as we can, to give him a chance. He tried the bait several times, once picked it up in his long, thick, flesh-coloured beak, dropped it, and then swallowed it, but he didn't like the cold of 'sailies'' hook inside it, so he rejected it. We have not caught him yet, and we are beginning to wonder if he is quite such a fool as he looks.

Saturday.—Did nothing all day but try to catch the albatross that scratched its eye; another one has joined it—a younger bird with some dark feathers about its neck and head. Cold S.W. wind and no rest. Shipped a lot of water to-day'; going three and a half knots. Now we are accustomed to the heaving and the pitching, and understand the motions of this particular vessel, and feel as secure as if we were sailing a small boat. But you can't sleep much when each roll throws you from your back into a praying position on the side of your bunk, let alone the water gurgling and flopping about the floor.

Our jib blew away this morning—sails, reefed topsails, courses and staysails. A stormy sunset to-night; a ragged band of yellow sky between two banks of hard-edged purple cloud, a sombre blue-black sea with bursting grey sea-horses tipped with yellow sunlight; a dreary tract of storm-tossed ocean waves.

I nearly lost my Ossian to-day—my much-thumbed, travelled, weather-worn, dog-eared Ossian. I was making pencil notes for illustrations against the day I meet a Gaelic Rothschild or a publisher of my mind, when a lump of green sea came aboard and turned my notes into water colours. It is a unique sensation getting solid water on your back—a very depressing sensation.

Ossian, to my mind, is the only poet you can listen to in the open air. In this fine wild weather, when the wind rises and sings, you cannot hear other poets at all. He is the poet for sailors and soldiers and hunters, for all men who have lived under open skies and slept on the earth's bare breast. His are the tales that mothers read to their children if they would rear heroes and noble daughters—of the days when our fathers drove the Romans from behind their stone walls, of the days when men were few and great in soul and body, and lived full lives, with music and art and hunting and fishing, when the land was unploughed, nor yet plagued with cities and overrun with a too prolific people. Here in the rolling

forties, where the driving rain-clouds sweep the sea with their dark trailing skirts, where the gloom of the hailstorm alternates with flashes of sunlight and rainbow, where the sound of many waters is always, here one can read Ossian, his words increase in meaning as the wind rises and hums through the rigging. . . . Long his voice has sounded through the dim aisles of the past. Hard it is to understand at first, meaningless as wind in mountain tops. Then as we listen our souls rise and the hero bard speaks from his cloud, far distant, filling our hearts with joy, with the glory of the past, listening to the tales of the times of old, to the deeds of other years.

Nomme des nommes! We have let her up in the wind with a vengeance. Hard up it is then, and back to our course again.

We had fried flying fish to-day and found them delicious—something between herring and mackerel—wish we had more. Now we are getting rather far south for them. There is generally a rush to get hold of them when they jump on board. They usually arrive at night, and flapper on the wet decks, so that we in our bunks can hear them and jump out and catch them. You can imitate the flapping sound exactly by beating the palms of your hands alternately on the wet deck. Most of us have been taken in by this imitation at some time, and have come rushing on deck to get hold of the expected fish.

CHAPTER XI

SUNDAY . . . A day of loafing and yarns. We had yarns at breakfast, pawky stories about Scotch Sabbatarian hypocrisy, yarns at dinner and tea, and, between meals, sketches and yarns. No wonder sailors can tell stories so well. Our first mate, Mr. Adams, is master at the art of spinning yarns. The descendant of generations of sea-captains, he has inherited an inexhaustible supply suited to all audiences. It fairly takes one's breath away to hear him drop from the broad Dundonian accent to that of a Cockney jarvie, then change to soft Inverness, pigeon-English or Glasgie sing-song, always winding up with the harsh Dundee accent for company's sake, I suppose. It is a positively dangerous accent this last, or rather manner of speech I should call it. A stranger in Dundee on hearing it for the first time instinctively stands on guard—left hand in advance, right fore-arm over the mark. 'Edinburrie' is comparatively pleasant and soothing. We have representatives of all our Scotch accents on board and some English. Curiously our professor of Cockney is a Campbell. This afternoon I listened to pure Peterhead accent, it is melancholy, the notes are those of the yellow-hammer several octaves lower, a sustained note in the minor dropping a semi-tone at the end of the sentence. The speaker made my teeth water with his descriptions of the sport in

Davis Straits,—fishing and shooting that we in Scotland would give our ears for.

Why do our traders not go up to the Straits and make settlements, and tin salmon, and trade in skins? On the south-east side of Greenland there are a few Danish settlements, but the east coast of the Strait is practically unhunted, only two Peterhead men spend the winter there with the natives. Surely fortunes are to be made where you can get a white bear-skin or a narwhal's horn for a dozen cartridges or a rifle dog-head, where you can fill a ship with reindeer hams or land hundreds of salmon at a haul. What think ye of this last, you seringe-netting, poaching yachtsmen (with whom I sympathise), you who risk fines and ignominy for a basket of sea-trout?

Wednesday, 16th.—Lat. 34.2 ; long. 39.16. We caught three stormy petrels to-day with a Tweed-cast and finished them with chloroform. I consider myself a fairly lucky fisherman usually, but the albatross beats me altogether. A salmon fly he broke and threw aside in scorn, and a cod hook he hung on to with his hard beak till he bent it straight, and then went off chuckling and swallowed the bait. Seeing the hand of fate in this, I wound up my line and left the albatross-catching to others, and by-and-bye the same bird came circling round, and seeing a tempting strip of bacon fat he sat down beside it and picked it up. This time it had the sail-maker's hook inside the bacon, something like a large button hook with a sharp point, and this caught in the curved tip of his great bill, and willy-nilly he had to come on board. He did look ridiculous being towed through the water like a wet rag, with his bill gaping wide open, showing a pink throat : on deck his wings were crossed and so locked behind him. He measured ten feet across his outstretched wings. This was quite a small one, I have heard of one that was caught measuring fifteen feet from tip to tip. The skin being possibly of 'commurrcial vallye' was stowed away, and the doctor gave me a lecture on its internal economy. The lightness of the bones is very remarkable, those of a twenty-pound albatross only weigh two and a half pounds; they look as if they would weigh much more. The men use the radius bone of the forearm for a pipe stem, and the skin of their feet makes a very pretty tobacco pouch.

Our thoughts are now concentrated on the Falklands, longing to see land of any kind, rocks and earth, green grass and trees, something to jump on that is not everlastingly on the move. There is nothing more delightful by contrast than the gentle roll of a sailing craft, but continued for nearly three months it becomes tiresome. How we long, too, for milk and green food, and for fresh water especially!

A fortnight of fine weather ought to bring us to the islands, but fine weather is hardly what we can expect down in these stormy latitudes.

To-day the cook's galley was taken down and stowed below, and now Peter cooks in the focsle. This has the advantage of keeping the focsle warm and dry, but it makes the place very crowded ; there are some thirty-seven living there, lying on shelves, two on each shelf ; what with their chests and wet clothes, want of light and air, and the vermin and smells from the bilge, it's a wonder to me the men can live. One can scarcely stand upright in it, yet they make merry over the miserable housing. They had the option of staying at home, of course, and starving. I would be ashamed to keep a dog in the place myself.

So far as Peter is concerned it is a change for the better, for he and the galley have been once or twice nearly washed away, but I miss seeing him on deck. He was an interesting figure in the ship's company, a tall thin man with a bushy beard and a somewhat severe aspect, his shirt-sleeves were always turned up, and every now and then he popped his head out of the square house and made the men on deck squirm with laughter by his jests and snatches of funny songs.

The boys rather score by having Peter and the galley below. In the night watches they can go below and warm themselves, light their pipes and forage round, and then when the mate comes down the main hatch they nip up the forescuttle, or *vice versa*.

I must not forget to give a sketch of our ship's dog. The cook and she are great allies and play at hide-and-seek round the galley whenever there's a moment to spare. If the cook is busy Fanny is given a leg up to the galley roof and sits there with the ship in charge. When it—she, correctly speaking—came on board, it was nothing but an insignificant black ball with protuberances where its legs were to be; and it used to roll across the decks at every lurch, now it has grown long legs, rickety from want of milk, I suppose, and has developed signs of its retriever, gordon-setter, and other ancestors. Though physically weak it is intellectually a giant. Forty-five able-bodied seamen and boys have devoted themselves to her education, so what she does not know of ship's life is not worth mentioning. I am afraid, however, her morals are lax. Yesterday I saw her with her head in a beef tin which I am sure did not belong to her mess. She had

apparently got into the tin leisurely and wanted to get out in a hurry. After running round the fore-deck backwards she succeeded in this and went off on another foray; then she found the Spectioneer's tin of marmalade open, and puppy-like plunged her head in and lapped it up, till fate, in the form of a sea-boot, caught her in the ribs; she scratched her nose on the ragged tin as she

extracted her head, and bolted up the fore-hatch woo-
hooing. It is a hard life at sea, but it has its pleasures.

Wednesday, 23rd.—Lat. 41.13; long. 49.9. It is blowing a living gale this morning, S. by W., and we
are lying close-hauled under a scrap of main-topsail and
fore and main-staysail. It is a wonder they hold in the
bolt ropes with such a strain. It is a nasty place to meet
with a gale, one has heard so often of vessels hammering
for months against head-winds down this road that we
fear lest we have the same fate. Miles and miles of white-
capped rollers come charging down on us. What dreary
wide valleys lie between them! As each huge crest
rushes past us the Balæna shakes herself as if with relief
at danger past, pulls herself together, and sinks down into
the long valley before her and steadily rises again to the
top of the next hill of water, now and then the crest of
a sea comes thundering on to our fore decks, throwing
the hard white foam high over our foretop. Cold, clear
patches of blue show at times through the grey sky, and
transient gleams of faint sunlight fall on our foaming
decks, and cheer our spirits for a moment, then pass
away to leeward, lighting up endless ranks of angry
white-headed seas. . . . Now the sky has darkened, and
the rain has come up with the wind. It makes the seas
easier. We can only see the first three ranks of the waves
rising and falling, their white heads threatening us like
ghosts out of the gloom of mist and spray to windward.
The Balæna is light now, as we have burnt a good deal
of our coal, and she rises to the sea almost as easily as

the petrels that flutter in our wake. One wandering albatross keeps us company and hangs calmly on the gale looking down at our troubles.

For several days past we have had the monotony of an empty horizon broken by a vessel on the same course as ourselves.

To any one who has not been for months at sea, shut off from the rest of the world by a circle of empty horizon, it must be difficult to realise the pleasure there is in meeting another ship. It makes the little world on board feel it is still related to the lands where people live far away over that grey wall of sea. A great longing comes over us to go alongside to speak to the people on board, and see new people, perhaps friends. But all we do is to nod a distant good-day with our flags, as stiffly as the two Englishmen on Mont Blanc. Even signalling the most simple salute causes great excitement on board, suppressed excitement, not noticeable by any on board of the other ship, we trust, unless, perhaps, when the flag halyards carry away, or the code blows overboard, or the flags get mixed up with the backstays or topping lift. I think no one on board knows much about signalling except our first mate. He succeeds in replying in great style, as quickly as any vessel we have met as yet.

This barque, like most of those going Capewards, overtook us, and passed us to windward close-hauled. We exchanged compliments in passing. *Guy Mannering* was her name, from the Tyne, bound round the Horn for Calloa or Frisco. Then the wind went round to the other tack and we found ourselves again to windward, and the Guy Mannering hull down to leeward. But she soon made up on us, and passed to windward a mile or two astern, and now we begin to feel quite old acquaintances.

Then on Saturday it blew hard, and we got away ahead again by dint of carrying on whilst the Guy Mannering lay-to under topsails and staysails. Her lying-to made us think she had ladies on board, or that something was the matter, and on Sunday she came up to us again and signalled, 'Have you a doctor on board?' and asked us to send him if possible. This was next to impossible as there was a tremendous kick-up of a sea after the gale, and a boat would have been smashed if lowered, so we stood by each other rolling our keels out and waited till the sea went down.

After dinner the starboard whale-boat on our quarter was manned, and 'the doctor's carriage stops the way' was the cry. The doctor was titivating himself in his bunk, so the carriage hung a-waiting in mid-air. When he appeared at last we were all greatly pleased. Lately his habiliments have been sketchy, merely a few ragged white flannels in the middle of some long mahogany-brown extremities, causing some remark. Willie Watson whispered to me the other day on this subject, 'Guide us, sir, 'twad gar the folks at hame look gash gin the doctur gaed doon the Hayne i' thae duds.' On this occasion the habiliments were beautiful, and did the ship and his profession credit. It is no easy thing to turn out neatly rigged on board ship, especially on a whaler, but it can be done,—the doctor proved it.

There was a pretty girl on board the Guy Mannering. This was perhaps why the doctor took such trouble.

We saw her with the glasses, a wicked thing in blue fishing albatross, on Sunday.[1] We could hardly see her face but she was pretty— we were all quite sure of that, possibly because she was the first of her kind we had seen for months.

The Guy Mannering was showing us a bird's-eye view of her white decks and brasswork alternately with the barnacles on her lowest plates, and as we were rolling heavily too, it was just a trifle risky getting the boat away. When everything was ready in the boat, the men in their seats, the oars looked to, the doctor seated on a stretcher, and George standing with his long steering oar shipped, she was lowered from the davits a few feet, then as we rose from a roll to windward the falls were let go and the boat and crew dropped on to the swell with a slight splash and immedi-

---

[1] I have since heard the Guy Mannering was wrecked about a fortnight later in the Magellan Straits. All hands got ashore in the boats. Poor thing, I do hope she was not frightened.

ately she was shoved clear. Out went five long black spidery oars, and away went the graceful white boat, suddenly come to life, lifting over the long swell as lightly as a white sea-bird, leaking like a sieve, with two men bailing for all they were worth. Of all beautiful boats these Yankee carvel-built whale-boats are far away the most graceful that I have ever seen. I had often admired the exquisite flow of their lines as they hung on the davits at our quarters. Our native whale-boats forward on the skids are really pretty, but they won't compare with these American boats for grace.

I made a jotting of the doctor's visit. The Guy Mannering hove-to with mainyard aback, her white sails dark against a pearly grey sky. It is easy to draw something like the barque, but as impossible to catch the movement and lines of the whale-boat as to catch the expression of the Milo.

Next to the difficulty of getting off a ship in a sea-way is the difficulty of getting on board one. This was managed all right, and we saw the doctor scramble up the Guy Mannering's chains and disappear under the poop, and then the boat backed off, and all hands set to work bailing her. We were disappointed with the doctor as our ambassador. When he came back he told us he had scarcely seen the blue dress, and had paid all his attention to its father, the master of the ship, who was unwell.

We then wished each other a prosperous voyage in the language of the mercantile marine, dipped our ensigns very slowly, and went on our ways, the fair one waving us adieu with a tiny handkerchief. We quarrelled for the rest of the day for whom her salute was intended.

But who can write about blue dresses, and draw ships with this dismal gale again howling through our rigging and the poor Balæna trembling all over? This afternoon a sea struck us, that would have carried away an ordinary ship's bulwarks in splinters. It burst clean over our fore-yard! The watch were lying out on it, reefing the fore-sail, and they had their boots filled! Another burst over our quarter, and enough went down the funnel to make things uncomfortable in the engine-room. As I write in my bunk, the water swishes from side to side as we roll, gurgling round my sea-boots. All the sail we have set is a close-reefed main-topsail, and our diminutive main staysail, a mere rag. Last night the sky and sea were as wild and ugly-looking as one could conceive, the sea was tossing wildly in dreary vistas of huge billows lit with the fitful gleams of cold sunset. There was one most extraordinary cloud effect, that I have never seen before, a canopy of cloud covered the sky, from the horizon almost to the zenith, this was dull blue-grey beneath, and showed white where its ragged edge met the blue above our heads. As we looked, out of the lower dark side there grew downwards some eight or nine extraordinary forms like fungi or fingers of a dull white colour, in no way beautiful, but ominous and uncanny in the extreme, and the like of which none on board had ever seen. The colour of the sea is green now, not the clear bottle-green we see in our seas at home, where there is sandy bottom, but an opaque olive colour like absinthe, and here and there are bits of brown sea-weed possibly brought out by La Plata current.

Thursday, 24th Nov.—Lat. 40.39; long. 48.57. Light wind. This morning some whales lay close alongside us. They were big fellows, over forty feet long. They heaved their black pectoral fins and enormous tails high above the surface, and churned the water  white, rolling, grunting, and blowing, in smothered bliss. The sailors say they were love-making. They paid no attention to their namesake, the Balæna, though she was nearly on the top of them. They were possibly the Pacific hunch-backs, but I could not be sure. Certainly they were not the *Balæna mysticetus* that we are in search of, so we let them be.

We saw many hundreds of small whales or porpoises the night before this last gale. They came up from the N.W., and passed us swimming S.E., travelling in companies of seven or eight, plunging half out of the seas, and tossing up spirts of white water. They were about seven feet in length, with black round heads and a white patch over the eye. Some had patches of grey-white on their backs. They resembled the American drawings of the pigmy sperm, but had a larger dorsal fin.[1]

Saturday, 26th Nov.—We are making a course to the East of the Falkland Islands. We intended to keep down the Patagonian coast, but these south-westerly gales have driven us to the eastward. Every hour, and on all sides, there are grand cloud effects, towering white clouds with purple rain skirts-trailing across the cold blue sky, and rough green sea with blinding hail-showers, alternating with sudden gleams of sunlight, and broken shafts of rainbow. There is but one man I know, Sinclair, one of our Edinburgh artists, who can paint the grandeur of

---

[1] We saw the same kind of whales in the following March, when we were on our voyage home, and nearly in the same position. They were travelling northward then in thousands, going about six knots, and considerably slower than the rate at which they were swimming south. They were accompanied by their young suckers, these were about three feet long. Almost all the whales and porpoises we saw south of the line on our voyage out were travelling south or south-east, and those we saw on the voyage home were travelling north with their young. I conclude they have a grand nursery down in the ice, where they bring forth their young in the Antarctic summer, and come north when the winter sets in.

such wild skies. We have much the same effects in the north, without the long seas; but as ninety per cent. of people are indoors or under umbrellas at the time, they do not understand pictures of such effects, they prefer Nature in her pretty moods.

There is still a heavy cross sea running, but without much wind. Last night we brought down the royal yards. They will not be needed for some time to come, for we have left the region of light winds.

Weddell, in his voyage to the Antarctic in 1823, describes many of his crew being laid up with colds from the constant wetting by rain and sea-water, and here we are in 1892 in the same neighbourhood, having just the same experience.

Sunday.—Last night we spent lying-to, under close-reefed main-top-sail and stay-sail, with a strong gale from the south, with furious hail-showers, and an enormous sea running. Sleep there was for none of us. Men thought of their souls' welfare, or dreamt of the curtained room at home, and the easy-chair by the fireside, each thought of what he valued most and would lose, if one of those seas boarded us. I thought of my sketches, and how they would spoil so easily, Bruce of his notes and instruments, and Jack in the focsle thought of his new sea-boots, his two months' pay, and the store of baccy he has won at whist. Each has a stake he would be loth to lose, even though we are tired to death with this endless tossing.

Thanks to the strength of the Balæna, and the skill of

those who built her, we pulled through the night all right. The day has passed, a gloomy day of sudden squalls and stinging hail-showers.

At night we turned our thoughts to serious things, as who would not in such heavy weather? We read some

'*Sunday books*,' which had been supplied by the same wholesale firm in Liverpool that supplied our ship's biscuits. The biscuits are good, but the literature is not. The tract I read to-day wound up with this exhortation: 'I hope this story will make my young readers kinder to cats. It is sinful and cruel to throw stones at them. It is far better to do as the little rhyme says:—

"I love little pussy, its coat is so warm,
And if I don't hurt her, she'll do me no harm."'

There is a good deal of common sense and pictorial suggestiveness in 'the little rhyme,' but it does not come up to the quality of the biscuits. People who send these papers on board should bear in mind that there are not always cats on board ship, and seldom stones to throw at them. We had a cat—I have referred to it already; it was treated with the greatest consideration to the last, and we have got nothing but gales for our kindness.

Watching her take it green.

CHAPTER XII

M ONDAY, 28*th Nov.*—Lat. 43.2; long. 50.24. Fine weather again.

Through my port under the break of the poop I can see the sun shining on our flesh-coloured mainmast, with purple shadows from the rigging encircling it. The sunlight and the dry warm air make hope revive in us again. Men are busied about the decks doing odd jobs, and on the deck overhead I hear the boys chipping and scraping the white paint off the renaissance rail that runs round our poop, preparing it for a fresh coat of paint.

There is a pleasant, gentle, to-and-fro roll that tells of a following wind. Now a chantie is started as the crew haul on the main topsail halyards. Lately the chanties have been few, and half drowned by the racket of the storm and hail-showers; but this morning there is a ring of triumph in the hearty voices, and the white sails that have been imprisoned so long seem to signal to the gale as they unfurl that we have beaten it, and are ready to face it again.

It is a new chantie to me, this old song, which one of our harpooneers trolls out—sung in the ark, probably, when Noah hauled in the gangway. Marshall has an endless stock of these chanties, and brings out a new one when we get tired of the last.

Chantie man:	Ran-zo was a tailor,
All together:	Ranzo, boys, Ranzo!
Chantie man:	Now he's called a sailor,
All together:	Ranzo, boys, Ranzo!

The skipper was a dandy,
Ranzo, boys, Ranzo!
And was too fond of Brandy,
Ranzo, boys, Ranzo!

They call him now a sailor!
Ranzo, boys, Ranzo!
The master of a whaler!
Ranzo, boys, Ranzo!

There is a fine sudden ring in the chorus that goes well with the wind and squalls. 'Belay,' shouts the mate, and the crew repeat 'belay,' and the chantie stops in the middle of a Ran-zo. Away the men go forward laughing and

Skinning albatross

splashing and sliding along the wet decks to set the fore topgallant, and the chantie sounds far away. In the evening the wind rose again from squalls to a gale. For the last six days we have made but seventy miles. Thirteen albatross were killed to-day, the excuse being that 'they may be of value.'

1st December.—Still strong winds and gales from south and west, and we make no progress to speak of, but hammer away in the same place under close-reefed topsail and staysails. Saw a sea-swallow to-day—the first we have seen. It is the prettiest bird of the sea, I think —our halcyon of summer days in the north. It had a spot of white in the middle of its black cap.

We picked up some sea-weed to-day—a long, amber-coloured, round stem, with pear-shaped pendants, hanging like leaves, at intervals of a few inches. On the base of each pendant there were exquisite clusters of barnacles of delicate grey, violet, and white.

A great variety of birds are following us now, or rather flying about our neighbourhood; for we can scarcely be said to have been moving, but merely pounding up and down in the same hole, making nothing but lee way.

The most striking of the birds is the Molly Mauk—a powerful bird, somewhat like our great blackback, but many times larger. The old bird has a white head and body and black wing-covers, a black beak, and a dusky mark over its eye that gives it a keen, hawklike expression. Then there are usually four or five albatross within sight, in different stages of plumage, besides Cape pigeons and other petrels and sea-birds, the names of which I do not know, as, unfortunately, owing to my hurried exodus from Edinburgh, I was unable to bring books on bird life in the South Seas; we have in consequence to give our bird companions names that would scarcely be recognised by scientists at home.

Whilst sitting at tea to-night, trifling with salt junk and ship biscuits, and clinging to the legs of the table, we got on to the well-worn subject of the comparative merits of solid bullets *versus* shells for big game shooting. As an instance in point, I quoted a Ceylon yarn about Mr. ———, who brought down an elephant with a single ball, dead as he thought, but found it was very much the reverse of dead when he began to cut it up. There were details about this story which raised it high in the ranks of tall stories. But the story is not yet written that our mate could not cap with ease, and down he came on the top of this one with a yarn that would make the readers of *The Field* shudder.

'Hoots, that's naething,' he said. 'I ken a man Tod, Wullie Tod, ye'll hae heard tell o' him. Spectioneer o' the Arctic. I seed him mysel' pit aucht-an-twenty o' they expanseeve bullits intill a white she-bear an' it nane the waur. Ay, but it's fac' I'm tellin' ye. 'Twas in Disco Bay, the year the *Montrose* gaed doon. We warna sae far frae the same berth oorsels forbye. Ae nicht Tod and me was danderin' roon' the ship. We were fast grippit i' the flaw, ye ken, when what should we licht upon but a great muckle bear, raxin' hersel' i' the bield o' a hummock. Up went Wullie's gun, an' he let flee, straicht intill her lug. Ay, and would ye believe it, she jist gied a bit glint ower her shouther an' gaed on scartin' hersel',—never let on she heeded ava'. Man, but Wullie was fashed. He was aye ane o' they thochtless, venturesome chiels, so what would he dae but tak a' the caertritches I had in ma pooch an' gang richt up till the bear—he wadna be furthir frae her than you an' me—an' pit in ane bullit after anither—sax-and-twenty coontin' the first. Maybe ye wadna believe it, but, jist as fast as Wullie pit them in, the auld b—— spittit them a' oot agin!

'Hae ye ony mair caertritches?' quo' he, gey stunnert like.

'Twa,' says I. An' I hands them ower till him—twa auld yins I mindit i' ma waistkit pooch, ane wi' a hollow tappit bullit, tither a solid yin.

'Weel, the bear was haudin' awa' a wee thing, whiles girning ower her shouther, an' says I, Wull, ye 'll no shoot the noo; it's nae manner of gude ava'. 'Twas jist tempting providence; for they 're gey sensiteeve i' the hinner-ends they beasties, ye ken.

'Ay wull I,' says he, 'it'll gar her jump onyway.' Man, he was wud! Weel, he lets flee wi' the hollow tappit bullit, and he micht as weel hae fired intill a peat hag. for a' the bear minded. It jist gied a bit wallup, and gaed maybe a thocht faster, hirplin ower the snaw, leuching whiles till hersel'. She wad be guid twa hunnert yairds awa' when Wull pit the last caertritch intill his gun and let awa'—the solid yin, ye ken—and jist turned the auld besom tapsie-turvie in the snaw, as deid as Julius Caesar.

'Na, na, nane o' your fusionless toom tappit splattering bullits for me. Gie me the auld-fashioned yins for bears, solid yins wi' a guid pickle o' diamond poother ahint them'.

Once we begin bear stories there is no end, and before we finished our beef I had heard some half dozen unpublished adventures, all of them founded on fact, and my respect and fear for the great Polar Bear had nearly vanished. There was the funny tale of the bear and the football. How W. T. was saved by a speaking-trumpet. How one Waddell killed eight bears in a cave, and the story of the bear that raised 'cain' in Dundee. The ship is full of these yarns, fore and aft; some few are very old junk, but others are of incidents in the last few years.

George, our second mate, has the reputation of being a great bear-slayer. When he and the second engineer came in to the second tea, I asked him if it was true that, last year, he had driven two wounded bears over a floe to the boats to save the crew the trouble of dragging them. George is a big man, tremendously energetic, and yet very gentle; he has light hair, and a yellow beard, with a suggestion of the berserker about him. He smiled with pleasure at the recollection, showing a set of ivories that would make a wise bear thoughtful; but he was too busy with tea to go into details, and not a good yarner at best, all he found time to say was: 'Ay, but I was gey nearly finished that time—I wadna do the like again for a guid deal.' He and Petrie, our bo'sun, so the story goes on board, wounded two full-grown bears, somewhere in the fore-quarters, and drove them five miles over pack ice to the boats to save themselves the trouble of dragging them, prodding them with an ice pick when they wanted to turn back. Just at the boats George grew too rash and prodded too hard, stumbled, and had the bear on the top of him in a twinkling. Petrie was just in time to put a bullet in the right place. This is gospel, and happened somewhere in 80° N. latitude last summer: you can buy white bear skins in Dundee for five or six pounds. But they must soon become scarce if so few ships continue to go to the whaling.

Saturday, 3rd December.—Lat. 46.14; long. ——. This is the first day for a fortnight fit to put one's nose out of a sleeping-bag. The cold grey hills of water, whose summits were distant from each other 'a long drive,' are at last levelled down into a regular, white-capped sea, the white crests about a half iron shot apart.

. . . We are on our course again! The sun shining brightly, the wind blowing from the S.E., a light and pleasant breeze, but sharp and chill like the wind that shakes down the yellow oak leaves at home in October. Here, it is by way of summer. Flocks of little fleecy clouds are racing across the pale blue sky, throwing strips of purple shadows across the crisp olive-green sea. On our poop the boys are sitting in the lee alleyway in a patch of sunlight, working at the mats and grommets for the oars against the time when we go whaling.

George has brought his grey linnet on deck, such a small pet for such a big man! He has placed its cage on the engine-room skylight, where the little chap flirts his wings in the sunlight and sings a long, thready tune, without beginning or end, all about summer, and love, and flowers, and green loanings. Surely he knows that we are nearing land, and perhaps, 'Only two more days from the Falklands' is the refrain of his song. All through the tropics and the Doldrums he only twittered very quietly; now he is singing his little throat sore. George, as he sprinkles fresh sand in the cage, is humming 'Only two more days for Johnnie, two more days,' and we at the pumps are singing the chantie with hope in our hearts:

> 'Only two more days of pumping,
> Two more days.
> Oh! rock, and roll me over,
> Only two more days.

Two more days till we jump on to firm ground and stretch our weather-beaten limbs and drink milk and eat fresh food.

How we long for land! The water is done, so we must of necessity land and fill the tanks. The salt beef holds out, but we are very tired of it. There is any amount of it below, so we are told, in the 'tween-decks, pickled in brine in great casks. They say there are cows and sheep in the Falklands. What nice animals they are! What a world of suggestion in the mere word *Cow*—of milk, and cream, and the sweet fragrance of juicy steak!

Not till this moment did we realise with Keats what 'A thing of beauty' is the 'simple sheep.' How full of sweet dreams, and health, and the pleasant sound of frizzling chops.

It is this diet of pork and salt horse, I suppose, that makes us so poetical. The men are even getting poetical over their *menus*, and the tenor of their minstrelsy is :—

> 'Pork and peas, as much as you please,
> Beef and duff, not half enough!'

The fair wind fell this evening, and we got up steam, for which every one was thankful, especially those who reside in the neighbourhood of the engines, for the heat dries our bunks, and we can get our bedding and clothes dried in the stoke-hole. The engine-room has been as cold and wet as a cellar lately, coals being considered much too valuable to allow of the engineers keeping the place dry and warm, so the engineers have had a bad time lately. Our worthy chief engineer is nearly doubled up with rheumatics. Bruce recommended a course of massage to him, but he does not care for 'they new-fangled medicines.' He has a cure of his own 'as guid as Sequah's prairie ile.'

It seems as if we were never going to get to those Falkland Islands. The two days which we thought would bring us into Stanley Harbour have come and gone, and still our little screw is drilling away.

The men are going about borrowing envelopes and writing paper, and testing rusty nibs on tarry thumb-nails. It is unlucky to write before you make your port; but we have not much faith in our luck, so we write away.

last wills and testaments, 'billy-doos,' and letters to the auld folks at hame. I have lettered some bags and chests lately, so Jack believes that I can write, and in consequence I am asked to address a number of these letters, but I think of the shock there would be at home when my writing appeared instead of the well-known, long-expected, familiar fist, and sternly refuse. However, I supply Indian ink and a quill, and look on with admiration at the bold Runic inscriptions that fill the envelopes from side to side.

. . . Every day the air grows keener and more bracing, and after the heat of the tropics we feel it just a trifle too cold now; there is no more comfortable napping on deck in the hot nights, and the men have to march up and down in pea-jackets and mufflers to keep warm. When there is a chance they steal down the fore-hatch and brew coffee on the embers of the galley fire, and smoke their pipes, and tell yarns in low voices, so as not to disturb the slumbers of the watch below, who lie in the dark shelves on either side of them. I went to the galley to-night to get hot water to make cocoa in the doctor's bunk. The talk there was about the grog the men intend to have when they go ashore at the Falklands—an interesting subject, judging from the way they linger over it. Charlie L—— gave his mind on it. He is a soldierly-looking fellow, and sat bolt upright on his sea-chest with his arms crossed, his cap over his right eye, and his sunburned, lined face half lit by the light of a smoking flare lamp. He has not told us that he has been in the ranks, but we have our suspicions. His half Cockney, half colonial drawl makes rather a pleasant change from the perpetual guttural Doric of which we have so much.

'No beer for me,' he remarks, 'not wot they makes in the Colonies anyway,—wouldn't take it as a prisint.... Why not? and wot do I know? Why, I've worked in a brewery,—in Caipe town for nigh on two months, so I *orter* know.' Here there was a pause, and you could hear the men sucking their short pipes and the breathing of the sleepers in the shelves. Charlie took the silence to mean interest, and continued his experiences. 'Went there from Sydney, in a barquantine—nice sort of a barquantine she was. There were only four 'ands and miself in the focsle—sundowners they were, too—new chums a trying to get back to their 'omes agin! It was precious nearly never seeing 'ome, I can tell yer. We was pumping 'er out two 'alves of every watch. Talk o' feedin' and wermin! Woi, I've sailed in a few of the 'ome lines, and they are 'ungrie enough, but this 'ere barquantine were the very 'ungriest ship I ever did see. 'Ow no, not quite so 'ungry as this 'ere poor's-'ouse—'ardly! woi, the *Berleener* ain't got enough food aboard 'er to feed a cockroach. Never sawr a ship before what couldn't erford to keep a few cockroaches.

'Well, as I was sayin', the old man 'e drank—somethin' awful, and the mate 'e came aboard dizzy, and were blind the 'ole way acrost, so the old man and me did all the navergatin'—queer navergatin' it war, too. When we comes to Caipe Town, thinks I to miself, it's about time for you to leave 'ere, mi boy, so I leaves, and looks hout for another job. There was plenty o' work goin' and 'igh wages, but a bloomin' serciety was a-goin' round, prewentin' deserters gettin' any. I tried the perlice first—the mounted perlice they was gettin' up to send up the country to do some fightin', but I couldn't join for the serciety. So I tried at a brewery, and I gets a job there,—it wurn't very nice, fur they was mostly blacks working, but we w'ites and the blacks lived separate, in coorse. I 'ad twenty-eight bob a week ; it was good paiy, but I was near goin' to the rats there— wery near. We 'ad one hour every morning to drink beer, just as much as ever we could 'old—and at night we 'ad each eight or twelve bottles to take 'ome in a baskit,—'ad to return the bottles, ye know, and the baskits in the mornin'—'ad two months of the brewery, and it was gettin' wery bad.—Oh, but it was hawrful—'ad the 'orrors every mornin'! Well, one Sunday mornin' me and my mate starts early and goes for a long walk into the country— and we 'ad some beer with us. Well, my mate 'e sits down by the roadside, 'e was wery tired and couldn't go on nohow, so I goes on till I caime to Newlands, and goes into the town, and I 'adn't gone wery far when I comes to a place where there was singin' goin' on. One o' them rewivalist meetin's as they 'as there, so I goes in, feelin' wery tired, and sits down in the back of the 'all, and I puts my 'at on the floor and leans my 'ead on mi 'ands and was feelin' hawrful. After a while an old man with a w'ite beard comes acrost an' sits down alongside of me and sez 'e : " Ere you saved ? " wery civil and perlite, and I was feelin' wery bad, so I sez yis. Well, hi gets up, and sings out glory allelulyer as loud 's yer like, and the president as was hadressin' the meetin' 'e stops 'is preachin' and 'e comes up the 'all and sez 'e : " Ere you saved, my friend ? " and I sez yez. Well, sez 'e, will you hadress a few words to the meetin', and say as 'ow you was saved. So I gits me 'at in my 'and and gits up and says a few words, as 'ow I was wery glad to find a place like this 'ere, and 'ow I was only a sailor man. Oh, I was feelin' wery blue, ye know. So they gave me 'arf a crown, and got me to 'elp them in the street preachin', and promised me a job.

'Well, I 'elped them preachin' for a week, a singing 'yms an' talkin' in the street, and saved some souls. I was livin' with a laidy of colour while we was preachin', and was gettin' wery 'ard up, and 'ad spent all the few quid I came to Newlands with, hall but a shillin' or two. So, thinks I, it's about time they gave me that employment they was speakin' of. So I asks them, but they 'ad honly been a thinkin' of it, and I must wait a little, they sez. Well, I 'ad to go and sleep houtside the town in the country, and was 'alf froze with the cold, and 'ad nothin' to eat. So I comes to the president of the serciety, and sez I, wery 'umble, Mr. President, sez I, I's come to see if you 'ave got that hemployment you was talkin of, for I was 'ard up, I sez, and 'adn't 'ad any pay for a fortnight. 'E 'adn't any hemployment! 'E was still a thinkin' of it! So, sez I, Mr. President, would yer like ter know wot I thinks of you and yer serciety? I don't know what ye thinks, sez 'e, but I know what we hare. Well, sez I, I thinks that you and yer serciety are a bloomin' set o' frauds. I went back to Caipe Town after that, and got work breakin' up an old man-o'-war.'

And so he yarns on, a very slight remark setting him off again when he comes to a pause. His experiences in the bush are more interesting than in the Cape. He looks back with longing to sheep-shearing time, to the riding across country from station to station, working like blazes amongst crowds of shearers one day, riding through the silent bush the next, with a chum, a swag, and a billie, to the lonely still nights under the stars after a fill of mutton chops and tea, with no man to call master. Ah me, would that I too were lying under the stars, far from here, perhaps amongst grey stones and warm heather, listening to the grass growing, waiting in the grey of the morning for the trail of the otter as he steals across the quiet water from the islands to his secret chamber in the cairn.

But I am wandering, whilst Charlie is giving his opinion of New Zealand craft, telling of white squalls and high wages. These are subjects with which several of us are familiar, so there is all round discussion, and many incidents are quoted. Now he is off to Frisco, and gets wrecked off the Horn, and spends two weeks in the boats; but this part of his experiences I have heard of already; it is a gruesome matter to write about. At Frisco he gets into boarders' hands, and is Shanghaied on to an American whaler, then sails from Frisco 'ome, but where 'ome is, I have never found out. I had thought it was Australia some time ago; this time it is apparently in the British Isles, where he acts as artillery officer's yachtsman. Then he sails from Dundee on a whaler to the Arctic regions. Last June he was in 82 north, and is now on the road to the Antarctic. Poor old Charlie! I'm afraid, as you say, 'you ain't been brort up as you orter 'a been,' and how much you, or the women, or your faulty molecular construction are to blame I would not venture to affirm. But here comes Mr. Adams down the hatch, through the half dark focsle to break up our congress, which I dare say he would as soon join, but that discipline must be maintained even on a whaler. 'Wha's the best man here afore I cam doon?' he shouts in a whisper. 'What! half the watch below here! What, eh! call yourselves sailors, div you, crooning roond the fire like a wheen bletherin' auld wives —gie's a licht, ma pipe's oot. When I served my time,' he continues, and a grin goes round the company, for this remark generally prefaces some hair-curling yarn. The old men smile, because when our first mate served his time was such a short while ago. But, though they smile, men and boys would walk overboard for him. He is young, but he is also the biggest man on board, and the best all-round seaman, and they serve him with absolute obedience, not from fear, but from love and respect. So the skulkers bundle up on deck, just for appearance sake, for we have about twenty hands on each of the two watches, whereas an ordinary merchantman of our size would have but six or seven. It is considered no great matter if some of the watch go below for a pull at their pipes when the night is fine.

This is becoming a long day's reckoning. I must wind it up, for my candle burns low, and it's time for a last pipe. Now the stillness of the night is broken—the mate has just shouted, 'Lay aft here and lower the mizzentop staysail.' From below I hear the clanging of the fireman's shovel, as he swings the furnace door open and shovels on coal, so I know we are getting up steam, and the black smoke must be curling overhead into the cold night air, blackening our mizzentop. The engine begins its gentle throbbing, and we go steadily on; it is such a very small engine that, even with my bunk right on top of it, the vibration is rather pleasant than otherwise, the more so now that every twist of the screw sends us nearer land. Now to bed with this parting advice: if you want to lie snug and warm get between the folds of a Jaeger's camel-hair sleeping-bag.

Wednesday, 7th December.—We ought to have seen land to-day, and I beg to apologise to the reader for the unavoidable delay. These southerly gales, and latterly these calms, have caused us much disappointment; but if the reader will just wait one moment till that curtain of mist rises, we will have a beautiful view of the land on our starboard bow from where we are just now. We are almost sure that it cannot be more than ten or fifteen miles off. To judge from the amount of sea-weed floating about, we might be within twenty yards of the beach; some patches are so thick, and so like the tangle on rocks, that it makes us feel uncomfortable to see the ship running dead on to them.

Long ago people thought there was land to the north and east of the Falklands. It was reported by one or two early navigators and was never seen again; now it is believed that what was taken for land was only floating sea-weed. La Roche was the first to observe this supposed island. He discovered South Georgia in 1675, and it was after leaving that island, which lies about two degrees east of the Falklands, that he discovered this lost land.

The Spanish author who gives the abstract from La Roche's voyage says that, 'after leaving South Georgia, and sailing one whole day to the N.W., the wind came so violently at south that he stood N. for three days more, till they were got into 46° south, when, thinking themselves then secure, they relate that, directing their course for the Bahia de Todos Santos, in Brazil, they found in 45° south a very large and pleasant island, with a good port towards the eastern part; in which they found wood, water, and fish. They saw no people, notwithstanding they stayed there six days.'

Captain Colnett, R.N., in H.M.S. *Rattler*, searched for the Isle Grand, as La Roche called it, in 1793; he expected to find it about lat. 45 south, and long. 34.21 west. 'This,' he says, 'I had often heard my old commander, Captain Cook, mention, as the position of the Isle of Grand.' But all Captain Colnett saw was a great quantity of feathers and birch twigs on the water, which was of a greenish hue. His men saw sand-larks, and a large species of curlew. Was there another deluge thereaway in the eighteenth century, and we in the Northern Hemisphere in complete ignorance? Has the Southern Continent, as it was called, gone down with all hands? If it has gone down, it has gone down deep, for the Royal Scottish Geographical Society's maps put the depth there at 4000 fathoms.

. . . That mist is long in rising. It is glassy calm, and we lie waiting to see where we are before we go on. We know the land is close at hand, from our soundings, and feel chirpy in consequence. A pair of penguins have put in an appearance. All the other birds have gone except our faithful stormy petrels. The penguins followed us under our counter for some time, swimming under water after the manner of their kind. Occasionally they put their heads into our atmosphere and looked about them, then dived and followed, looking up at us from below the water. But more of penguins anon. We hope to see them in their thousands when we get into the Antarctic ice, and many other strange birds besides.

On the fore-deck the crew are ranging the cable, and the mate and his watch are getting the anchors off the focsle-head, heaving them with handspike and tackle till they hang at the catheads ready to let go. Viewed from the poop, this makes a splendid picture. Immediately beneath me there is the wet deck and glistering bulwarks running up into perspective; and on the focsle-head stands a group of dark figures, blurred in the mist, and framed in by the great folds of the clewed-up mainsail, that hang in grand sculpturesque folds. There is a feeling of sunlight in the mist, and up aloft a faint air flaps the damp sails at times, and brings down showers of rain-drops from the wet shrouds and yards.

CHAPTER XIII

THURSDAY Morning.—At last a light cold air comes off the land on our starboard bow and lifts the edge of the mist veil from the smooth leaden-coloured sea, leaving a long band of faint yellow. In this we can see a line of low hills. . . . It is land at last, vague and hazy, but still land, and we gaze at it, longing to feel the rocks and the earth under foot. . . .

The mist falls again, and it is almost a relief. The land is there all right, and all hands talk and laugh, and blow big smokes. There is a time when your feelings are too comfortable for expression—that is when you see land after three months of sea; and undoubtedly another is the time when you put foot on that land.

The light air hardened to a fresh breeze, which rippled the greenish sea into many white-crested wavelets, and made the penguins' black heads go bobbing.

Now we have quite a distinct view of the lower parts of the land about nine miles to the south of us; but the mist is lying so low on the hills that it is no easy matter to fix our exact position, especially as the profile view on the Admiralty chart is very small and indistinct. Through a lift in the mist we catch a glimpse of a beacon on a low rocky point, slightly to the eastward, then the mist falls, and we steam ahead, assured of our position. Once more the mist rises, and we see Stanley lighthouse on Cape

Pembroke, the most easterly point of the Falkland Islands.

The appearance of the coast was, to us, very homely, and reminded us of the Shetlands, or the shores of Mull or Jura. The hills were, perhaps, a little lower and sharper. They rose inland from wide sweeps of dun-coloured grass, and brown moorland. This moorland met the beach in white sand-dunes and low stretches of black rock.

Here is a small map of Port William roadstead. The harbour of Port Stanley opens off the south side of the roadstead. The entrance to the harbour, called the Narrows, is about three hundred yards wide, and the channel is marked five and a half fathoms. Port William can be entered in any weather, and the prevailing wind, which blows across the Narrows, is a fair wind for a vessel entering the harbour. Once into Port Stanley harbour, blow high or low, a ship can lie as snug as in Dundee dry dock. The bottom is soft green mud.

There was no pilot beating about, so we did without one, and trusted to the chart. Whalers are accustomed to do without charts or pilots, and pick up rocks and shoals by running on to them, usually coming off without much harm done, except, perhaps, to the rocks. But our great iron merchantmen, which a tap on a rock sends to the bottom, must be prevented calling here, when they would otherwise do so, by the want of proper pilotage. Yet these islands were occupied by Britain with the ostensible reason of making them of use as places of call for our merchantmen. I am told that, at the time when there were two companies on the islands, the pilotage was all that could be wished, owing to the competition; vessels were then seen in plenty of time, and were sure to find proper pilotage whenever they made the islands.

On entering the Narrows we thought that a pilot would surely appear, for our masts could be seen from the harbour over the low land on either side, and the intended visit of the whalers must long have been expected. But no sign of pilot or pilot's boat appeared.

As we turned the bend in the Narrows, the houses of Stanley and the vessels in the harbour came into view, and we eagerly scanned the latter to see if any of the Dundee whalers had arrived before us; but no patent reefing yards appeared; only the regular merchantmen's tall masts and double topsails, that dwarf our little sticks to the size of matches. Almost all the vessels we could see had suffered from the Horn weather. But what interested me more than anything else was the strange bird-life round us ; hundreds of divers and ducks scurried over the dull green water, splashing and diving—waiting at times till we were nearly on the top of them before they moved away. Gulls and petrels flew from the shores and circled round our masts—strange, unfamiliar, silent birds, with a quaint, old-world look and odd colours, as if they had been designed for a pantomime, or had just flown out of a Noah's Ark. Some of them were the gigantic petrel, I think—big, clumsy birds, nearly as large as albatross, with coarse feathers of a raw chocolate colour, and big, yellowish beaks ; some of these birds were almost entirely white. Some of the gulls were like our black-backed gulls, with a band of red on their yellow beaks. There were also molly mauks, and a pretty gull of a French grey colour, with black wing-covers with white edges, and brilliant red beak and legs. Besides the petrel and gulls there were many kinds of divers and ducks, white-breasted shags, and several varieties of penguins. The last only showed their heads above water, as our cormorants sometimes do at home. Sometimes schools of them leapt clean out of the water, making black-and-white half circles in the air, popping in again with hardly a splash. Such an island is a naturalist's paradise ; and already I begin to regret that we shall have so little time to stay here.

As we entered the loch we saw that the ships lying at

anchor were almost all old hulks or dismantled vessels.
Three or four seemed still to be of this ocean life, but they
were sadly the worse of weather; one had her foremast
gone, and her bulwarks smashed, another was having new
yards hauled aloft. A pretty white schooner we passed
alongside showed only the two stumps of her masts and
looked damaged about the hull.[1] All told of storm and
gale and narrow escape,—the dismal side of sea life.

Stanley lay opposite us on the south side of the loch,

some eighty small white wooden houses with corrugated
iron roofs, scattered along a low hill-side that rose behind
the town some 400 feet. But for the want of trees,

---

[1] The *Foam*. Registered from Waterford in 1862; 65 tons, owned by
Lord Dufferin. She was once within 100 miles of being as far north as any
sailing vessel of her time (see *Letters from High Latitudes*, by Lord Dufferin),
has since been owned by the Falkland Island Government, went on a reef
in S.W. gale, May 1890. *Requiescat in pace.*

its general appearance resembled that of a Norwegian town.

Along the beach we could see several larger buildings, the most conspicuous being a Gothic church of grey stone, the corners of red freestone, and the spire still unfinished; to the left of that was a long, low, white house, marked in very large letters Falkland Island Company, and near that again a large shed with convex iron roof, that we found was the Company's forge.

It would be hard to express the feeling of perfect contentment and rest that came over us as we lay in this sheltered loch waiting to drop our anchor. The peat smoke blowing off shore on the keen south wind gave us a pleasant feeling of home-coming, rather than of visiting a distant colony. We had to wait about an hour before any one came off to show us our berth. At last, after much blowing on our fog-horn, we saw a man come down the shore, get into a dingy and row off to us with great vigour. This was the pilot—I may here say to those unfamiliar with the ways of the sea, that this is not the usual way of picking up a pilot! When on board he explained why all the flags were hoisted in Stanley, and the reason was so flattering to our vanity, that it was put down as against his slowness in coming off. The people had taken us for one of her Majesty's ships of war,—our buff funnel had misled them. We felt extremely complimented, but could not but feel that distance in these parts must have a peculiarly enchanting effect. The pilot had not been told of our arrival! And besides, he could not have breakfast on shore and pilot us into harbour at the same time. This we quite grasped, but failed to see why, after finding our own way into this natural harbour at our own risk, we should be obliged to give the pilot £7, 10s. for standing by while we dropped anchor.

The anchor down, we procured two or three tumblersful of water and some Sunlight soap, and had a superb wash. Then we pulled on our least disreputable and mildewed finery, plying our pilot meanwhile with many questions about his country: 'Can we get tobacco on shore?—milk?—butter?' all these we could get. 'Whisky?' 'Yes, wiskie too.' He was a Sassenach, poor man, quite 'appy with wiskie without an h! 'Price?' Something fabulous! beyond a Rothschild's means. 'Cigars?' Alas! at ransom. Everything apparently cost three times the price charged at home, from a pound of tobacco at 24s. to a main yard at £3000. However, it would have taken more heaped up sorrows than these to depress us, so we got into our finery and stepped on deck beaming with soap, sunburn, and anticipation. It was a queer turn out we made—a feeble attempt at respectability. The attempt that most nearly reached this standard was the master's son James or Jim, as he is commonly called. He appeared in the garb of his profession of bank clerk—a costume that was really superb. How he managed to preserve an immaculate white stand-up collar and a bowler through these storms and troubles was what none of us could make out. But our doctor's costume was a poem, a work of art full of suggestion of the Past, the Present, To-morrow, and the Future, both of the man and of the clothes. The morning-coat and the mildewed trousers recalled the Past—the days of yore when my friend was still a medical student: years and years ago it seems now, when I look back over these 7000 miles of ocean and these ninety days at sea. A piece of packthread-sewing in the nether garments was suggestive of the Lately, and the immediate future as well. But it was the ensemble of flowing mackintosh, vasculum, geological hammer, Jaeger snow-cap and shooting-boots, that suggested the present medicine-man of scientific tastes, and the Antarctic Pytheas of time to come.

Now, to be fair, I should let the doctor sketch me; but he is scientific, and so might be realistic, and realism is so out of date nowadays. My own impression, received from two inches of bad looking-glass, was that my appearance might have been described as seedy, or very seedy, and rather complex, this latter effect was produced by the many properties I had to encumber myself with. There were my gun and cartridges to shoot specimens for the Scientist, and a bag to carry them in, besides sketch-books, water-colours, and various other trifles.

One of our whale-boats at the quarter was lowered, and the shore party got into it, and five minutes after were standing with solid stones and earth under heel, as happy as schoolboys on the first day of the holidays. Along the beach there were some five dilapidated hulks; some of these were connected by gangways with the shore, and formed small piers. The hulk we landed at was once called the *Snow Squall*. She had encountered the *Alabama* in her early days. The Alabama chased her into Stanley, and there she has stopped ever since. Why, my informant did not explain.

There may be said to be no loafers in Stanley; even the arrival of the first of the Dundee whaling expedition could only muster a crowd of some half dozen thin, sunburnt boys. Amongst these there was one elderly person, a tall, clerical-looking gentleman, wearing a white straw hat. This we found was the Rev. Mr. H——, who came to Dundee after we had left, to try and get a berth on board one of the four ships. Finding they had sailed, he had come on here by steamer to see if there were still a chance of finding a passage to the Antarctic.

We then called at the office of the Falkland Island Company to see if there was any news of our companion vessels. We thought that since we had been so unlucky in our weather they might have got out before us; but greatly to our surprise and delight we found that we were the first out. We heard word of the 'Diana'; she started with us and followed us round Cape Wrath, but had to put into Queenstown for repairs. The Polar Star, that left Dundee the day after us, had not been heard of, and the Active had coaled at Madeira, so we expected to see her soon. A Norwegian barque, the *Jason*, that started from Norway at the same time as we did, with the intention of hunting the right whale in our company, had taken 200 tons of coal at Madeira, and was supposed to be steaming most of the way out, but since Madeira she had not been heard of.

Mr. Baillon, the Falkland Island Company's colonial agent, who gave us this information, received us in a very comfortable little office that looked out on the loch. He seemed more anxious about the Company's coal ship, 101 days overdue, than about the affairs of the Dundee whaler—naturally enough! The possibility of the Falkland Islands becoming a whaling- or sealing- station can be no pleasant prospect to the Falkland Island Company. They at present have the trade of the islands in their hands, and cannot look forward with pleasure to Dundee whalers bringing settlers who will live independently of the Company and possibly compete with them in all branches of trade. To the Company's shareholders such an Antarctic whaling-station would probably mean a loss, but in my opinion the poorer colonists would greatly benefit by the competition that would result.

We would have taken coals here, but the price was £3 a ton; yet shipping freights were so low when we left Dundee that we could have had coals sent from Dundee as ballast to some of the South American ports and picked it up at actually the same price it cost at the pit mouth.

We next proceeded to the lodging where the Rev. Mr. H—— was camping to see the natural history specimens he had collected, likewise to enjoy a shore spread. The doctor and I had made up our minds to go right off into the country the moment we landed, with gun and vasculum; but once in a comfortable room with pleasant company, fresh food, and usquebaugh, we found it hard to move. Then we were hospitably entertained by the consul and his wife in a cosy little German drawing-room. How we did enjoy seeing new faces and listening to new voices! The feeling of soft carpet was quite a new sensation; we luxuriated in cushioned chairs, lingered over books, and inhaled German cigars with delight. Even the obstructions customary in small drawing-rooms, things you trip over and knock down, had become a pleasure to us, and if our hosts could only know what intense gratification those creature comforts gave to our souls they would feel they had not lived in vain.

We were so blissfully contented at the consul's that we almost forgot about Natural History, and only remembered the letters we had called for as we were going away. None of the pile we overhauled were for us. Most of them were addressed in lilac ink and feminine hands to the Jason's crew. To Sigurdsons, Boernsons, and other high-sounding classic names—doubtless from fond Brunhildas in Gammel Norge.

We next went to the Company's stores. All the Falkland Island life gravitates there, and we did not attempt to resist the attraction, but went and bought all sorts of things and paid absurd prices for everything excepting for sketch-books, which were half the price they cost in London! I always did think artists' colourmen laid it on.

From the Company's stores to the Company's bar is but a step, and the invitation from some of our crew who were there was too pressing for either the doctor or myself to resist, even if we had tried. We found them getting rapidly mellow, making up against time for three months' total abstinence. A very small amount of liquor seemed to affect them, owing, I suppose, to their meagre diet. But a jollier, finer set of men one could not wish to see—roughly clothed, tanned, tarred, and weather-beaten,—pulling together on board and on shore in a way that did one good to see. It was a great sight that bar—one of the pictures on the voyage that I shall not forget. The eager, jovial crowd of sailors filling the rough colonial bar, each with his glass in his fist and his pipe in the corner of his mouth, talking away freely for once of the events of the past three months. The few colonials were almost crowded out of their usual haunt, and looked on in silence, listening to those whalers from the North. Braidy, of the grey eyes and the fair hair, got hold of a melodeon and played jolly Irish tunes till some began dancing; the second engineer gave us 'Wacht am Rhein' meanwhile, with tremendous force, and the rafters rang and the smoke trembled in the air with the din of the talk and the singing and the dancers' boots on the floor. At last the doctor and I made our escape out of the smoke and the racket and went in pursuit of science. Some of the crew rowed us across the loch to the north side of the harbour, about a mile across, passing the Balæna on the way.

The Rev. Mr. H——, not being a good walker, we rather unfeelingly left him on the beach picking mosses and lichens, and went ahead. Bruce dropped out next to chip off pieces of the grey quartzite rock that crops out through the peat, and to collect botanical specimens, while H.'s man, a Swede, and the writer, pelted over the low hills to the bay on the north of Port Stanley after wild-fowl. On the ridge we could see lots of ducks and geese feeding along the water edge. But they seemed too exposed to let us come near them, and we were in too great a hurry to try to circumvent them. Near the shore I picked up a couple of small birds of the lark family and one a little like our yellow bunting. I had No. 8 shot, so they were fit for specimens; we placed them on a high stone and signalled to the doctor to pick them up, and pegged on, over

rocks, peat, and bog. Just as we got within shot of the beach a heron of some kind got up and I straightway let drive, and the wretched beast fell out in the sea. It was an unfamiliar heron to me, of a brownish colour, with a very long yellow crest, with the ermine-like neck feathers of a yellow tint, a little like our night heron, and the only way to get it was to swim for it. My word, it was cold! and the sensation of swimming through the kelp with the heron in tow was anything but pleasant. The scientist now came up in great glee; he had been having a splendid *quart d'heure* revelling in strange mosses and lichens, and bent under enough specimens to start a museum; besides, in one hand he carried a huge red handkerchief filled with stones, and in the other a bundle of shag's corpses, all bones and feathers. We sat down on the heather and compared notes, and came to the conclusion that this country is good and fair to see, and very like dear old Scotland, and that Darwin must have written about it when he was suffering from one of his frequent attacks of sea-sickness. I forget what words the great naturalist used, but they were to the effect that the Falkland Islands were a howling wilderness, waste, wet, cold, inhospitable, and unfit for man or beast. We would have given a great deal just to pitch a tent where we were and stop for months.

I have written heather, but it was not heather on which we reposed, but *Empetrum rubrum*, which is much the same at a distance, and is a sort of crowberry, and has little red fruit. It grows about eighteen or twenty inches high, and its roots are wide-spread and form half the peat on the islands. Diddle Dee is its local name. I have a list of the other plants of the islands—splendid names—*Giamardia Australis*, *Bostkovia grandiflora*, and the like, and I feel tempted to throw in a number here, but refrain. Neither does my companion approve of such inexpressive, unpopular names. Science is meant for all, not the few, he says, and we should call a spade a spade and not a bally shovel as the Bishop remarked.

The next addition we made to our collection was an entirely black oyster-catcher, with the usual red sealing-wax bill and flesh-coloured legs, like a hen's; then I shot two small waders, rather like our ring-dotterel—shot them running, I confess—did not even, like the knowing French chasseur and the pheasant, 'vait till he did stop.' But it was getting dark, and I could not have seen them flying unless against the sea. Crossing the hill, on our way back, we shot two curious little green birds of the linnet tribe; they had stayed out late, and flew up against the light in the way of some No. 8 shot. One more item

made up our mixed bag. Just as we got to the north shore of Port Stanley, and were stumbling over the stones and peat-hags along the shore, there was a great flapper-flapper-splash-splash, and a big goose, as I thought, went scurrying out of the bank. Bang went my left with No. 8, and it fell in its feathers. This turned out to be one of the most curious ducks one could well set eyes on. I should think he must have weighed twelve or thirteen pounds, perhaps more. Its head was the colour of a widgeon, and very large and strong, as also were its yellow-webbed feet, but its wings were small as a flapper's, and not large enough to lift it off the water, so its only means of progression was to flap along the surface, splashing with its wings and feet. The feathers were hard and short, of a granite grey on the back, changing to a marble yellow on the breast. This duck makes such a noise and spluttering going over the water that it has been called the steamer-duck, or sometimes the loggerhead, from its large, heavy head.

On the beach we found the Rev. Mr. H—— patiently waiting for us. The Balæna lay opposite, in the middle of the harbour, her topmasts and yards black against the red evening sky, her hull and lower rigging lost and blended into the dark hill-side beyond. A light or two peeped out from the Stanley houses, the water was smooth as silver, and the air full of the sweet smell of burning peat. We felt as if we were standing on the shores of some sea loch in our Western Highlands.

We raided the pantry when we got on board,—now it is really worth raiding—and made a spread of fresh mutton and fruit pies on the doctor's chest. That meal of fresh food formed an episode in our lives. I think we were tired as Londoners after a Twelfth. The three months on board ship had put us completely out of training, but there was to be no rest. Some people in the cabin, and a company from the neighbouring ships the *Hyderabad* and the *Old Kensington*,[1] that the mate was entertaining in his abode,

---

[1] The *Old Kensington* had been here since the previous May getting damages repaired. She had been generally smashed up coming round the

were going ashore to visit the foreman of the Company's forge, with whom the Rev. Mr. H—— was lodging, and we had to join this party, sleepy and tired as we were, and had to take the pipes too. The whale-boat was pretty well loaded when we were all aboard. The piper was put in the bow, and had to play all he knew. We rowed round the two neighbouring ships, both here to repair damage received from Cape Horn weather, and great was the excitement. The crew of the Hyderabad stood on the anchor-deck, silhouetted against the primrose evening sky, and each asked for his favourite tune : ' Please will she play piobrach " Dhoal Dhubh,"' a north country man would ask, and 'Hi, mon, gie's the "Glenda Ruil Hielanders,"' would shout one frae Glasgie. She was a Glasgow ship undoubtedly, so I played pibroch laments and marches till my cheeks ached, for the pipes were 'stiff,' and then we played ashore and landed, and played up the road in the dark to the house of Chaplin, the master of the forge. Chaplin hailed from Dunkeld, and was greatly stirred in spirit when he heard his native music. As a lad he had served as smith on a Dundee whaler in the Arctic, now he is foreman of the Company's engineering shop here, with a dozen men under him ; a tall, clean-limbed man, with small head and long arms, the picture of an athlete, the best in the colony at throwing the hammer, and running the mile. . . . What a glorious evening we had!

Horn—foremast and some yards gone, and bulwarks damaged. Still from May 28 to November is a long time to take to refit, and the skipper expected to have to stay several months longer. The bill to pay the Company was something astonishing.

Burns was in the chair, and the English clergyman and Peter White, cook of the Balæna, were croupiers. . . . It was after midnight, not to be too accurate, when we turned in. On the way to the beds the Chaplins had provided for us, we looked stealthily into a half lamp-lit room, and saw a glimpse of the child life of the island. Asleep in a row, on the same bed on the floor, their heads resting softly on the same pillow, bathed in rosy sleep, four little golden-haired angels lay, with rosy lips and dark eyelashes closed on warm cheeks,—sound asleep,— 'full of sweet dreams and health and quiet breathing.' They had been turned out of their own beds to make room for us seafarers.

In the morning the four fair-haired ones would have me pipe to them endless tunes. They made a pretty audience; the eighteen-month cherub sat half-dressed in his small sister's arms, with a blue-eyed fairy on each side. With what rapt attention they listened to the tunes of the olden times! It is strange how Highland children love the pipes. I have seen a small child when it heard the pipes stop crying and forget all the pains of teething, and listen motionless with wide eyes till it dropped asleep; an English child would have run to its mother's arms crying. Is it not strange, this hereditary 'association of ideas'? I wonder what vague associations are stirred in the child's mind by our ancient tunes. Does the new memory go back to the old past, and listen again to the piping on the galley of Pytheas as he came sailing up the firth on his Government's Scientific Expedition, or does it see the people stringing across the wet sands of the Red Sea and hear again the clear notes of Gilla Callum?[1]

Chaplin's house is typical of all the other Stanley houses. It is built with horizontal boards (clinker-built, if I may apply the term to a house), with a red brick foundation, the roof of grey slate—most of the other houses have corrugated iron roofs—with five small windows, with brightly-coloured sashes and a glass porch in the middle of the front. In this there are geraniums and roses; only few flowers grow out of doors on account of the strong winds, so the colonists make up for this by cultivating them indoors.

Of the interior of the houses there is little to be said; all the furnishings are machine-made, mostly sent from Britain, that grand factory of cheap, ugly things. Alas and alack-a-day, when will taste drive our machinery, and the capabilities of a machine cease to be the limit of our taste?

After breakfast we were requested to play our landlord down to the forge. We played the 'Perthshire Highlanders' through the potato patch in great style. The forge is a large corrugated iron shed, about 150 feet long, at the foot of the garden. There were about a dozen big sinewy men working at some heavy iron work for a dismasted vessel that lay opposite in the loch. The steam-hammer was pounding away, and the sparks were flying. The pipes ringing in the vaulted iron roof and the clanging of the anvil made a most infernal din.

---

[1] Tradition says that Gilla Callum was the tune Moses asked his piper to play on this occasion. It is a tune well adapted for those who would walk hastily.

One of the Scotsmen there had been on the island since the old days—thirty years ago is about the time of the old days here; then there was no Government to speak of, and cattle and Spaniards went wild. He had had lively times, and varied sport. But now the wild cattle are almost killed out, and the Spaniards are few and tame.

. . . There are trout in the streams of the islands. He described a stream that made me long to be off to fish it:

The Proprietor of 'The First and Last' Bar plays us tunes of many Nations.

a stream of pools and rapids running amongst rocks and peat banks, and full of trout. Unfortunately it was a day's ride out into the 'Camp,' as the interior of the island is called, so I could not have started with less than three days before me, and we were told the Balæna might leave any moment. My informant described the trout as striped trout, like mackerel, very plentiful and easy to catch, raw meat apparently being the best bait. From the hand-and-forearm measurement used, I should judge them to run from a quarter to two pounds weight.[1] As we talked of these things fishy, there came one running who told us there was yet another whaling ship; and we went forth, and lo, as he said, there was another—at least we could see the spars of a ship that looked like a whaler appearing opposite us over the low land on either side of the narrow entrance to the loch. As we looked a whale-boat came rowing through the Narrows. In it was Captain Robertson of the Active. They had also come in without a pilot but had dropped their anchor in the roadstead. They had made the passage in ninety days some odd hours, a trifle less than the time we had taken—two record passages for slowness, I should think. But they had suffered more than we had off the Irish coast. They lost two boats and their mizzen topmast and had the galley smashed up with a heavy sea. What we envied them for was that they had called at Madeira for coals, and had surfeited on fruit, and at sea they caught a turtle that kept them in fresh meat for weeks.

Dr. Donald, whom Bruce and I had last seen at University Hall, Edinburgh, was in the boat, so we held a great palaver. We then went to pay our respects at Government House. I think His Excellency Sir Roger Tuckworth Goldsworthy must have been rather appalled when he saw the eighteen feet five inches of piratical-

---

[1] These trout do not belong to the true *Salmonidae*, but to an allied family, the *Haplochitonidae*, which in the south represents the trout of the northern hemisphere. See Captain J. Cumming Dewar's interesting account of the voyage of his yacht the *Nyanza*.

looking whalers coming down on him just before lunch-time.

Government House is towards the west end of the bay. It is built of wood, yet without any of the flimsiness one associates with wooden buildings, but solid and substantial and suggestive of interior comforts. It was the hospitality and comfort inside that went straight to our hearts. The low, harmonious colouring, the narrow

square-paned windows, and the wide hearths with ruddy peat fires reminded me of the interior of a Burgomeister's house in the Netherlands; and the view from the windows looking up the bay to the west recalled Kilchoan in Ardnamurchan and the view looking up the road to Benhiant and Loch Meudal.

Before we left we were shown through the garden, and were astonished, after the accounts we had read of the poverty of the soil, to find all the usual garden vegetables, as far as I can judge, in a flourishing state. Strawberries were in full blossom. There was spinach, lettuce, pease, potatoes, and many other green things; and under glass were marrows, cucumbers, and tomatoes. Round the outside of the garden there was a splendid yellow blow of furze that filled the whole air with perfume. I noticed a bird in the gooseberries somewhat resembling our thrush in colour and movements, with a red waxy bill. Lady Goldsworthy told me afterwards that these birds sing beautifully, and that this one in particular was a favourite of hers. Providentially, we did not shoot! When we went on a scientific whaling expedition we left all sporting instincts behind us, and are really unfit for civilisation now, which is proved by the following event. Just as we were saying good-bye to His Excellency, an upland goose came down feet first on the field in front of the house, looked round, and up at the British flag that was flying close by, and then began to eat the short grass. Here was a chance, we thought. This goose evidently longed for immortality and a glass case, so we asked His Excellency's sanction and proceeded to secure it. Our doctor had never fired a shot in grim earnest, so I gave him my gun with a couple of No. 3's. He grasped it with the nervous tension of a first shot, and I knew the goose was doomed.

We advised him to circumvent the goose by following a path that crossed the field, and to walk just like a harmless botanist with the gun hidden down his right side, and then to wheel to his left when a little beyond the goose. Of course a wild goose at home would have seen through this stratagem at three miles off, almost before it was conceived—any one who has had dealings with them will bear me out in this; but the Falkland Islands geese are—geese!

The doctor followed the path as we advised with a jaunty, careless step, looking in front with a smile that was pensive and childlike, then suddenly wheeled to the left, brought the gun to the present, and advanced rapidly with long strides and flying coat-tails.

The goose looked round, but showed no fear; it was beguiled, no doubt, by the doctor's scientific get-up of satchel and hammer and vasculum. Nearer and nearer the doctor approached, the strides growing longer and faster. At thirty yards the goose looked round and saw the two black muzzles of the twelve bore and the doctor's eye gleaming above them, and there was something about the expression it did not like, so it began to put one yellow leg before the other, walking away in the manner peculiar to geese, looking behind it at the same time to see our friend. Then it stumbled and picked itself up and our doctor gained some yards. The British flag was now fluttering directly above the goose, and to this emblem of freedom the goose raised a pathetic eye, and as it did so the doctor pressed the trigger—both triggers, rather—and there was a fearful explosion!

... A cloud of feathers floated in the smoke-laden air, and the goose lay a soft white heap on the grass.

I never shall forget the expression of boyish happiness on B.'s face as he came up smiling with what remained of his first shot. In the house Lady Goldsworthy heard the discharge and came out, and Bruce waved the shattered remains. . . . It was our hostess's *own favourite wild goose.*

 . . . . We went away in a very dejected condition. Bruce towed the beast for some time; then we hid it in a peat bog, and when we stole back for it in the evening, laden with real wild-fowl, it was gone!

Our next proceeding was to go along the coast to try for wild-fowl. We had not to go very far before we spotted a flight of about twenty duck feeding in shallow water near the shore; these we decided to circumvent, trusting that their insular stupidity would serve us in better stead than the ground, which was nearly level and unsuited for stalking. As we came in sight the ducks cleared out into the open water, and when we sat down they came to the shore again. This, to me, was a charming exhibition of faith in a duck that I had not looked to see, and we advanced with confidence till within about four hundred yards, when the ducks decided it best to keep in deep water till we showed our colours. Then we executed a manœuvre that has been resorted to in cases of extreme emergency with our wild-fowl at home; but with them it requires almost superhuman patience.

The doctor sat down and I began to approach them in a serpentine manner, shoving my gun along in front of me, following after it at full length on my face through the heather, but always in sight of the ducks. If you do this slowly enough, leaving something, a cap or bag at your starting-point to divide the ducks' interest, the effect is sometimes surprising, always so if the ground is peaty and you have light clothes. When I got the length of the stony beach and became too evident, the ducks cleared off. Then I waved my legs from behind a stone, and with the corner of my eye saw them swimming nearer. Again I wriggled ten yards nearer, with my heart pumping as if there was a Royal within fifty yards, and waved my legs from behind another stone. The ducks had gone a long way off this time, but the queer fish on the beach was altogether too new and interesting, and they slowly sailed back to between thirty-five or forty yards. Then I jumped up and ran in ten yards or so, and let drive right and left as they rose, and brought down five.

Bruce had agreed to go in for any I might kill, as I had risked my life for Science the day before. I did not envy him stumbling over the stony bottom waist deep in the cold water, with showers of sleet making dressing uncomfortable. We got four of the five; the fifth drifted out of reach. They were huge ducks, in first-rate condition for eating, and made splendid scouse,—so the crew said afterwards.

There is such a quantity of fish, wild-fowl, and rabbits about these islands that all a man needs to live well is a boat, a net, and a gun; but a mere punt costs £15, and a seine net that would cost 30s. at home would cost £4 or £5 here. With a good seine or trammel one could catch a ton of fish in the two tides in front of Stanley; and in the season the wild geese are very plentiful and even more tame than the Governor's goose.

The people are so dependent on the Company and they

have got so much into the way of finding all their wants
supplied at the Company's stores that they do little to
supply themselves. I met one man who was making an
effort to live independently, and I believe with a certain
amount of success. As an instance of the unthriftiness
of the people in this way, this man could sell a plucked
goose for 1s. 6d., and a goose with its feathers on for 1s.;
with the feathers he could fill a mattress in a week and
sell it for £1 or more. Almost all the people's supplies
are bought from the Company. They have nothing but
tin milk and imported butter as far as I could see, when
there is no reason against their having their own cows but
that the land immediately round the township is the Company's land; at least this was the reason given me by the
people I met.

By evening we had quite a collection of strange birds.
As I had some small shot the smaller skins were quite
suited for preserving. It was late when we returned to
Stanley, and the lights in the cottages were all out;
only in two or three of the taverns were there signs
of life. In one of these I found five of the young
fellows of our crew getting very festive, and with some
difficulty managed to get them off to the ship, while the
doctor went on to call at the Rev. Mr. H——'s. As we
pulled across the loch in the moonlight it was agreed
not to talk or make a row as we came alongside the
ship, so as not to disturb the sleepers on board; but
the first thing our jolly tars did was to run full tilt into
the Balæna's counter. 'Bow' hit 'Two' on the head with
the butt of his oar; 'Two' swore; 'Three' told him to

shut up; 'Four' chipped in, and I thought the whole ship's company would turn out to see what the racket was about; but old Bonnar was the only man we found on deck when we climbed through the chains. The lads toddled away to their bunks, and old B. and I smoked and spun yarns, and the boat swung astern by her painter.

One of the Boys.

Early next morning we were ashore again to see the Governor's trammel net overhauled before breakfast. There were only a few fish in, and they resembled mullet, and are very good to eat, in taste rather like cod, but softer, and not so white. Those we caught on this occasion were about one pound weight, but we afterwards saw great quantities caught in a net, averaging I should think, five or six pounds. These the fisherman told us could be caught in enormous quantities round the coast. He told us of a loch which is dry at low tide, where, if a net is set across the mouth, there are such heaps of these mullet left on the sand at low water that a schooner might twice fill her hold in the day with them. But only the one man makes an industry of the fishing.

It would possibly make a profitable industry to take these fish and cure them and send them to the South

American markets, where there are many Roman Catholics. The fish cure well, though not quite so well as cod, for they absorb rather more salt.

We had still some time before breakfast to collect natural history specimens, so I went up the loch in the punt, whilst Bruce naturalised generally along the shore. In about two hours I had five different kinds of birds: Loggerhead, Black-back, King Shags, large reddish-brown Gulls, with spotted legs and deep wings, and Grey Gulls.

Life, it is said, is made up of small things. Breakfast at Government House was not one of these. Lady Goldsworthy had prepared us a Scotch breakfast suited to men doing twenty miles a day for ten brace, or fresh from the rolling forties. We attacked it like savages, and appreciated details like epicures. The pleasant society, the warmth and comfort, and the large rooms with the faint perfume of peat and oat-cake were in delightful contrast to our late life. There must be many who recall similar pleasant memories of this kindly oasis on the lonely islands of the stormy South Atlantic.

The solitude of these islands is prettily expressed by the name the Spaniards gave them—the Malvinas. Malvina is a lonely, sad heroine in Celtic poetry, the widow of Oscar, Ossian's son. To her in his old age Ossian sings his songs. I read, and I am told positively, that the Spaniards who took the islands forcibly from the French called them 'Malvinas' because the first French settlers who came there were supposed to have come from St. Malo. Is this probable? Is it not much more likely that the Spaniards, instead of coining Malvina from St.

Malo, used the name 'Malvina,' that had existed long before the Maloese or any one else had ever heard of the islands—a name which is, besides, a Spanish name? Malvina was a Spanish princess, so our ancient poems tell us. I do not here refer to Ossian's poems. Of course every one knows they are unreliable—a fat Cockney said so! At any rate I intend to believe my own derivation of the name till some one gives me another that I like better. . . .

After partaking of the Governor's hospitality we visited the Lord Chief-Justice—a genial Scot, who had served his time in our Parliament House. With him we enjoyed the feast of shells and drank the golden streams of Islay and Jura and Skye, and met Government and Company employees in the afternoon. Afterwards we met a sociable sheep farmer with whom we had forgathered the previous night in a bar. He took us to see some nests—they were much like the skylark's,—and he also showed us molly mauks' and penguins' eggs; and in the evening he took us to his house and entertained us hospitably.

The room he showed us into was a large farm kitchen, with plenty of firelight and deep shadows, built when the Falklands were still a young colony, and British manufactures were hard to get. His old mother, a dark-haired, black-eyed Celt, was serving a tall, fair-haired son with tea when we came in, and we were asked to sit down by the lamp-lit table and fall-to. It was a typical colonial station meal, splendid mutton, home-made bread, milk, and lashins of tea, and we enjoyed it thoroughly, although we are aware tea and meat is slow poison. Undoubtedly the people in this

colony are rapidly destroying their physique by their excess in this drink. Aggravated cases of indigestion are the most common complaints. Children and men show the effect of it in body and face.

Our old hostess had left Ireland when she was a mere child, but her accent was as soft and rich and as sweet to listen to as the sound of running water. She must have been eighty years old, at least, and seemed as active as a girl, and her memory, too, was clear. Much she spoke of the days when she first came to the islands with her German husband from Buenos Ayres. That was forty years ago. I would like to have remembered all the things she told me; but I was too much taken up with the interest of her face and the feeling of the light from the peat-fire glinting on the dark rafters to remember details of past events. One thing she was sure of, and all the other old colonists I met were decidedly of the same opinion, and that was that the climate here has steadily improved during the last twenty years or so.

These people had kept a bar before the Company absorbed that business, and in the far corner of the room was a recess with an ancient counter of dark, worn wood now used for dishes. Behind, in the shadow of the recess, hung old pewter measures, dusty and disused, dimly reflecting rays from the lamp, relics of the days when they clinked accompaniments to Spanish Fandangos or rattled encores to jolly Jack's sea-song. Round the room, against the simple plaster walls, hung pictures of the Saints in black frames—a pleasant tie in this new country to the old stories of our northern lands.

The sons were tall men—rather wiry than muscular; they liked the life, and wisely desired no change; they

had been born and brought up on the islands, and, with the exception of short visits to the Brazilian coast, had seen no other land; yet they were quick and clever, and took interest in the affairs of the world abroad. Their voices were quiet, perhaps a little weak; but the accent was very pleasant and soft, a little like that of Inverness,—a blending of Irish and Spanish, with a faint colonial twang.

In their garden they showed us a flourishing potato crop and some gooseberry bushes with the fruit forming, and as a proof of the mildness of the climate they pointed out an apple tree five feet high on which six or seven blossoms were trying to blow.

The climate of the islands must not however be condemned because fruit-trees do not flourish and barley does not ripen, though the islands lie the same distance south of the equator that London does north. It is the absence of any continued heat and sunshine that prevents fruit ripening. In the two hottest months of the year, December and January, the average temperature is only 47°, varying from 40° to 65°, but in the two mid-winter months the temperature only varies from 30° to 50°, with an average of 37°.

Rain falls two hundred days in the year, but it only amounts to twenty inches, and the air is dry and invigorating, owing to the constant winds. The prevalent wind is southerly or sou'-westerly — the wind that brings our merchantmen home from the colonies round Cape Horn, and sends them bowling along the forties on their outward voyage round the Cape of Good Hope.

This may possibly be like one of the natives of the islands. It was just a glimpse of her I saw as she passed out of a store—marketing, I think.

And the following is another jotting of a Falkland Islander. Bruce and I met him on board a schooner that arrived in Stanley from 'The Coast,' as the Islanders call the east coast of South America. The schooner had come across with horses on board, and open hatches! This man

Hantz was the first-class passenger. He left the Falklands some years ago, and went gold-digging on Sandy Point. The gold-digging there is for alluvial gold. The diggers club together, get a boat, a tent, and provisions, land on a likely beach, and grub away. This man had made what for him was quite a little pile; he showed us some of the gold—brought it out of his pocket in a piece of cloth tied up with string. It was in little flakes about the size of linseed. He described the life to us as we drank beer at the Companies' bar, described it vividly, the hungering, and the cold, and excitement.

I drew him as he was describing a find. Words failed him to express the excitement, 'God damn—when you're turning it up two inches deep!' was all he could get out; but his face expressed the fun of the thing.

CHAPTER XIV

SUNDAY, 11*th Dec.*—Leave the Falklands. We blew our fog-horn continuously, but no pilot answered our signal. So we sat down to breakfast, and after we had done the pilot appeared. He had been hunting for a boat to take him off! Who ever heard of a pilot hunting for his boat? He had not far to take us—only about one thousand yards through the Narrows; but he took our letters ashore, so he was of some use.

As we steamed out of the Narrows and turned to our right, up Port William, we passed the Active at anchor, and our men gave her three cheers and three cheers more, and the Active's crew climbed into their shrouds and answered with much feeling. I felt sorry for the poor crew of the C—— B——, a Glasgow ship, lying all dishevelled, the rust trickling down her grey sides and white ports, and all her gear adrift. Her crew were all down with that hideous disease scurvy. They must have turned very sadly in their bunks as they heard the full-throated shouting as we passed and left them in the solitude of that lonely loch. Poor fellows! they were dying one by one: the accounts we heard of their sufferings were most distressing. Yet there are those who would not have men unite to protect themselves from such awful ills, who would have men and boys, with their women and families, still dependent on the sweet wills of even humane owners and masters.

As we steamed round the westerly point of Port William, to the south, past the lighthouse, the Active got under weigh and followed us. Then we set all sail, and once more started for the south for the country where, as Jack has it:—

> 'There's ice and there's snow,
> And the stormy winds do blow,
> And the daylight's never done, brave boys.'

Wednesday, 14th Dec.—We have spent many good hours in these last days reading newspapers that are dated up to the end of last October, and feel in no way the better for it. The Lord be praised we are free of social interests for a time at least, and a newspaper is only valuable as paper. B. is occupied in his berth skinning birds, pressing flowers, and arranging innumerable specimens. I have an idea that he walks the deck all night; if he doesn't, he must sleep on the top of his bird-skins and rocks.

Mr. Adams shot a molly mauk to-day. It was flying alongside to windward, and it fell into our waist. It is a very handsome bird, of much more grace and beauty of form than the uncouth albatross.

... *Thursday.*—Course again S.E.; wind S.W. to S.; a hot sun and a thin mist coming up with the wind.

Nineteen white, soft, Swedish steel harpoons are laid out in the sunlight on the poop. Each harpoon is about four feet long, and each has Balæna engraved on the steel, to let all know who meet a whale north or south with such a harpoon in its back that it has known its namesake at one time.

The harpooneers are busy splicing foregoes to the ring that travels on the shaft of the harpoon. The forego is a length of six fathoms of soft, pliable, two-inch rope, so pliable that it offers no resistance when the harpoon is shot out of the gun at the whale. To the inner end of the forego the whale line is spliced. The whale line is one hundred and twenty fathoms of two-inch rope (two-inches in circumference), and each boat has three of these ready to splice together as they run out. But more of these technicalities when the whales turn up.

We have not come away empty-handed from the Falklands. Mutton there cost $2\frac{1}{2}$d. a lb., so we have a supply of fresh meat for the cabin which is very welcome. There are legs of beef hanging at the mizzentop and clusters of sheep at the quarter-boat davits, enough to keep the cabin at least in fresh food for some time; besides, we have some fresh vegetables which His Excellency the Governor of the islands gave to us out of his own garden. Without these we should have had to do without vegetables, as the people had none for sale—evidently an enterprising gardener would do well there! The ships that call would take a considerable supply, and as most of the colonists—there are six hundred and ninety in Port Stanley alone—are busily engaged with other occupations, there would be enough sale amongst them and the farms in the Camp to make things pay well.

Three of our men left us at the Falklands without any formality. They said they couldn't stand the food; but I expect they had plans of bettering their fortune. Certainly if I had been quite in their position I would have left too. They were seized by Government and treated to half a day's imprisonment, with fresh food. How they must have enjoyed the change! One was a sailor and bird-stuffer, and another was a tall, smart young fellow, a rigger by trade. He was the most awful swearer I ever heard, so we were somewhat surprised afterwards to hear from the Diana that he had got a berth on a Missionary schooner, and was off to convert the Fuegians. I think he is rather missed on board, not for his swearing, but in other ways he was well liked, and even one man leaving a ship's company makes a noticeable gap. The third was a young man of apparently not less than thirty summers,—a first-class sparrer. His mother brought him on board at Dundee with a tearful request to our mate to take care of her dear son. The mate is about two years his junior. Probably he is now taking care of simple sheep out in the Camp at £1, 10s. a week, which is better any day than serving either before or aft the main-mast.

This evening Mason's head popped into my bunk when I was dabbling in water-colours, getting on a touch at each roll. 'There's some doos fleein' aboot the fore-mast,' he said, 'get yer gun, sir, and co'wae forrart.' I was prepared for any sort of bird, as we were getting into strange waters. Some time ago I was seriously informed that a cuckoo was flying over our stern, yet I hardly expected to see doos; but I went forward, and fairly gasped with astonishment, for there were four pretty white birds, exactly like fantails, fluttering above our fore-mast. They flew about the mast-head for a little, as if they were going to light, then dropped into the sea, where they floated as land birds do when they fall into water, with their wings spread out and partly submerged, then they rose and fluttered round us again and went away. They did not come far enough to windward, so I had not a good chance of bringing one down. I suppose they must have been Chionis, sheathbills, but I never heard that sheathbills could swim.

Friday, 16th Dec.—At 8 A.M. this morning the thermometer was at 35°, so I take it we are getting near ice. There is a heavy mist, and when it lifts we see thousands of sea birds on the waves. Molly mauks are flying around us, and we hear whales blowing in the mist. This afternoon we are making a course between the South Shetlands and South Orkneys—the Orkneys rather closer on our lee than we care for, as a strong current to the east is helping us to make lee-way.

We had our first glimpse of the Polar world this afternoon: a thin mist rose from the sea and showed us a huge island of ice at some miles distant, white and glittering in the faint sunlight. I should think it was about half a mile long and about two hundred feet high; the top was as level as a billiard table and absolutely white. The precipitous sides were of a faint grey blue, with great sea-worn green caves shaped like Gothic arches; in these we could see the swell rising and falling and bursting out in soft foam hundreds of feet in the air.

Between us and the berg the sea had the appearance of a slack-water, as if the tide was running towards us from either side of the berg. On this were countless myriads of Cape pigeons and blue petrels; each wave was speckled with them, about a yard apart, all heading towards the distant berg and against the breeze. As we sailed past the birds, those closest to us rose and circled round us for a little, then joined the others on the water. To make a foreground to this Antarctic picture three enormous

whales rolled their black backs through the grey sea with ponderous, irresistible force, throwing up blasts of fine spray, which hung in the air for a few seconds, and then vanished above their white wake. They were of a grey-black colour, with a sheen of purple-brown—'finners,' we called them. Whenever they rose to blow a flight of blue petrels came and hovered over them.

We caught about a dozen Cape pigeons this afternoon for the larder: they make excellent scouse, and we had great fun catching them. First of all I caught about a dozen with a cast of loch flies baited with fat; but this was rather slow work, so one of the crew rigged a thing resembling a landing-net on the end of a boat-hook. A second man threw in scraps of food at the bow. The pigeons came tumbling over each other for the food as it passed alongside, and he with the net bailed them on board. All hands had quite a gay time at this in the dog watch. Every one had a try at it, it looked so easy to catch some of the scores of birds that came down; but they were cautious though they were eager, and the long pole was difficult to handle with accuracy.

Just before dark we could make out another berg down to leeward. As the barometer was going down we were anxious to get to the south of the Shetlands, which islands ought to be to the westward of us now, in case of a gale from the south-west.

. . . There is a fresh wind, cold and damp, with a swell running from the westward. The sky looks threatening—

leaden-coloured with rags of purple-grey cloud driving up from the west. In places the upper grey sky is ribbed like sea sand.

The sun sets now far to the southward, and scarcely dips below the horizon. To-night it has left a long band of cold orange between the sea and the level canopy of cloud.

Ahead of us to the east and west are two icebergs, forming what seems to us a wide porch to the unknown Antarctic seas.

Saturday, 17th Dec.—The fog came down thick last night, and when it cleared up this morning with a fresh nor'wester we found we had made a passage somehow or other between a number of large bergs. A few large

ragged pieces of ice, like the roots of huge teeth, are rolling about in the swell, with the grey sea surging over them and pouring down their sides in white streams. The men call these detached pieces of ice 'growlers,' from their unpleasant nature and the sound the sea makes breaking over them. To us they can do little harm; but many an iron ship has had her sides ripped by these wandering rocks.

A few penguins are swimming round us. Now and then they put their heads above water and quangk—a sudden, melancholy, strange call, sounding sad and lonely in the mist.

This morning we saw a seal alongside, apparently sleeping. I bolted for my rifle and managed to put a bullet in its head. We drifted down on it; but we had nothing ready to hook into it; a boat-hook would not

hold, and a running bowline we got round it slipped over its after end, just as we had hauled it up to the rail. Fortunately it was shot before it had time to contract its muscles, so it floated.[1]

It would have been an unlucky thing to lose the first blood of the cruise, so the starboard quarter-boat was lowered and after some hunting the seal was picked up.

---

[1] I hold that the contraction of the muscle—the panniculus carnosus—has more to do with a seal's sinking than the state of its lungs when it is shot.

Again I was struck by the exquisite beauty of our white Yankee whale-boat. With its black, spidery oars lifting it over the grey seas, it seemed the very embodiment of strength, grace, and speed. After pulling about in the mist for a few minutes the crew came upon the seal, rowed alongside, and climbed on board, whilst we on deck hauled the boat up to the davits.

Then the seal was laid on deck, and we all examined it with much interest, for it was very different from those of

the north. It measured seven feet from its nose to the end of its hind flipper. Its colour was nearly black, with a tinge of brown and a silvery-grey sheen; beneath it was of a yellow umber colour, spotted with the dark colour of its back; its head, with its large teeth and narrow, shark-like eyes, somewhat resembled that of a Danish hound. Its circumference was small for its length, and the blubber very thin, so we concluded it had either come through the breeding season or travelled far.

Just after killing the seal there was a shout amongst the men forward, 'A Uni! A Uni!'—the whalers' term for a Narwhale. Several men said they saw their horns.

The crow's-nest was sent aloft to-day. It is a cask, about five feet deep, painted white, with iron clamps that clasp on to the main-topgallant mast. In the bottom there is a trap-door. To get into the nest you climb up a Jacob's ladder— wooden ratlins rigged on two  backstays that run from the top-gallant mast-head to the cross-trees; these run through the bottom of the tub. You climb up these and shove the trap open with your head, and when you are right into the tub you let the trap shut below you, and stand on it, and enjoy the extensive view. If you prefer it, you can sit on a shelf-seat fixed in the back of the tub—a sheltered, quiet place, far removed from the troubles of the little world below: round the top of the tub there is a small iron balustrade, on which a screen runs, so as to shelter the watcher from the wind.

. . . The boats were all lowered from the skids to the

deck to-day and slung out on to wooden davits that are fixed to the outside of the bulwarks.

The mist still hangs over us, and we expect to meet the ice every hour. The growlers are more frequent, and we hear the surge rolling over them; now and then they show through the mist, faint pearly-grey and white and dull green, with the swell spurning white down their worn sides. They are slowly drifting, on their funereal voyage to the warm waters of the north. . . .

All day we steamed southwards through the black, smooth water, with the mist hanging round us brown and damp. At two o'clock it grew a little lighter, and the folds of the mist curtain were drawn up a little, as if by hands from above, and beneath the veil we saw the edge of the Antarctic ice close to us, white against a dark sky beyond.

I felt as if the weariness and the fret of many years of voyaging would be repaid by the first glimpse of this strange white land, by the sensation of quietly stealing under the mist veil into this secret white chamber of great Nature. The blocks of ice and snow that formed the floating shore were varied with many faint tints, pale violets, creamy whites, and silky greens; and the shapes were as beautiful and unexpected by me as the delicacy and variety of the colours. It was as if a Doric temple built in dreamland of Carrara marble had been thrown down, and lay floating calmly on the dark, still water. Yet with all the strangeness of the fantastic shapes, of capitols, columns, and shattered carvings, there was still a decision in the sculpture of the blocks and masses, and a certainty in the working out of each detail, in the form of the icicles hanging from goblin mushrooms, in the green fret-work supporting white tables, that made us marvel at the skill of the design, and wonder what it was in this stillness that owned and enjoyed such grand and delicate beauty. Whilst we skirted this floating snow-land, the crew watched it from the black bulwarks, and were awed into silence by its unfamiliar beauty. The silence was broken by a whale rising between us and the ice; he was about seventy feet long, I should guess. He spouted a jet of steam into the mist and went down. Some one called, 'He's a Bowhead!' and every one forgot all about the ice and thought of whalebone and blubber and great profits. All the men who were not already on deck crowded on to the focsle-head at the shout, and waited to see the whale come up again—a silent group of intensely expectant figures, with the mist hanging grey on their clothes and beards. A second time he rose quite close to us, spouted, sighed heavily, rolled slowly over, and went down without showing enough of his back to let us know whether he was a finner or a right whale. Certainly his colour was not quite right—it was not black enough for a Bowhead; still, the colour would not matter, we thought, if he had no fin on his back. The third time he rose higher, and just as he was going down a diminutive fin appeared, and a shout of laughter echoed in the misty stillness, and every one bundled off to his work jeering at the man who 'couldn't tell a Bowhead from a bl—y finner.'

Think of all the dreary melancholy, the blank hopelessness described by writers about the Arctic, and you can have but a faint idea of the sad, inhuman feeling of solitude there is in this world of white cliffs and black sea. Take all the grace, softness, and mystery of form and colour together, that they have written of, and you can scarcely dream of the delicate beauty of the forms, or the infinite subtlety of the harmonies in white, and silver, and green, and pale yellow and blue that we have seen in these last few hours

steaming along the pack edge—an endless fairy picture, painted on silk, with a ghostly brush from a palette of pearl.

To give more than a suggestion of colouring is as impossible in colour as in words. The bloom on a child's cheek can be reproduced in paints, but these high-toned schemes of variously-tinted white are infinitely more difficult. Their unfamiliarness is at once their difficulty and their charm. One feels in looking at them as if developing a new sense of sight, with each new effect of colour, so that the thought of attempting to reproduce the tints at the time is crowded out of mind.

All the effects that I can hope to give here as illustrations are merely the most evident—those that may be expressed in grim black and white—but any delicacy of light and shade and tint that I attempt to reproduce in colour, is certainly beyond the reproductive powers of our patent photographic engraving processes.

To-night Nick laid out five tumblers, five spoons, and the sugar-bowl on the cabin table, with a considerable amount of solemnity, and the master brought out his rum, and we in the cabin were invited to celebrate the occasion of our reaching the ice with a modest glass of rum hot! Taking the total distance N.S.E. and W., we have sailed about 9000 miles, and come through much bad weather, with no loss but a few sails and one spar. So the occasion quite well warranted the excuse for a glass.

Sunday, 18th Dec.—The mist came down over us again this morning, and hid the bergs—which are now very numerous, from our view. A few Cape pigeons are flying round us; they show their black-and-white chequered backs as they fly under our stern, and fade away in the mist, where they seem as much at home as we feel strange.

When there is a lift in the mist we take advantage of it, and steer south by west, making a course along the ice edge for Erebus and Terror Gulf, in Louis Philippe Land, where Sir James Ross saw the right whales in 1842, and where we expect to meet our consorts. We expected to see Clarence Island, the eastmost of the South Shetlands, but the fog was too thick; so the first land we can see now is Joinville Land, or the small islands that lie to the N.E. of it.

We passed a large berg this afternoon, probably a little more than a hundred feet high. I guessed it was eight miles long, and by compass bearings we made it seven and three-quarters. To our Arctic sailors this was an extraordinary sight, as a berg a mile long in the north is considered huge. But the impression of size is not received from enlargement of an object in one direction, so this ice cliff, eight miles long by a hundred feet, was not particularly impressive. The most imposing effect I have yet seen was a mere chip off one of these bergs; it loomed out of a bank of mist, and grey surges climbed up its ice cliffs and burst, and the spray vanished in the mist above.

The melancholy of this grey Sabbath amongst the bergs was broken this afternoon by the cry of 'A sail!' Though we expected every hour to fall in with one of our consorts, it came as a great surprise to us. It seemed so improbable, at first hearing, to see another vessel here. Just for a few moments we saw it during a lift in the mist; it was a mile or two astern of us. Then the north wind brought the fog down again and hid it, before we could do more than guess which of our consorts it might be.

Monday, 19th Dec.—The weather has been so thick that it has not been possible to shoot the sun for the last two or three days, so we trust to dead reckoning. Last night the fog fell so thickly that we could not see the end of the jibboom—a nice position to be in with bergs to windward and bergs to leeward, drifting goodness knows where! Fortunately the wind, that had been blowing pretty fresh, fell at night, and our case was not so bad as it might have been. It was queer work as it was, and we thanked our stars we had steam power to get us out of the way of the ice islands when they heaved in sight. All night the men were peering out into the mist, and every now and then you heard a shout from the vague figure at the bow: 'Berg right ahead!' Then a shout from aft: 'Berg astern!' and 'Berg to port!' 'Berg to starboard!' till we thought we were completely hemmed in. In the morning the mist lifted suddenly, and the welcome sun shone out. Then we saw the grisly company in which we had spent the night. White cliffs were shimmering in the sunlight in every direction—very beautiful they were, but we did not linger in our leave-taking.

To-day the air is pleasant and warm, and the thermometer stands at 40°. I have managed to make half-a-dozen ice-sketches. The difficulty in doing so was the number of subjects, also the blaze of white light on the snow made me quite blind when I went below to work out my notes. It was so dazzling, too, when I came up on deck again, that the forms of the ice were invisible for some time.

The glass went down rapidly to-day, and a N.E. gale sprang up in the afternoon. From twelve o'clock midday till six we steamed and sailed with the gale on our quarter, along the side of what appeared to be an endless berg. When we reached the south end of the cliff, we turned and sailed S.W. for a few miles, and lay in the shelter of the ice cliff, with the wind howling through our rigging, till the masts trembled down to the cabin floor. We calculated the side of the berg we sailed past was at least thirty miles long, with an even height of little more than a hundred feet. There was but one break in the dead level line of its top, where it rose to perhaps two hundred feet or rather less, in the shape of something like an inverted bowl, with part of the front cut away. It appeared to me that this may have been raised by the berg grounding on a submarine peak. There were, however, no splits to suggest any sudden upheaval; the curves were soft and gradual, and suggestive of a gradual accumulation rather than an upheaval.

Tuesday, 20th Dec.—Last night we lay sheltering behind the berg—driving to leeward and steaming up to it again. A cold, strong gale is blowing on us over the top of the table-land of ice. It whistles through our rigging and brings stinging snow-showers. Snow and mist come down together, and blot out our sheltering berg from view. Masts and rigging are white with snow and ice—a wintry picture—yet this is the middle of the Ant-

Swell on the Ice Edge.

arctic summer! I think the climate here is probably worse than farther south, where the temperature may be lower but less changeable. In the afternoon the sun shone out clearly, and we went on our course again. A great swell was running from the N.W., and the sea was bright blue and littered all over with small fragments of white snow and ice, through which we ploughed our way. This small ice was perhaps the cause of the great length of the swell, which was not deep, but from top to top of each low hill was so long, that any guess I could make would scarcely sound credible to one who had not seen such a swell on the ice edge. A berg to the south of us, about three miles long, seemed to extend over only five or six of these low hills. When they rose and burst out of the caves the towers of spray were magnificent, and must have risen three hundred feet in the air. I give a drawing of this berg. It was apparently breaking up. Large portions seemed as if they had been undermined, and had fallen into the sea. The ship, which I have inserted, had to be made many times too large to be visible.

It was only for a few hours we enjoyed the sunshine. The mist came down again in the afternoon; it was so thick and heavy that even the Cape pigeons seemed to lose their way, and fluttered quite close to us for company's sake.

The engine-room on such an evening is the most comfortable place in the ship. After the snow and cold mist on deck it is pleasant to sit down there in the warm gloom and watch the gleam of the yellow firelight on the oily pistons as they slowly rise and fall. It is but a small engine, and one engineer and a fireman can meet all its wants during the watch; still, it gives a feeling of civilisation that to our degenerate nature is almost welcome in this far land.

The engineers, like their engines, have more of modern thought than the whale-killers in the cabin—how we value them now, when we cannot see a ship's-length ahead, with bergs everywhere, and land anywhere.

When we are not steaming up to the shelter of a berg, or steaming clear of one to leeward, we play dominoes for imaginary stakes, and tell yarns, and I learn here, as any one may learn by reading Kipling's 'Bolivar,' that there is as much of the Romance of the Sea, to use a rather pretty term, in the stoke-hole of a Whaler or an ocean tramp as in any of the old South Spainers.

We have been taking soundings, for, by dead reckoning, we ought to be in the neighbourhood of the Danger Islands, which Sir James Ross discovered in 1842. We have no wish to land on them suddenly with this big swell running.

We use Sir William Thomson's (Lord Kelvin) deep-sea sounding-line; and the doctor has managed to have Dr. H. R. Mill's deep-sea thermometer attached to it—an interesting combination of two scientists' inventions, which we feel they would have much pleasure in working themselves were they here.

In fine weather it is somewhat aggravating to hear our whaling friends talking big of practical seamen, and of 'thae scienteefic chaps wha stay at hame and ken naethin' aboot the sea ava''—ignoring their entire dependence on such trifles as the compass, sextant, chronometer, etc.; and it is equally satisfactory to see them here, in a tight place, using the scientists' inventions for the sake of dear life.

There is much ice round us to-night, and every now and then, as I draw in my bunk, comes a crash and a shuddering, tearing sound, as if our thirty-two inches of timber were being crushed like a straw hat; it is a bad place, this, for weak nerves. In the silence that follows we cannot but wonder whether the next rasping will be the edge of a growler rubbing off the barnacles, or the first touch of the green ice-cliff that lay to leeward when we turned in.

Wednesday, 21st Dec.—No change in the weather. The sun shines feebly through the mist. There is nothing to be seen from deck, and we lie idly rolling, waiting for a lift.

A seal appeared under our stern and the mate shot it, but the bullet went a trifle behind its skull and it sank. Apparently it was the same as the last we saw. Later, some penguins jumped on to an ice island and we shot three of them. We are to have them for Christmas dinner, but sincerely trust there may be something besides. These were the first we had seen close at hand, and our astonishment at their appearance was great.

At 4 o'clock it cleared up, and we had at last an open view. Sailing round a long point of bergs and pack ice we headed S.W. with a light breeze in the N.E. The colour of the water has changed to the colour whalers like —a raw umber tint, caused by minute colourless jellies, the size of small shot, each speckled with brown spots.

The grey, streaky sky has opened in the N.E., leaving a

long band of primrose along the horizon, a pleasant change from the wet and mist that we have had so much of lately. In all directions great whales are showing their black backs and blowing up jets of hot, wet breath. The puffs rise as from an escape steam-pipe, and float away with the wind down the yellow ribbon of light, and seem to melt into the low canopy of grey clouds.

There was quite an impressive ceremony to-night. All hands were called aft to the break of the poop and divided into three watches—the master and the two mates picking men alternately; so the crew is now divided into three watches, and the day is divided into three eight-hour watches. This division of the day is adopted on reaching whaling-ground, instead of the four hours on and four off usual at sea; this is to suit the long spells in the boats that the men may be expected to have.

Thursday, 22nd Dec.—Were there natives in this part of the world I suppose that they would call this a fine day. We can see quite a mile on each side, now, sometimes even two or three when the mist rises. There must be about a score of icebergs round us—huge fellows—grim companions; we are under the belief that their feet are resting on the green, muddy bottom, for we see about one hundred and fifty feet of them above water, and the depth by sounding is something under two hundred fathoms, so that would allow their depth below water to be as is usually supposed nine times that of their height above the surface. They ought to be well anchored, and the more firmly fixed they are the better for us. A S.E. wind is blowing down on us over their tops, humming as it does in mountain tops before a storm; snow fine as dust and as hard as flint is driven along with it, stinging our faces till they burn. It has filled up all the nooks and crannies about the decks, and lies in the folds of our furled sails. We can make no progress, can do nothing but dodge about in the lee of a big berg and keep out of harm's way: the few men on deck are getting the whale lances

and knives ready, giving them all a touch-up on the grindstone. It is midsummer, but the Balæna looks like a Christmas-card, and we feel the blazing stove in the cabin none too warm.

As I have already mentioned, one of our hands who did haircutting and bird-skinning left us at the Falklands, so the doctor has taken up bird-skinning in his place, and what with attending to the sailors' boils and various complaints, arising from this inhospitable climate, and making his hourly observations, his hands are full. I should like to give a drawing of the doctor at work in his bunk, overwhelmed with skins, bottles, and apparatus, but perhaps there would be '*trop de choses*,' as the great Carolus used to say.

Wind S.E. We thought we saw land to-night to the westward.

Friday, 23rd Dec.—Hurrah! we've made the land at last—the islands of the Antarctic Continent. At seven this morning the mist rose and we found ourselves almost exactly where our dead reckoning put us, but rather nearer the most northerly of the group of Danger Islands than we cared to be. Sir James Ross discovered them fifty years ago, and I suppose they have not been seen since. Beyond them to the west lay the N.E. end of Joinville Land, seen by Admiral d'Urville from the N.W. in 1838. What we saw of it was a sweep of snow that rose in a very gradual slope to between two or three thousand feet, then fading almost imperceptibly into the clouds. At times the sun shone through the whisps of cloud and chased shadows along the glacier slopes; I thought the faint lines I could trace on the snow might be crevasses. Not a sign of a rock or any kind of land showed through the glacier slopes. Sir James Ross saw some rocks like warty excrescences breaking abruptly from the snow on the top, and Captain Crozier and his officers in the *Terror* believed they saw smoke issuing from the top, but owing to the wreaths of cloud we could not see the rocks, neither did we see any smoke.

I made several profile views of the land and the Danger Islands of the useful, if not altogether of the ornamental, kind of art. Some of the islands we found had not been charted by Sir James Ross; probably he did not see them owing to their being surrounded by icebergs. The largest was called Darwin Island. It has blue-black precipitous sides, with a table-top covered with snow. Some of the islets were low and flat, without snow, others rose like

Danger Islands.

broken pillars abruptly from the sea, and these also had no snow on their flat tops. I failed to find a reason why the snow should lie on some of the islands and not on others.

This has been a tremendous day of business: both watches have been coiling the whale lines into their compartments in the whale-boats. This is a mighty careful process. They have to be laid down so that they can run out when the whale sounds, without a hitch. One line is coiled down in the stern-sheets in a triangular shape—the steersman stands on this, when it is not running out—another is coiled in a box amidships, and the third is coiled in the bow. There has been some demur about coiling the lines on a Friday; but so many instances are quoted of full ships as the result of lines being coiled on a Friday, that the work goes on merrily, and as each crew lays down the last fathom they give a cheer, and the men in the neighbouring boats growl at each other for their slowness. Every one is in a state of great expectation: to-morrow we ought to be amongst the 'great numbers of the largest-sized black whales' that Ross wrote about.

One of our harpooneers, the slayer of hundreds of leviathans—perhaps the oldest and most energetic of our crew—has not coiled his lines down yet. He has kept out of sight in his bunk, whistling to his dicky-bird, waiting till twelve o'clock, the end of the nautical day, when there will be time enough, as he says. Nothing will induce him to equip his boat, and nothing will make him confess that it is on account of its being Friday. The harpoon-guns too are being fixed in the bullet-heads on the boats' bows. They are rather like short-barrelled duck-punt guns—muzzle-loaders with a pistol stock supported on a crutch and a swivel-pin that turns in the bullet-head; a few inches behind this bullet-head there is a second bullet or timber-head, round which the line is hitched as it runs out over the stem.

Soon after passing Danger Islets we saw the southern extremity of Joinville Land, called by Ross Cape Purvis. Off this point lay Paulet Island, 750 feet high, as estimated by Ross—I should have thought it only about 600. Its sides rise precipitously from the sea, then slope gradually into a truncated cone. The only snow on the island lay in a gully down the middle of the cone. I could see no reason why the snow did not lie on this island, as there were steeper slopes on the other islands on which the snow lay. The snow on the islands and the snow on the land to the eastward was of a slightly different tint from that on the pack-ice and bergs. It had a yellowish, creamy tinge, whilst that on the pack and bergs was cold absolute white. The difference was very slight, but remarkable. It would be interesting to know the cause.

Captain Davidson of the Active discovered that Joinville Land does not continue to Cape Fitzroy, but is separated from the land to the South by a strait through which he navigated the Active. Captain Davidson called the land Dundee Island, and the strait the Firth of Tay.

As we steamed south the views of the land and icebergs and islands and birds became so numerous and interesting that we felt at a loss which to look at first. The number of penguins increased as we sailed towards Erebus Gulf. They jumped on to the ice-cakes in family parties, and looked at us as we passed, striking quaint attitudes on the snow; then a new kind of tern appeared, and some snowy petrels—an exquisitely beautiful, pure white bird, never found far from the ice; they are about the size of a common tern, with black beak and eyes and feet.

About midday we saw a long, pale, brown figure lying on the snow, and all eyes were bent on it; at first, owing to the blinding white light, it was difficult to see

what it was, but as we came close we found it to be a
great seal, of such a light colour, that if it had not been
for the contrast with the snow we would have called it
white. We passed within a few yards of it, and wakened
it, but it gave us very little attention, merely raised its
head, with some snow sticking to the hair, and looked over
its shoulder at us, then closed its black eyes and lay down
to sleep again; it seemed to ignore the presence of us

poor creatures who require a ship and engines and all
sorts of things to come and sail in its country, where it
can supply all its own wants and spend the whole day in
glorious repose on the snow in the faint sunlight. We
lowered a boat after we had passed it, and several hands,
mostly Johnnie Raws, tumbled in. Whalers are not
born, and some of the young chaps who got into the boat
had much to learn. The smith and the cooper got amid-

ships, sat facing each other, and pulled, each his own way. Such a 'how to do' I never did see. I had expected some rather smart boat work in a whaler, but on this occasion there was enough excitement to launch an ark. Every one pulled his own stroke; they bucketed, rolled, and pulled out of time, but they pulled hard, and at thirty yards the men in the bow began blazing away at the astonished seal. It would have been as easy to hit as a haystack, but the excitement was such that it took seven shots before the seal was hit. Then we jumped on to the snow and despatched the poor beast with ice-picks, and rolled it into the boat, using the oars as a gangway, and it was no light work doing this, for the seal was full twelve feet, with girth in proportion. Later in the day we saw many more of these 'white seals,' as we called them ; we did not stop to kill them, but steamed ahead to reach our rendezvous in Erebus and Terror Gulf.

The bergs have become so numerous that we have been sailing through aisles of ice-cliffs, the beauty of which was beyond description. Now and then our passage was blocked by barriers of floe-ice, twenty feet thick, soft and white on top, but under water hard and green. We ran into these and drove them aside, and it

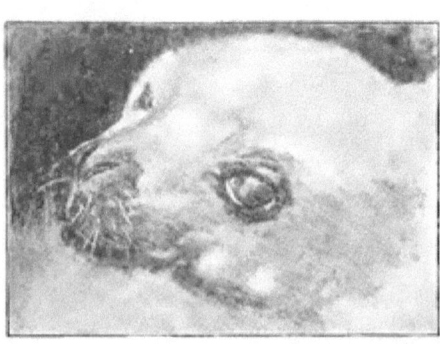

was altogether a novel sensation to me this running a ship intentionally against what appeared to be solid ice islands. Sometimes an island would not break or shove aside, then we backed, and steamed against it again full tilt, and the sensation we felt in the Balæna was as if we were inside a hamper and some one had jumped on it. As we jammed slowly through between the pieces they tore along our sides, and took off something more than the barnacles we brought from the tropics.

It seems strange that the penguins should jump out of the water on to the snow at our approach, instead of into

the water off the snow. They scurry over the snow in an upright position, like little fat men in black coats and white silk waistcoats. Their bare pink feet show just beneath their waistcoats, but for all that they look as respectable as can be. When they reach the middle of the ice islands they toddle up some mound of snow and wave their flippers to us with most ridiculous *empressement*. I am sure they discuss the new arrivals in their country; though 'quangk-quangk,' is the only word I distinguish, their attitudes are as expressive as a Shakespearian vocabulary. When they are not engaged making a living below water they come up and play games on the snow—have little debating societies, and King of the Castle and other games, and sometimes when they are in great numbers they have military manœuvres. The men say they are the only things worth coming to see in the Antarctic, and no matter how melancholy a man may feel, if he sees one of these jolly little fellows he cheers up.

An hour or two ago I saw an elderly tar with rather a sad face, looking over the bulwarks across the ice in a dreamy sort of way, thinking perhaps of his home and his family. Just in front of him a penguin popped out of the water on to the ice, then turned and looked down to see how high it had jumped—it was good three feet—then put its head in the air and waddled away over the snow, with its toes pointed out, and an expression that said

'A precious good jump that for me anyway.' At this little episode a wintry smile stirred the lines on my friend's face; and when a second penguin, a friend of the first, missed the jump and hit his head against the ice-ledge and fell back into the water, the smile changed to a broad grin. Penguin No. 2 was not to be daunted, however, but made another attempt, and got up and waddled after his friend, expostulating with him loudly for not offering him a hand-up, and the melancholy man filled full of laughter, and rolled away forward to the focsle, to discuss 'thae blasted funny wee beggars,' with his mates.

To-night we steamed into Erebus and Terror Gulf—the place where it was arranged the four consorts were to meet—and within four hours of each other three of the four turned up. The Active, which we had a glimpse of a few days ago, came up from the ice to the eastward, and a few hours afterwards the Diana's topsails appeared above the ice in the north. Half-an-hour afterwards the three black barques lay alongside each other, in a pool of open water, with the Union Jacks flying apeak. The sun at midnight just dipped below the horizon of ice and rose again, tinging the level bands of clouds with a faint lemon yellow. Near us a square berg, with round buttresses rising at its corners, stood dark and grey against the sky. We only wanted the little Polar Star to make the picture complete.

CHAPTER XV

SATURDAY, 24*th Dec.*—Now for the whales, if there are any! Every one is on the look-out for the black back of the finless whale that carries the gold in its mouth.[1] Looking back on our course we see Paulet Island to the N.E., surrounded with loose ice and small bergs, and to the south the horizon is broken with bergs and loose ice; above us there is delicate grey sky that lifts at times, showing a yellow band of light in the east. To the west the snow-clad land comes out towards us, terminating in what, I suppose, is Cape Gordon; then it stretches back, west and south, till we can just make out the entrance to Admiralty Inlet—a deep opening into the snow-clad land, fortified on either side by black precipitous cliffs, which rise one above the other in terraces till they are lost in the clouds. The inlet reminds me somewhat of the entrance to Loch Huron or some Norwegian fiord. In front of the entrance there are some low islands of a reddish, chocolate colour, with almost no snow on them. Between us and the land, in the open water of the gulf, we see our two companion vessels. They help us to form an idea of the height of the mountains. Mount Haddington lies west, slightly north of Admiralty Inlet, but on account of the low clouds we cannot see its top.

---

[1] Whalebone was worth £2500 per ton when we left Dundee. A big whale has a ton of bone in its mouth.

Glaciers cover the whole slopes of the land, in some places sweeping down to the sea and in others ending abruptly at the edge of some black cliff. Immediately to the north of Admiralty Inlet we can see a deep bight in the snow slope that seems to form a horse-shoe bay, with steep white sides, sloping into the sea, which terminate above in a circle of glacier-capped cliffs. We are filled with an intense longing to land and make a closer acquaintance with these shores, which have but once before been seen by man. What might we not discover? and what a glorious view to the south we could have from the top of Mount Haddington! When the clouds lifted we could lay out the chart over leagues of undiscovered lands. But blubber is apparently to be the only interest, and we steer away south-east—away from the land—in search of it. The progress of Sir James Ross to the south was here stopped by the loose pack-ice—the sort of ice that offers no impediment to our vessels. To the south we see loose ice, and beyond it blue sky and open water. With our steam power and well-protected hulls we could push right through it, as easily as what we have already come through —south or south-east, for who can tell how far, without risk. We are in an unknown world, and we stop—for *blubber.* . . .

We are steering to the south-east, the three ships in line; the Balæna leads, the Active and Diana follow. We are leaving the open water in Erebus and Terror Gulf, threading our way through the loose pack between aisles of many bergs. The water is calm and dark,

almost inky, with a lilac shimmer on its surface, and on either side of us the cliffs rise high above our masts, their splintered sides hung with gauzy whisps of vapour that float motionless in the cold, sunny air. The side of the bergs near us are of a transparent leaden colour, dusted with snow. Occasionally we pass greeny-blue clefts in the cliffs, which seem to lead far into the berg to fairy chambers in the white palaces. Above, the sky is of the most delicate lapis-lazuli blue, crossed with soft bands of dull white cloud and flecked with cirri. As the bergs recede into perspective behind us, they take faint, rosy, purple tints. In this colourless illustration you see the Active and the Diana, with her broken mizzen, following in our course. They are on the north side of the ice fiord, and the sunlight pouring over the ice-cliffs lights their flesh-coloured spars; their black hulls are in shadow and set off the delicate pearly colouring of the bergs. We are on the south side of the canal, in the shadow of the cliffs, forcing our way through belts of snow-ice that bar our passage. Sometimes we have to shove an ice island out of our course; our black bows crunch into its soft, snowy surface, and break into the green undercut caves, and the shock brings down showers of clinking icicles, and the piece is shoved aside. As we pass, black-backed penguins jump out of the water, and scurry about on the dazzling, white snow.

The black penguins set off the white tints; but there is red in the picture as well, to contrast with the blots of intense blue in the snow—vivid splashes of scarlet, where the warm carcases of seals which we have killed in

our course lie quivering on the snow. A few nellies—
large brown birds—dance round them very awkwardly,
with their big, webbed feet. They peck at each other,
and then gobble up the warm meat. It is a hideous thing
this sealing, and most awfully bloody and cruel. Some
of the seals were killed with the ice-picks—a short staff
of natural wood about four feet long with a steel pick-
head; others were shot. Sport there was none. I would
sooner stalk a bunny with a pea-rifle, behind a dyke,

than shoot a score of these splendid, dark-eyed seals.
They showed not the least surprise at our presence—just
raised their heads, and sometimes snarled at us. In
killing them with the picks there was the faintest element
of risk, as the snow was deep, and hard on the surface in
some places, and soft in others. Sometimes we plunged in
waist deep when delivering a blow, and found ourselves
unpleasantly close to the seal's gaping jaws. Their huge

bear-like teeth do not look pleasant at close quarters.' But the poor beasts only acted on the defensive; if they had had the good sense to attack us or take to the water instead of taking to the centre of the ice-cakes, there would have been trouble. They evidently consider the centre of the snow pieces their refuge from danger; probably the Orca or Grampus treats them here as it does the seals in the north.[1] We found some of the seals very much scarred with long parallel wounds almost encircling their bodies. I think these were marks left by the grampus; the smaller cuts about their necks and shoulders were signs of domestic worries.

In the evening we steamed gently up against the edge of a large pack some miles long, which bounded the comparatively open water of the gulf to the south-east. Our bows struck softly against its edge, and the screw went on revolving, while some men dropped from the martingale and made two wire hawsers fast to spikes driven deep into the snow. This position was within a mile of the spot where Sir James Ross brought in the New Year of 1843.

The Diana and Active followed, running their black bows over the snow-edge, one on each side of us, and distant a few hundred yards. Some of the boats were lowered, and the masters of the ships met and had one of their 'mollies,' and the men of the three vessels had an opportunity of speaking to each other on the snow. It

---

[1] An Orca or Grampus, twenty feet long, was found on the Danish coast with the remains of fourteen seals and two porpoise inside it. See Rae Society.

was tremendously hard work walking on the snow—a hundred yards quite pumped us.

The pack seemed to consist of collected blocks of broken snow-ice levelled up with soft snow, so walking on it was most fatiguing. For a few paces we succeeded in walking on the surface, then the crust broke and we plunged through waist-deep, often jamming our feet between blocks below the snow. With a sledge and dogs we could have travelled over this pack fairly well. The greatest obstruction to sledging would have been the little pinnacles of ice, of the shape of the stumps in a burned forest. These stood up all over the level snow in numbers. In the inside of each point there was a core of hard ice.

Here we found some of the large king or emperor penguins. They landed on the snow just as we brought up against the floe edge, and waddled towards the interior of the pack, and the stillness of the white evening was broken by the shouts of men and boys in pursuit. The penguins took it all very quietly, and easily outdistanced us on the snow. When in a hurry they dropped on their breasts and shoved along with their feet, paddling with their flippers, looking rather like turtles in this attitude. The track their feet left resembled a dog's, and when you saw these tracks on the snow, following and between the flipper marks, it looked exactly like the track of a dog in pursuit of some other animal.

We never could have caught any had they so chosen. But at times they stopped to observe our movements, climbed on to some snow mound, and looked at us first with one eye then the other whilst we stumbled up.

We crept up to them, partly surrounded them, and let drive with our picks. We got a few, but the remainder led us wild chases over the snow, giving us many a tumble and matter for infinite mirth to those looking on from the focsle-head.

I made a drawing of one of these extraordinary birds as it stood calmly on our poop after many vain attempts on the part of the crew to kill it. Driving a hole through its brain only saddened it, and all the most killing treatment usually applied to other animals only seemed to add to its expression of calm, eternal resignation. They stand about four feet four inches high, but their bulk in pro-

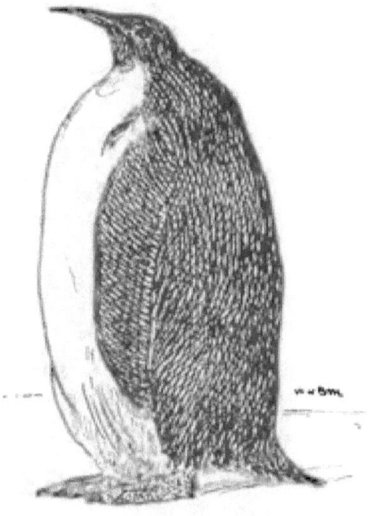

portion is something enormous. They are twice the thickness of any drawings of the species that I have ever seen in books. Either the draughtsmen of these must have drawn from stuffed specimens, whose skin had shrunk in width, or this is some new kind. Their beak is black, with a bright patch of yellow fading into lake, and is long, narrow, and curved. There are some golden yellow feathers on its neck immediately under its black throat. Its back feathers and rudimentary wing-feathers are black, with a slate-grey touch in the centre of each—quills would be a better name than feathers, as they resemble a scale frayed at the edges rather than feathers. They are very stiff, short, and hard, and seem to be scarcely fitting protection from the cold. I expected to find a great quantity of protective oil beneath the skin, but found there was little more than on our guillemots and divers at home.

... Days such as this are few in a lifetime, so full of interest has it been, and so fatiguing. Since early morning, rather since yesterday, for there was no night and no morning, we have been constantly marvelling at most astonishing and beautiful spectacles. We have been bathed in red blood, and for hours and hours we have rowed in the boats and plunged over miles of soft snow dragging sealskins, and I have been drawing hard in the times between the boat excursions; but the air is exhilarating, and we feel equal to almost any amount of work. Sun and snow-showers alternate—fine hard snow it is, that makes our faces burn as if before a fire. It is very cold sketching, and incidents and effects follow each other so rapidly that there is time to make little more than mental notes.

Christmas Eve.

Those who have felt the peace of a summer night in Norway or Iceland, where the day sleeps with wide-open eyes, can fancy the quiet beauty of such a night among the white floes of the Antarctic.

To-day has passed, glistering in silky white, decked with sparkling jewels of blue and green, and we thought surely we had seen the last of Nature's white harmonies; then evening came, pensive, and soothing, and grey, and all the white world changed into soft violet, pale yellow, and rose. . . .

A dreamy stillness fills the air. To the south the sun has dipped behind a bank of pale grey cloud, and the sky above is touched with primrose light. Far to the north the dark, smooth sea is bounded by two low bergs, that stretch across the horizon. The nearest is cold violet

white, and the sunlight strikes the furthest, making it shine like a wall of gold. The sky above them is of a leaden, peacock blue, with rosy cloudlets hanging against it—such colouring as I have never before seen or heard described. To the westward, across the gulf, we can just distinguish the blue-black crags jutting from the snowy lomonds. Little clouds touched with gold and rose lie nestling in the black corries, and gather round the snowy peaks. To the south, in the centre of the floe, some bergs lie, cold and grey in the shadow of the bank of cloud. They look like Greek temples imprisoned for ever in a field of snow. A faint cold air comes stealing to us over the floe; it ripples the yellow sky reflection at the ice-edge for a moment, and falls away. In the distance a seal is barking—a low muffled sound that travels far over the calm water, and occasionally a slight splash breaks the silence, as a piece of snow separates from the field and joins its companion pieces that are floating quietly past our stern to the north, —a mysterious, silent procession of soft, white spirits, each perfectly reflected in the lavender sea.

Nature sleeps—breathlessly—silent; perhaps she dreams of the spirit-world, that seems to draw so close to her on such a night.

By midnight the tired crew were all below and sound asleep in their stuffy bunks. But the doctor and I found it impossible to leave the quiet decks and the mysterious daylight, so we prowled about and brewed coffee in the deserted galley. Then we watched the sun pass behind the grey bergs in the south for a few seconds, and appear again, refreshed, with a cool silvery light. A few flakes of snow floated in the clear, cold air, and two snowy petrels, white as the snow itself, flitted along the ice-edge.

. . . A cold, dreamy, white Christmas morning,— beautiful beyond expression.

CHAPTER XVI

CHRISTMAS DAY.—We rose this morning tired as dogs. The air is so overpowering here, that if you turn in for a pipe and forty winks you may waken a day or two later and growl at having to get up so early. Like the seals here, or schoolboys anywhere, we have to be fairly bullied awake. But though the air makes us sleepy, we all agree that it has not so much of the tonic effect as the air of the Arctic regions—that atmospheric champagne on which men can work all day and night without fatigue.

We still lie with our bow over the pack, and a rope ladder hangs from the bowsprit, so that we can go 'ashore' whenever we like. Occasionally seals come on to the ice in our neighbourhood, and though the day has been given the men as a holiday, a boat's crew generally goes off to secure them. A few Emperor penguins arrived, and they were also captured and brought to the ship.

We had an opportunity to-day of meeting our friend Dr. Donald of the Active. To put it mildly, we were extremely glad to meet another man of our own kidney, and wandered away over the snow-field, and held a great palaver behind a hummock, stretched on the snow, enjoying the blaze of sunlight.

We had many notes about bird-life to compare, and knotty questions in medicine to discuss, to the solving of which, as assistant surgeon, I lent my most attentive hearing, and all three bewailed the utter commercialism of the expedition. Is it not a hideous marvel that Dundonians should show such splendid enterprise as to send four ships out here for whales, and at the same time show total disregard for the scientific possibilities of such a cruise?

Our walk over the snow was short and warm. A thousand yards over deep, soft snow, under a blazing sun, did us brown. D. tried barrel-staves as skis. They might have supported an average-sized man, but in this case they only sank deep blue trenches in the snow, which we following found of use.

Much to our regret, we had no opportunity at this time of meeting Dr. Campbell of the Diana. He, we understand, has been more fortunate than we on the Balæna, for Captain Davidson gives him every opportunity of collecting specimens. If we lay hold of glacier rocks or birds' skins we raise a whirlwind of objections, and an endless reiteration of the painfully evident truth that 'this is no a scientuffic expedeetion.' A most painful state of things this, to see common albatross skins collected by the score, and rare penguins killed by the hundred, their bodies eaten, and their skins chucked overboard. Emperor penguins, king penguins, an endless variety of birds, some unheard of, all go over the side because they are supposed to be of no commercial value. To the whaling skipper, animal life beyond his own and the Bowheads is absolutely uninteresting. His knowledge is limited by immediate necessity. In bird-life he can distinguish a hen from a kittiwake, because the one is worth money and is good to eat; and amongst cetaceans he can pick out a Bowhead for the sake of its bone and blubber, but in all the other endless list of birds and whales, which have surrounded him from boyhood, he takes not the least interest, consequently the information he can impart is extremely limited. If you ask him the difference between a right whale and, say, a 'finner,' his explanation is, 'a richt whale and a finner? Oh, there's nae mistakin' them—ye ken a richt whale's a'-the-gither duffrent frae a finner. There's nae resemblance ava. Na, na; there's nae mistakin' the twa when ye see them; a bairn could tell the duffrence.' I verily believe that some of these whales here might be stuffed to the throat with bone, and these men would pass them by, if they were not facsimiles of the whale they know in the north.

We celebrated the evening of Christmas Day in the doctor's bunk,—a tight fit for three long men with their pipes, but we enjoyed ourselves mightily. Donald and I curled into the hole used for a bed, whilst Bruce brewed our treasured cocoa, which we brought from the Falklands for great occasions. Later on we joined the skippers in the cabin, and listened to tales of deeds of other years —of the killing of great whales, and how the depraved skippers, in the old days, drank themselves fuddled on a Saturday night, and served out lashins of rum to all hands when they killed a big fish, and were not ashamed. Nowadays, praise be to God, they are all so very much improved, and the crew on these occasions have tea.

When we turned out of the cabin in the clear morning

air to see our friend off we found the black water of the gulf was covered with a thin coating of ice-needles. The water gradually changed to a delicate, rosy tint of lavender as it receded into the distance, and lay so still that the ice islands were scarcely distinguishable from their reflections. I would willingly give my left hand to have the power to paint or describe this one scene of divine beauty. Last night filled us with awed admiration; but the purity and heavenly colouring of this still morning is almost oppressively beautiful. We feel our black ship's hull and our sombre clothes in painful discordance with this land of white and rainbow colouring.

Monday, 26th.—Lat. 64.30 S.; long. 55.28 W. A clear, fine morning, with a bracing wind from the S.E. The thermometer at 31°. We left the pack-edge this morning.

The three vessels are beating about in the open water in the gulf between Trinity Land and the somewhat closely-

FROM EDINBURGH TO THE ANTARCTIC

packed ice to the east and south of us. We are waiting for the whales to turn up; the water is just the kind they like—brown, the colour of a peat stream, thick with diatoms that tinge the water-worn tongues and roots of the ice islands with the colour of weak tea—a pleasant contrast this yellow to the blue and green of the undercut snow ledges. This morning we made out a sail to the S.E., and had great hopes that it might be our little friend the Polar Star. It however proved to be the Jason, the Norwegian barque that has come out to keep us company in the search for whales. They met the ice some time before us, and have been sealing between this and in the ice south of the Orkneys for about twenty days. They have had splendid weather, and have collected some 500 seals, but they have not seen the right whale.

In the afternoon I went out with a crew and had two hours' pulling, which is about equal to six with decent oars. We have a few fairly good American ash oars on board, but the others are merely Norwegian fir poles, flattened at one end, with as much resemblance to a properly-balanced oar as a Castle Connel has to a Norse fishing-pole.

The first seal we came across was a very large one. He was lying on the snow on his back and would not budge, but turned on us, snarling, showing his formidable teeth and red throat. George stood for me for a few seconds whilst I elaborated some instantaneous eye exposures with pencil and paper, which you have here reproduced. The figure on the right tried to kill him with his pick, and gave a welt or two at his head that would have killed an ox, but only added to the seal's savage expression. A bullet at two yards ended his days. He was about fourteen feet long, dark on the back, yellowish-green below, with coal-black

spots overlapping lower light parts. His canine teeth were very large and formidable-looking, but the three-pronged molars were much decayed. I should much like to see

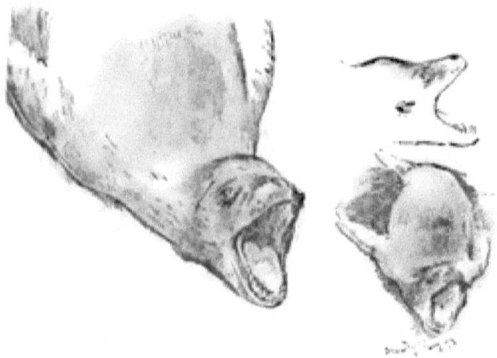

the kind of fish these seals capture. Some of the men saw one with a large fish in its mouth above water; they said it was like a conger-eel. It is very remarkable that we very rarely see these seals swimming with their heads above water like our northern seals.[1] To-night we had our first fricassee of the small penguins. They were stewed in curry; the meat was black and unpleasant to look at, but we voted it good. It tasted rather like jugged hare with a flavouring of oysters. It is a great thing for all hands that they are good eating, as it ensures us an endless supply of fresh meat.

Monday evening.—Still beating about under sail in the open water, with plenty of whales blowing all round, but still no right whales.

We are sailing in smooth water amongst scattered ice islands. It takes some careful steering to avoid running into them, and upsetting Nick's cups and saucers. At tea there was a crash, and the Balæna stopped and seemed to collapse like wicker-work. It was nothing— merely an acre of ice in the way, probably about twenty feet thick; such trifles are of no consequence to a whaler. Some advice, however, was passed up the scuttle to the steersman.

. . . Called on my friend 'The Chief' to-night. 'The Chief' is the title of Mr. Broch, our first engineer, who lives below with the second engineer in the dark engine-room —a life apart from the sailors. We play dominoes down there by the light of a smoking miner's lamp. The temperature is pleasant and warm, and we discuss matters of high import. To-night we went right through Scotch

---

[1] During our long stay in the ice I saw the seals swimming with their heads above water only on four or five occasions.

history, dating and discussing the Stuarts from the sons of Banquo to Queen Victoria. Broch must have left school half a century ago, yet he knew far more about the subject than I did, and I have been grinding at it for months. So much for the education of our old country schools.

Tuesday, 27th.—Barometer 29·6 in. ; thermometer up at 31°,—this is about our average glass here. Fresh wind from the S.E. The air is damp, and we feel as if the temperature was far below freezing-point. In the 'tween-decks the men are making-off the blubber from the skins and throwing it into the iron tanks that occupy the lower part of our hull.

Evening.—No whales yet ; but every one has one ear pricked for the long-expected shout 'A fall!'—a shout that will make us tumble neck and crop into the boats. Even in our bunks we are ready to jump up at a moment's notice. We sleep with our clothes beside us, tied up in a bundle, so that when the time comes we can jump into the boats and dress as we row.

The excitement when a whale is seen is almost beyond belief. Men have been known after long spells of whale-chasing in the boats, to go almost off their heads. On the shout of 'Tumble up and go to the boats' they have been known to rush on deck with their bundles and throw them into the water instead of the boats, from sheer nervousness. Once a boat's crew rushed on deck, threw their bundles over the side into the boat, as they thought, and followed themselves ; but there was no boat!

So at least I am told. One necessary precaution for sealing or whaling is to have a pair of spare mits sewed to the inside of one's jacket, and tobacco and matches you put into the pockets overnight.

We have been close enough to the land to enable us to distinguish the colouring and form of the rocks. The low, reddish-coloured islands seem to be crossed by fissures running into each other obliquely, with a little snow in the crevices ; but there is not the least sign of lichen or moss.

It is a marvel that no scientific expedition has been sent down here since the days of Ross. If one is sent in future it ought to bring some good Alpine men who would climb Mount Haddington and take bird's-eye views of the lie of the land and ice to the south. The ascent would not be difficult as far as the steepness goes. We cannot be sure whether there are crevasses or not.

It is almost unbearable to see the land so close and yet have no means to land on it. We feel tempted to jump overboard and swim. All our boats hang idle on the davits, yet we are not allowed one to land with. Snowy petrels and penguins of all kinds evidently breed there. Captain Larsen of the Jason has landed, and he tells us he found beds of fossils on the beach, shells, and tree trunks. Some of the fossil shells he showed us resembled very large cockles.

Wednesday, 28th.—A cold, dreary day. The N.E. wind is driving the pack about, causing us some uneasiness. It threatens to hem us into the gulf. Whalers, however, make little of such things. They say that once into the ice they never look over their shoulder, and we hang on to this ground, supposing it to be the most likely for whales. There is as much dour patience needed in whaling as in salmon-fishing. There is little choice left us what to do. If we try back the road we

have come, heavy seas and fogs and the swell in the pack await us; land blocks us on the west and south, and to the east the sea is a mass of driving bergs and pack-ice jamming together. We hope the wind will turn round to S.W. again, and give us a chance to get out.

The Jason came up astern to-night, and Bruce went on board to doctor a sailor who is ill. In the evening Captain Larsen came on board, followed later by his 'Steersman' or first mate, and we had a jolly evening in the cabin, smoking and yarning.

We gave them a parting salute on the pipes as their two boats rowed away to the Jason in the early morning.

Thursday, 29th.—Tired of drawing icebergs, and loafed about waiting for seals to come in sight. One has to look pretty sharp to get into one of the two boats at present used for sealing, for whenever they are ordered to be lowered there is a rush of about twice as many men as the boat will hold; at least this is so in the morning. By the afternoon, when most of the crew have been out, there is not the same competition. We soon saw three seals a mile or so to windward, and lowered away. Allan, the Spectioneer (Spec, Dutch for fat or blubber), was Bow, Two and Three were boys, and Braidy, a jolly Irishman, stood at the steer-oar. It was cold work rowing at first, and coats and mits were none too warm for the first mile.

Seal number one was asleep, and allowed Bow to shoot it without moving its head. We were anxious to bring some of these big seals' skins and anatomy home for museums,[1] so we pulled this one into the boat holus-bolus, in the hope that it might be preserved. The difficulty in doing so can be understood when it took ten men with a tackle to haul it on board-ship. With a lot

---

[1] I understand that none of these were brought home. They were destroyed or thrown overboard on the return voyage.

of pulling we managed to get its head into the boat, but there it stuck. Then we lugged it on to the snow again, and this time brought the boat's gunwale to a low ice-edge and rolled the carcass on board over the oar handles—no easy matter, as besides its weight there was the boat to hold in, and the ice-edge was weak and gave way under our weight. This large seal is undoubtedly one of the most

horrid-looking animals. Its huge, lizard-like head and long body reminded me of the prints of antediluvian monsters. This was not one of the largest, but it measured ten feet seven inches from the tip of its nose to end of the hind flippers. Its internal economy, excepting a green fluid, was as empty as a whistle. How these seals sleep so comfortably on the cold snow, on an empty stomach, puzzles us.

The men say that owing to their recent domestic

troubles their appetites have quite gone. This lady had some fresh teeth-marks about her neck and shoulders.

The next seal lay in the middle of a flat pan of snow-ice. On to this ice we jumped, into the blaze of white light that fairly dazed us, the seal's soul went out at a bullet-hole and his skin was off before he stopped jumping. It was a new kind to us—what Allan called a fresh-water seal, for the reason of its resemblance to a seal in the Arctic of that name. It was shorter than the first by two feet, with a thicker body, and had more blubber. Its skin was dappled, with a red brown and yellow-ochre colour along its sides, with dark umber and grey hairs on its back. Its head was short and cat-like. There was a large supply of fish inside it, resembling something between

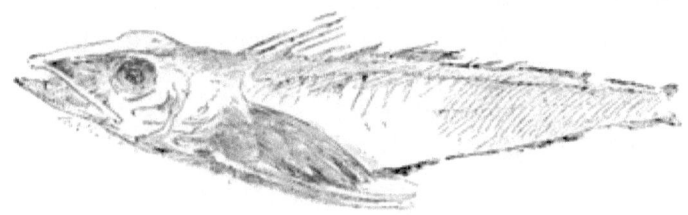

a small whiting and a gurnard. Here is a drawing that I made of one less digested than the others. The smell of these fish was strong! Just as we had pulled his skin into the boat, another seal, a huge fellow of the black kind, put his head above water about a hundred yards off, and, either attracted by the fish or bent on revenge, came down on us, diving and bouncing half out of the water, making a wake like a penny steamer. Two dives brought him within fifty yards of the boat. The next time he bounced up alongside and looked horridly unpleasant; but a bullet through his neck made him vanish instantly.

We got back to the ship after several hours' pulling, with a boat-load of skins, and as tired with lugging at these clumsy oars as if we had rowed all day.

Friday, 30th Dec.—Spent the afternoon in my bunk attempting to paint ice-effects,—shut my ears to all interesting sounds of life on deck. After our midday meal my conscience went to rest and my body needed exercise, so I stood by for the first boat. The doctor has been skinning one of the Emperor penguins; this is a most difficult task, and takes no end of patience. The body is to appear as a goose at New Year's dinner, and its skin will delight the eye of the public in some museum in far-away Scotland. There is a great quantity of muscle on its anatomy, which itself is slight compared with its bulk. Its pectoral muscles alone weighed fourteen pounds; they must surely have other use than working its flippers. I have noticed they have great power in increasing or decreasing their bulk—I expect a good deal of the chest muscle is applied to this.

It would be interesting to know to what depths they dive to find their food. I am inclined to believe that they feed on the soft bottom, and at great depths, from their having a long delicate beak, their enormous structural strength, and by reason of our never seeing them on the surface of the water. When we do see them they are on the snow islands, apparently resting, and these islands are in places where the depth is from ninety to two hundred fathoms.

We found stones and red shrimps inside the penguins; and penguins, red shrimps, and stones inside the seals. May good digestion wait on the grampus that swallows the lot!

About midday one of the boats was ordered off for seals, and five of us scrambled into it and were lowered away. Bonnar weighed down the bow, the Cockney steered, I stroked, and two boys rowed Three and Four. Bonnar is a stout, good-natured, middle-aged Irishman, as round as an egg, with bearded face, a model for a Sancho Panza: one moment he is the picture of fat woe, the next he is shaking all over with infectious, gurgling laughter. All hands enjoy getting away from the ship just now, as the life is made miserable for those left on board by one man. Away in the boats we shake off the gloom and work like niggers, and enjoy life like schoolboys in the country.

Once we have shoved off from the black ship's side and begin to row in and out amongst the ice islands we feel more at home, as if we, as well as the seals and penguins, had a share in this quiet world. Our appearance I am afraid is rather against such a claim—dark worn clothes, soiled with blood, are hardly in keeping with the brilliant opal and amethyst-coloured surroundings. The exercise in the keen, pure air puts us all in good humour, and we get away for a mile or so in splendid whaling form. Then Bonnar gets puffed, so we say, and lets his oar swing in, and stands in the bow and begins to see

R

'swales.' 'Och, mi bhoys,' he says, 'the swales is just all round us, an' thur's wan to windward about a mile an' a half away, an' thur's another away down to leeward. Pull away, mi lads. Shure, an' the old —— has his eye on ye; three more strokes and she's there. An' jist bae so kind as to put her up another point, Mr. Campbell, and kape her so.' And he takes his oar again, much to our relief, as it is only a four-oared boat, and when Bow gets up Three has more than his share of pulling. His remark to Campbell was pointed. Campbell rather prides himself on his steering, for which reason, I suppose, a report got up that he was one day found at the wheel with the Balæna three points off her course. We draw him on this and other subjects as he stands in the stern steering with the long steer-oar. To-day he waxed eloquent about our Christmas dinner, and had an appreciative audience. Campbell, notwithstanding his name, is a thorough Englishman as regards food, and the Christmas dinner was really a painful memory to him. 'Call that duff,' he said, almost with tears, 'woi, that wurn't no duff. Oi've bin at sea for a lorng wile, and I never saw duff like that before. Plum duff, they calls it! 'Oo ever 'eard o' plum duff made with *currints*! Woi, the currints war as separate as King's Crorse and St. Pancras. Oi've been in many a 'ungry ship in mi toime, but s'help me bob, oi never was on a ship w'ere ye didn't 'ave yer grog on a Christmas daiy.'

We all jumped on to the snow when we reached the ice-piece where the seal was lying absorbing the sun, and Bonnar slowly laboured through the snow, bent double, as if he were stalking an educated seal of the north. Bonnar has been so long at the Newfoundland sealing that he deems this style of approach necessary here; we try to chaff him out of it without success.

The seal was one of the large whity-yellow fellows with small, dog-like head and grand black eyes. I made a jotting of the men flinching him; as a piece of colour the effect was gorgeous—masses of scarlet, dazzling white, and the blue sea. The snuffling of the seal, and the sound of the blood spouting and fizzling into the snow, with the crisp sound of the steel in the quivering flesh was hardly nice, and when the red carcase sat up and looked at itself, I looked up to see if God's eye was looking.

Just as Bonnar and Campbell were going to heave the skin into the boat with one great lift, the edge of the ice broke, and they both went into the water. They clutched at the snow ledge and the gunwale of the boat, and we pulled them out. Campbell had to come out over the top of the gory blubber, and looked a sorry spectacle, as he dripped on the snow. He didn't 'moind the wettin''; what he objected to was 'the bloomin' blood all over his bloomin' clothes.' What difference it made I could not see, as we had been up to the eyes in gore for weeks past.

We only picked up a few seals, and had a great deal of rowing, and got back to the ship with appetites that made the black penguin mess delicious.

The skipper is on board the Jason to-night, and she is lying about a mile or two to windward. In the evening we had a great function on board. All the way out there has been a talk of burning some one's effigy, but nothing came of it till to-night.

We, the doctor and I and the skipper's son, were luxuriating before the cabin-stove, reading and brewing coffee, enjoying a well-earned repose, when two men came aft, and asked me in a mysterious way if I would come down the 'tween-decks, and bring my sketch-book and bagpipes; they wanted to have a portrait taken. I followed them down the main-hatch into the dusk of the 'tween-decks, and there I saw a ghastly spectacle. A man's figure hung by the neck from one of the beams. His eyes were real seal's eyes, pinned on to a canvas face, his nose was made of wood, and he wore spectacles, and a goatee beard. Some one had supplied a very ancient dungaree suit, and this was stuffed with shavings and rope-ends. The whole figure bore a ghastly resemblance to one of our company. Braidy supported him on one side, for his legs were weak, whilst Harvey added a few finishing touches to his face with the ship's paint. When they had finished him and made him as hideous as they possibly could, I was asked to draw his portrait. I have served my time at that trade, and have drawn many types; but, bar one, this was the ugliest of all my sitters, and, though I say it as shouldn't, my representation of their handiwork gave the greatest satisfaction. After the portrait was done, a procession was formed, Braidy led it, and played a wheezy march on the melodeon, the cook played the pipes, and Mason and Harvey supported the figure. All the rest of the crew followed in couples arm-in-arm, enjoying the fun like children. They marched round the deck till they came to the mate's cabin, under the break of the poop, and there the mate passed sentence of death on the unfortunate effigy, by hanging at the yard-arm. It was then marched round the deck once more, very solemnly and slowly, Peter trying hard to play 'Lochaber no more,' and Braidy squeezing out something like a funeral march. Under the fore-yard a running bow-line was drawn round the figure's neck, and a match put to a fuse at the foot of his trousers, and it was hauled up to the yard-arm to slow music, and the tune of 'Give

us some time to blow the man down,' sung slowly and with much feeling.

It looked gruesome and real, and the great goggle eyes glared down at us with a horrible expression. To and fro it swung at the yard-arm, with a thin thread of smoke waving from its foot against the white frosty sky. It was then riddled with Henry bullets, and each bullet as it pierced the corpse tore away pieces of rags and stuffing, which fell and floated smoking on the glassy sea. Finally, when the remains were all ablaze, and nearly consumed, a hand lay out on the yard, cut the line, and the figure fell into the water with a fizz.

We caught an Emperor penguin this evening. I was on deck enjoying the quiet and beauty of the white night when we saw it. The decks are quiet through the night watches; the crew walk quietly, and talk in hushed voices, partly subdued by the queer, still feeling round us, and partly from the reason that if they did make a noise, the watch below would turn out to know the reason why. Just as I was going to turn in, I spotted him on a piece of snow within two or three hundred yards. I was anxious to make a drawing from an Emperor penguin, so went aft, and let the mate know, and he ordered away a boat. The penguin was standing in the middle of a round pan of snow-ice about fifty yards in diameter, with a hummock at one side. We rowed up to this and put two men behind the hummock, and then rowed round to the other side, where three of us landed and spread out. Then we all five advanced, closing in with the penguin as centre of our circle. He got upon a mound of snow as we approached, and only looked slightly anxious as we drew in; then, evidently thinking that his position was dangerous, he tried to get away. He slid down the mound of snow on his breast, puddling away with his flippers and feet. One of our party made a successful rush over a hard piece of snow in pursuit, and fell on the bird and embraced it, and the penguin looked quite shocked, and threw him off with a sort of hitch with its shoulders; then it got up and stood on its feet again, and looked at us calmly as we struggled after it through the soft snow. When we got near it again, five of us made a rush at it, and the bo'sun got in first, and scragged it with both hands round its neck. The two rolled over together on the snow, and the penguin freed its neck and began to let drive with its beak at the bo'sun's head, but missed, fortunately. It had no chance, however; we fell on it altogether and made it 'have down.' Its strength astonished us. One man held its neck, other two got hold of a flipper a-piece, and two others held the legs.

With all our strength we could scarcely keep hold of it; and yet it did not seem to be in the least flurried, or put out—merely moved its flippers slowly, and drew up and extended its short legs, but that nearly twisted our arms off. It was too difficult to carry it to the boat this way, so we strapped him round the middle, with his flippers down by his side. We used the bo'sun's belt—a broad affair with a big brass buckle, and hauled till the penguin collapsed like a Gladstone bag. Then we made another belt fast round his short legs, and stood up and drew a breath of relief, and so did the penguin—a long sigh from the bottom of its chest, and the buckle burst, and it got up and hobbled away with the belt still round its legs; it actually hobbled with dignity. Then we all sat on it again without any ceremony, for we were angry—the penguin remained calmly dignified—and fastened him up with some fathoms of whale-line that happened to be in the boat, lashed him from his bill to his toes all the way down, with marline hitches, like a roll of beef, and carried him to the boat and dropped him in the line-chest. There he freed one flipper just to show what he could do if he tried, but made no other effort to escape. On deck the penguin preserved his sphinx-like dignity under very novel and trying circumstances. All the men stood round him, and marvelled at his strange, bulky form; but he did not take the least notice and there was a strange, far-away look in his little black eye, as if he saw right back to the days when these white shores were clad with the verdure of the tropics and there were no glaciers on the black rocks. Fanny, the ship's dog, tried to have a game with it—a most absurd idea! She danced round the penguin, bounced against it, and vainly tried to tumble it over. At first the penguin merely kept the dog off with its flippers, hitting round-arm blows with them so quickly that the movements were scarcely visible, and puzzled Fanny as to what the game was; then Fanny came too close, and the emperor's pencil-like beak went out with a flash and strength that would have punched holes in a steel plate, and off went Fanny in no end of a hurry, and never came near again, but walked round and round the deck as far away as the bulwarks would allow her.

It was thought the penguin would be in our way on

deck, or we would find ourselves in its way, which would have been worse, so it was condemned to death. It took four hours to kill it, 'and it wasn't dead then,' as some one remarked. It had holes driven through its skull, it was beaten with clubs, and it would not die. Then out of pity the doctor was called to put it out of pain. He sat on its back with confidence and worked at its brain, till it lay on the deck apparently lifeless. When we saw it two hours afterwards, it was waddling about with its head in the air as if it had neuralgia.

An Emperor Penguin Chase.

If they take such a very long time to die, they surely must have a very long time to live. They certainly look with their calm air of all-knowingness as if they were born long ages before man ever drew breath. We tried to eat these large penguins, but their flesh, even when cooked with strong curry, had a very unpleasant taste, rather like seal's flesh, both in taste and colour, but

I daresay, if one had to put in a winter here, that a taste for them might be developed.

... You can loaf in the Antarctic when the sun shines, just as well as at home, and you can loaf longer, for the sun does not set, neither does the dew fall and make you uncomfortable at night. I loafed all day, shamelessly, in the maintop, enjoying life to its full. From the ship's deck you have quite a limited view of the ice-floes; when you climb up the rigging it spreads and extends till the canals of open water, running in and out among the ice islands like purple veins, seem to grow narrower and narrower till at last they are lost in the distance, and the ice on the horizon seems to form a solid field.

The sea between the islands is of the most delicate warm lilac colour, and as smooth as crystal, excepting where faint cats'-paws tint the water with a darker violet. The scene is so utterly quiet and beautiful that it is perfect bliss to sit and look, and inhale the pure, sunny air.

To the west we have a clear view of the land, and see several unnamed islands. The Jason is keeping us company just now; she is a mile or two to the south, steering in and out amongst the ice. At times her black hull is hidden by the white blocks, then we see her all perfectly reflected. Her boats, like water-spiders, are flitting up and down the water lanes; one of them stops against an ice island, and the black spider divides into several black dots that go straggling over the snow, and a distant pop, popping of rifles tells of the death of seals.

The air is so intensely still that up here in the maintop

I can hear the mate's clock in his cabin ticking the seconds; the sound must travel up the taut shrouds and backstays. On deck, two or three men are sauntering up and down, their hands deep in their pockets, and high above me I see the bottom of the crow's-nest, and over its edge the telescope, ever on the watch for seals. I think we have killed about seventy-five seals to-night; but the great black whale we came for has not yet put in an appearance. Finners there are in any number—they all show the annoying fin on their backs, and none of them lie on the water's surface after the manner of the right whale.

A number of grampus were seen to-day; and we think that they are perhaps keeping the right whales far inside the ice, as they do in the north, where the whales will rather drown under the floes than venture into the neighbourhood of their deadly enemy.

A school of these sea pirates came swimming down on us from the northwards, their gaff-topsails, as Jack calls their dorsal fins, showing high above the water. Whales and penguins fled before them, the penguins leaping like shoals of mackerel, and the finners blowing along in great fright.  The penguins got on to the first ice they met, for safety, and toddled into the centre as fast as their little legs would carry them. Two of the finners passed under us; one put his black back out of water under our counter—I could have dropped on his back—

and the other went waggling below our keel. It was an uncanny-looking beast, down in the dark water, huge and long, of a greenish white colour; it was fully thirty yards long.

To-day we found another black seal full of fish and penguins. It is a wonder these penguins continue to exist with such powerful and numerous enemies. A few sheathbill came about the ship to-night; they seem to move about in the evening more than in the day, though we see them at all hours.

It is a strange sight to see such pretty white birds feeding on raw, bloody flesh. I have been told by the men that they had seen some with red breasts; but I rather think the red must have been caused by the blood of the seals. We often see them standing on the snow beside living seals. Fresh meat must surely be quite an exceptional diet with them.

This has been the most dismal New Year's Eve that I trust any of our ship's company have spent or ever will spend, but to go into the cause of the gloom would be here too long a matter.

CHAPTER XVII

SUNDAY, 1st Jan. 1893.—Of all the hypocritical, canting humbugs in the wide world the Lowland Scotch sectarian is out and away the worst. The bigotry without the justice of his covenanting forebears has surely come down to him wi' muckle aggrandisement. Would any one who knows what a Sunday in Dundee means, believe that a crew from that godly, radical town would be ordered to put aside the laws of God to work at seal-ing on the Sabbath day? Yet so it is, and we are told that for this Old Testament law-breaking we have the sanction of a worthy Presbyterian minister. Killing seals is to-day 'a wark o' na-cesseety,' and the crew who have been killing seals all week, day and night, are sent off dog-tired to paint the snow vermilion.

Though sealing is 'a wark o' nacesseety,' bawbees being gained thereby, 'drawing picturrs on the Lord's

Day o' Rest is an awfie-like thing!' This I am told very clearly and explicitly, and have to do reverence to the Creator's works by painting from memory in the privacy of my bunk, as represented in the sketch, cursing at the same time the length of my legs and the interference with the purest form of worship.

We steamed from Erebus and Terror Bay N.E. with a strong current from the N.E., that swung the ice along at four miles an hour. It was jammed together at one time, then drifted out in long streams, whirling past us round bergs, piled piece over piece. We have had thumping and crushing enough to crack the nether millstone, yet the boats were sent out sealing, though the Balæna could scarcely make her own way. How the men cursed! Just as one of the boats had managed to come up astern, some ragged snow islands of all sizes swept together and enclosed it. We thought to see her nipped

into nothing, but the crew jumped on to the ice and hauled her into a little space between the white teeth before they closed, where the boat was safe, though she could not get out. We left them there, as it was difficult enough to get the ship out of the jam, and by and bye the ice opened a little, and the black spot of struggling figures, by dint of much poling and shoving, made its escape and rowed up astern and got hold of a tow-line, and we steamed out of the swirling currents.

About six P.M. we were again in the neighbourhood of the Danger Islands. Before coming to them we had a good view of the high mountains in Louis Philippe Land; they seemed to me nearly as high as Mount Haddington, with sharp peaks and some small patches of black rock showing through the coating of glaciers. These were hidden by mist when we sailed south. As they are not put down by Ross in his chart, I suppose we are the first who have ever seen them. I made a drawing of them as they appeared— dull yellow against a clear band of primrose sky above them, a canopy of ridged grey clouds just touching one of the peaks. Their outlines reminded me of the peaks in Arran.

As we neared and passed Cape Fitzroy, I saw what I take to be the pillar that Sir James Ross called D'Urville's monument, after the French navigator. It resembled a lighthouse covered with snow, and rose from the sloping S.W. shore of Joinville Land; it was hidden by the high land on the south point of Joinville Land as we steamed north; I should think it was a little under a hundred feet high. I may say, however, that guessing heights and distances in these latitudes across water is more difficult here, owing to the atmospheric effects, than it is at home. I certainly would never have thought that Mount Haddington, which Ross puts down at 7050 feet, was nearly so high.

In his chart, Ross shows no island at the south end of Joinville Land where D'Urville marked an isle 'supposée.' He thought D'Urville had seen this point only and not the low land round it, and so assumed that there was an island. Ross finding, as he thought, D'Urville in error, gallantly named the pinnacle D'Urville's monument, 'in memory of that enterprising navigator.' But Captain Robertson of the Active, by sailing round this land, has proved the 'Isle Supposée' does exist; probably the Firth, called Firth of Tay by Captain Robertson, was filled with bergs when Ross passed, and so he would have no idea there was an island here.

In the evening we were about nine miles N.E. of the most southerly of the Danger islets. Here we were on comparatively open water, with only scattered pieces of pack-ice, and the bergs were few and low. These bergs, about fifty and eighty feet above water, had apparently come off the coast opposite us.

All night we steered about E. by N. At midnight we passed a small dome-shaped ice island, sea-washed and very slippery, with a regiment of penguins standing at attention on the top of it. As our game larder needed replenishing, we dropped a boat with two guns, and shot down the regiment. It was a very sad sight to see the poor beasts shot down; they had not the least idea how to escape this unfamiliar danger. Even when they were wounded and fell down the slippery ice-banks into the water, they immediately struggled to get on to the ice again to join their companions. The jumps they give out of the water are astonishingly high; three feet seems to be an easy jump, but I have often seen them fail at higher attempts.

At the same time I shot a tern of a kind that I have not seen elsewhere; but, much to my regret, there was no time to pick it up. I also shot two sheathbills that were either with the penguins at first, or came and joined the battle; they fed on the blood as we shot the penguins. These are the only land animals known to exist in the Antarctic; close at hand their dove-like characteristics disappear, and the flesh-eating character shows itself. They are about the size of a bantam hen, with grey-coloured, strong legs, and feet something like a hen's or an oyster-catcher's; the bill is deep, sharp-pointed, curved above and below, and strong, the colour, grey-green, and yellow. Over its base there is a sort of sheath that gives the bird its name; round the base of the sheath and round its beady black eye there is a whity-pink coloured wattle, something like that of a carrier-pigeon's. They have a bony excrescence at the joint of their wings that corresponds to the wrist. On skinning them I was astonished at the strength of their bones and muscles, and especially at the very small amount of fat and feathering they have to protect them from the cold. A common wood-pigeon has more feathers on it.

Monday, 2nd Jan.—Kept steaming along the pack-edge E. by N. all night, picking up seals. This morning they were very numerous—ten, twelve, and twenty on a piece; the men just walked in amongst them, tapped them on the back with the muzzle of their rifle until they lifted their heads and received the bullet.

We have found it necessary to take the whale-lines out of the boats; and now all the whaling-boats are working amongst the seals. They are constantly going off the ship and coming back gunwale deep with seal-skins and blubber.

Tuesday, 3rd.—Seals lying all round; the crew working like niggers! Every skin means the fraction of a farthing into their pockets, therefore they sweat at their oars and slash at the skins, half blind with blood, with the blaze of white light, and fatigue. Many of the seals are diseased, they have festering sores under the flippers and other parts. The men's hands are constantly being cut, and some of these cuts fester, probably with the matter from the sores. But we aft have not suffered, though cut often enough; the difference in our diets may account for this. The men call their sores 'pusey' fingers.

This afternoon the doctor and I worked the steam winch

for a change. As the boats come alongside we heave over some long strops into the boats. The men in the boat run these rope rings through the holes in the skins, where the flippers have been—the arm-holes of the seal's waist-coats, as it were—then both ends of the strop are looped over a hook that is fast to a line that runs through a block above the main-hatch and comes down to the drum of the winch at the foot of the mainmast. When the men in the boat shout, he at the winch lets steam on, and up comes the bunch of bloody skins which are flopped down on the main-deck; the second hand on deck then unhooks the strop, hauls it out of the seal-skins, runs to the bulwarks with it, and drops it over into the boat along with the line and hook. Done against time this means plenty of exercise: as the pile of skins rises higher and higher, the second man has to stumble up and down the heap of sliding skins to get hold of the strops. To-night the decks are piled some five feet high with skins.

Wednesday, 4th.—Just as we were beginning breakfast this morning, a hand came down the after-hatch and whispered with an awe-struck voice: 'There's a whale *lying* alongside, sir.' Whalers are only accustomed to see the Bowhead lying on the water, so you can imagine the excitement! Up the hatch every one went hatless into the wind and snow, and stared from the stern at the great beast's back. There it was *lying*, sure enough, with the dark ripple lapping against it; but there was an unmistakable spinal ridge down its back that the right whale does not have. It was just the colour and shape of an enormous elephant's back. After lying quite still for some time, it rolled over and showed a very small fin not far from his tail.

We wonder if Sir James Ross mistook these whales for the Bowhead; with his great experience in the Arctic we scarcely think it likely, and hold to the belief that he was right, and that the £3000 whale, with its round smooth black back, is still here could we but find it.

It is cold and damp, and the seals stay below water, so we have time to make off the blubber from the seal-skins on deck. Making off is the term for cutting the blubber from the skin. I daresay the drawing I have made shows how it is done better than my writing.

It is a busy scene that goes on all day on deck. Immediately after meals all hands turn up on deck with their pipes going; they are muffled up with cravats, and have their collars turned up and the ear-flaps of their caps pulled down. Then all get their knives out of their wooden sheaths, and there is a great rustling as they whet them on their steels, and every one sets to work. The old hands stand behind upright boards on which the seal-skins are hung, half on each side of the board, blubber side up. They cut from left to right, with a crisp, greasy, swish-swish at each sweep of the thin flat blade. The blubber curls off in yellow folds, and falls on deck, and a boy throws it with a small pitch-fork into the tanks. Other boys prepare the skins for the old hands; they catch the lumps of flesh that have been left on the blubber in the hasty skinning on the snow with a steel hook and cut it off. At first there is plenty of talk, and jests fly about, then gradually the talk quiets down, and there is little sound but the breathing of the knives and the clang of the blubber falling into the metal tanks.

... The men are very tired. Days of constant work with poor food, hastily swallowed, has told on them sadly—their faces are drawn and their eyes blood-shot;

they are tired, but they work away cheerily. They will have a share in the profits! Such a share, enough to keep one in cigarettes for a month. They don't like this work on deck so well as being out in the boats— they feel the cold more. Several of them are filled with rheumatism, and most have festering hands, and many have scanty clothing.

Each group of lads tries to make ready more skins than the neighbouring group, and the man at the board vies with the man next him in the number of skins he makes off. It is tedious, back-breaking, profitless work all this, and it astonishes me to see men take it all so easily. Is it not a fortunate thing for society that so much contentment comes with hard work?

To-night Mr. Adams and I went off with a crew in a four-oar Norwegian boat, belonging to the Jason, that was hanging astern, and picked up an unusually large white seal, one of the kind that we have killed so many of lately. There was something especially grand about this particular seal. He lay resting on a bank of low-toned snow, and behind him a purple black cloud formed a background, dark and soft as a velvet curtain. When we were within twenty yards he raised his head and shoulders above the snow-bank and looked down on us with calm wonder in his courageous black eyes. Near him was a family of penguins, with their backs toward us, taking not the least notice of our approach. The black lips, eyes, and nostrils of the seal, and the blue-black of the penguins' backs, were the black touches in this perfect picture of primeval peace. . . . Up went the rifle—crack—and the bullet entered the beautiful dog-like face, and the picture was ripped up.

How mean and ugly we of the world of people feel in this lovely world of white beauty, making bullets sing through the cold, silent air, fouling the snow with blood and soot. . . . All the majesty and beauty of the seal has gone; it is only pitiful now, lying on its back, its nostrils wide and quivering, its dark ox-like eyes trembling in agony as the knife tears down its white skin. Up and down slashes the merciless steel, between the hot black flesh and the yellow blubber, blood pours gurgling from the severed arteries and spirts in fine red spray at every cut, steaming in the frosty air. The poor stupid family of

penguins waddle away, looking over their shoulders at us, wondering what the deuce it all means.

Thursday, 5th Jan.—Another day of mist, soft as thistle-down. The ice looms faint and grey, a light wind comes from the north, and a few snow-flakes are falling, settling in the frozen folds of the grey sails. Icicles are formed on the black shrouds and stays, and fall at times, clashing on deck. There is no use keeping a look-out for seals from the crow's-nest to-day—the fog up there is thicker than on deck. So the Mjolnar[1] is allowed to drift south with the ice and snow, her head pointing east and her wheel lashed. Occasionally we steam up wind or ahead to clear ice. Tall bergs show faint and ghost-like through the mist to leeward.

I saw the Jason close alongside one of these bergs, and its height was fully twice that of her masts.

All hands are working hard at making off, and the pile of skins is reduced to a few feet high; the object is to get the decks cleared against the next sunny day, when the seals will come on to the ice to bask.

I am surprised there are so few birds about us, when

---

[1] Mjolnar is the name on our counter now. The Atlantic waves rubbed off the painted name Balæna, and washed the plaster of Paris out of the carving of our vessel's old name, so we are Thor's Hammer once again.

there is so much seals' flesh being constantly thrown over the side. Only a few Cape pigeons fly round us, picking up the scraps. One or two terns have passed, and a white bird, slightly bigger than a sheathbill, with black speckles on its back, is gorging on the seals' cran as it is thrown overboard. Only naturalists can appreciate how intensely aggravating it is to have these strange birds so near and yet to be unable to identify them for want of a boat. We greatly regret not having brought a Berthon boat for such purpose. Dr. Donald thought of this at

the Falklands, but the price of anything there that will float is prohibitive. A punt scarcely worth £3 on the Clyde was offered for £15.

Sunday, 8th Jan.—Went sealing in the Spectioneer's boat yesterday. What a glorious day we spent away from the ship in the dazzling white sunlight. Our first care in the morning was to see that the biscuit-keg and the water-breaker were full. Each boat has a keg, filled with biscuits and a piece of cheese, only to be opened in case of emergencies. We pulled away from the ship about 8 A.M. Allan rowed bow and told tales, as he pulled, with pawky

Scotch humour and the high Peterhead voice. Braidy steered, and bubbled over with Irish fun all the time, encouraging his crew to lay out. The warm sun had brought the seals up in numbers. We killed about thirty on one piece of ice. Hard and hot work it was flinching them and dragging their skins over the waist-deep snow.

By twelve o'clock we were down to the gunwale with skins and as hungry as hawks—a case of '*heros peut-être*

A Chip off an Antarctic Berg.

mais les ventres avant tout,' and the ship-biscuit that we could scarcely break at breakfast melted between our teeth, and how deliciously sweet the half frozen water tasted, sucked out of the bunghole of the breaker!

Several times we were jammed in the ice, and once the boat was nearly smashed up; as it was, the gunwales were squeezed in till they looked as if they would take the shape of a figure 8. We had been trying to get at three seals that lay on the top of an overhanging ledge of snow, and as we were struggling to climb on to this, the floe came up from behind and hemmed us in. The tongues of ice that project under water from the cakes overlapped each other, and we found ourselves squeezed out of the water. After about an hour's struggling the floe opened a little, and we at last managed to get out of the hole by dint of much shoving and pulling, and got away minus some rollock-pins plus a deck cargo of loaf-sugar snow.

A great number of whales were blowing in every direction, filling the air with the sound of sighing. All round the horizon the jets of steam puffed up from behind the white islands and hung in the air more like whiffs of cigarette smoke than the ponderous spouts you see in whaling pictures. Sometimes the black backs rolled so close as to threaten us with a capsize, and we had to put bullets into them to keep them off. By two o'clock we had sixty-five skins in the boat, and the water was lapping over the gunwale. As the ship seemed to have no intention of coming to us we had to go to it, and having so many skins on board we had to sit tailorwise on the top of them—an uncommonly awkward position to row in. After about two hours' pulling we came alongside and clambered on board by the chain-plates, and some of the men who had got back to the ship before us, and had swallowed their dinner, came into our boat and discharged the skins for us. About five minutes after, as it seemed to me, Allan came aft, and lost his good opinion of me when I absolutely refused to leave my penguin stew: not having even a fractional interest in the proceeds of the voyage, it seemed to me advisable to do a little drawing when life was possible on board ship. But my good intentions came to nothing: the other boats began coming in with their second loads, and with hungry, tired crews, and as all hands were working in the boats or laid up, Nick and I had to string the skins on to the strops whilst our scientific friend spent his time working the winch ; it was 8 P.M. by the time the last boat was emptied and hauled up on the davits, and I again turned my attention from blubber to æsthetics.

The evening was marvellously beautiful. North of us the floating ice was reflected in a calm grey sea ; each island delicately tinted with rose. In the south the sea was crossed and patched with ice streams and islands which showed purple against the reflected gold of the evening sky. Before bringing out paints I lit my pipe in my kennel and sat down, sea-boots, wet clothes, and all—just for three or four whiffs, and less than forty winks, and never moved an inch till I opened my eyes and heard Nick knocking and saying, ' Breakfast 's on the table, sir.'

Sunday, 15th January.—Heavy fog to-day, so there is no sealing. The crews are having a change of work; they are now busy clearing the coals out of the tanks to make room for blubber. Whales are sighing round us ; they seem to go in couples, and rise and breathe almost together, each making one half of a huge, weary, melancholy sigh, with about half a note between the two. We can only see the ice a few yards from the ship. Sometimes we can make out the penguins' black backs, whilst the snow beneath them is indistinguishable from the mist.

Monday.—Still wrapped in mist. . . . One of the boats is lost. The mist lifted a little, and some seals were seen and a boat sent off. It fell immediately, and we lost sight of the boat. For a time we heard the shots, and then they seemed utterly lost. . . . We keep the fog-horn booming its muffled note every two or three minutes. It seems hopeless to send sound through these misty walls. In the silence that follows, the white petrels flitting past us seem more silent and moth-like than usual.

Towards evening the thermometer went up to 35°, the highest point it has reached since we entered the ice. Later a faint air came from the south and soon brought it down below freezing again. As the cold air lifted the mist it showed us the foot of a berg a few hundred yards from us, its blue and grey sides wrinkled and puckered into many folds of pale blue and white. The lift in the mist helped us to pick up the boat.

The Polar Star has turned up at last. We thought she had turned back or foundered. As the mist rose she appeared on the pack-edge threading her way towards us under sail through the loose ice. We hauled up our ensign and steamed towards her, playing on the pipes, as is our wont here on great occasions. As she came alongside there was much cheering. Most of our men have acquaintances on board, and some have brothers. She left Dundee two days after us and went down the English Channel and escaped all the bad weather we started with. The master is Captain Davidson, called by the crew Polar Davidson, to distinguish him from—the other—Davidson of the Diana.

To-night the skins are being salted and rolled up and stowed away in the fore-peak—a mightily strong place, a labyrinth of huge beams and knees which support the ship to stand the shock of running into ice.

Tuesday, 10th.—The first good southerly breeze we have had since we made the ice; the light air we had last night from the S.E. has risen to a strong wind. Though it is blowing hard, the ice to the south shelters us and keeps the water so smooth that we scarcely roll enough to spill a glass of water. I made a picture this morning of the Active beside a large berg—a grounded berg, I believe.[1]

5 P.M.—Strong wind S. by W., yet the thermometer is at $33\frac{1}{2}°$. I should have thought a southerly wind here would be certainly very cold. The short, choppy waves are wearing away the edges of the ice-pans, and the sea is littered with the small pieces of ice that break off.

We are steaming S.W. to-night through the pack so as to get back to Erebus Gulf from the south and so avoid the strong currents about Danger Islands. It is most aggravating beating like this about the same ground. Unfortunately our instructions are to hunt for whales where Ross saw them, instead of far and wide, as I had hoped,

---

[1] The reader must draw on his fancy for the colouring: the clouds soft warm grey, the crags of the berg to the right a purple lead colour, the slope dull white; the berg to the left pale violet, with two or three upright clefts of deep blue, along the top an edge of pure white; between the bergs a third appears light emerald green. The floating ice in front, some parts creamy-white, like broken marrons, others dead marble-white, and two or three of vivid sky-blue, frosted with white; the sea an umber colour, with lavender sheen.

and to these instructions we attend almost to the letter; there may be whales within fifty miles, but we may not go in search of them. This southerly wind must be opening the pack far south, and I believe that were we to head in the direction of Weddell's track, which was a little to the east of us, we could reach far farther south than he ventured with his small, unprotected, sailing ship. He passed through a belt of pack-ice and bergs in the Sixties

and reached lat. 74°S., and found the air was as warm there as in 64°, also innumerable blue petrels and a sea free of ice!

9 P.M.—The wind is blowing up the mist from the southern horizon, leaving a long band of yellow under the canopy of grey. The rigging is freezing as hard as iron.

Wednesday, 11th.—A most beautiful morning—the air clear as crystal, sky pale blue, bordered and ribbed with soft grey clouds. The sea's surface is a pale, pinky violet. In the west we see Mount Haddington for the second time, but viewed from a more southerly point than before. For a few hours I kept myself at work sketching below in my bunk, then gave in to the temptation to merely enjoy nature without caricaturing her. I climbed up to the crow's-nest and enjoyed the view of wild rocks and black cliffs and glaciers. The land lay distant about eight miles, but the cliffs and snow slopes were so large and the air so clear that they seemed much closer. The Active lay underneath the mountain, close to the reddish-coloured rocky islands that lie to the south of the entrance to Admiralty Inlet ; she had stayed here waiting for whales whilst we were sealing. The view of these dark cliffs, each topped with its white ice cap, towering terrace above terrace till they disappeared in the overhanging clouds, was grand in the extreme. Feathery soft clouds hung like smoke on the black faces, and blew up the wild white gorges in fantastic swirls. The clouds hid the crags at about 4000 feet, but beneath them we could see part of the snow slope leading up to the greatest height.

We see the land stretching for some thirty miles to the S.W., low and undulating, covered with a white sheet of snow, with only two table-topped crags jutting out of the whiteness. This seems to extend some fifty miles, and sweeps into the sea in a very gradual slope, and then must sweep round to the west, giving me the impression that there is a deep inlet running west, or a strait into Hughes Bay. Farther to the S.E. a stretch of unbroken smooth ice extends some twenty miles in an easterly direction, with a fall of some thirty feet at its edge—the field-ice, probably, that Ross saw; but beyond it to the S.E. I can see open water.[1]

We have just had a glimpse of this land never seen by man, and now we are turning back again. Is it possible to conceive anything more heart-breaking? From what we see here, and before us, we feel confident we could sail S.E., or S. by E., without the least difficulty. The ice we have come through seems closer than that which lies before us. I think this ice that we have been in lately forms a long tail or stream of floes and bergs in the lee of Trinity, Joinville Land, and the South Shetlands, collected by currents through Bransfield Straits and the prevailing south-westerly winds and the currents from the South of Trinity Land. Once through this pack ice we could make the open water Weddell found to the east. This ice we are in just now, which barred the progress of Ross's sailing vessels, is no obstacle to us with our auxiliary steam power.

Is it not incomprehensible why so much interest has been shown in Arctic exploration, where all the difficulties of making progress are well known, where scientific questions are practically exhausted, whilst no general interest is taken in these Antarctic regions, where there are no difficulties known in the way of discovery, and the answers to the magnetic, meteorological, and geographical questions of the day are to be read by the first explorers?

Would that I owned this ship and this good crew even for three summer months in the Antarctic. Just such a

---
[1] The bearings in this paragraph are not from compass.

vessel as this could be chartered and fitted out with men, scientists, provisions, and all necessaries for a year's exploration for about £5000. If monetary profit was to be considered, 5 per cent. might be reasonably expected for seal skins and oil, and of course there is the chance of meeting Bowheads worth £3000 a piece. One vessel, or two in consort, could chart the whole of the unknown Southern Continent. Think of this, ye rich who dream of knighthood and more riches! For £10,000 this chance is going, cheap, I call it—a chance to write your names in Big Type on the maps of the world. Think of this, ye gentlemen of England who yacht at Cowes in case, the chance is going—going; and if you don't bid for the South Pole, some bold Yankee and his fair lady will be down there before you get under way, and then—there will be no new place under the sun!

There is a proposal at present to send a Government expedition—a great idea, let us all assist to promote it! But if, as has happened before, Government is laggard, let private effort come to its place in the front. Surely we have wealth enough and men enough. What is wanted is a man to put the two together.[1]

 . . . We make a party of four to-day in the ice. The

---

[1] If any one who reads this feels inclined to send or take such an expedition, I will be very glad to look out for one or two well-protected barques. I know of just the right sort of man for master, and a first-rate Scotch crew could be picked up easily. Practical young scientists of the newest school are waiting the chance. I have given a large estimate—a less expensive expedition might do great things and make profit. As this goes into print, I hear a Norwegian whaler is reported to have seen a Bowhead, or right whale, in the Antarctic.

Jason is lying alongside, the Diana has joined us, and the Polar Star came up from the south under canvas, sailing in and out amongst the ice, her topsails showing dark against the white sky; she has such small engines that she has generally to carry some sail. The Active has not come to the meeting; but the Diana's crew gave us an account of her doings in the early part of this day. For reasons unknown, one of her boats made fast to one of those whales that have been constantly blowing round us; probably the harpooneer was tired of waiting for the right whale, and felt that he must kill something, so let drive at the nearest finner. The result was that the whale went off in a bee-line with the three lines in the boat; a second boat followed and made fast, and again the whale made off, with three more lines, that is, with 720 fathoms in all, or 1440 yards of two-inch rope trailing behind it—beats salmon-fishing, doesn't it? To save the first lines a third boat fired another harpoon into the whale, and this time the line was brought on board ship; and the ends of the other two lines were also picked up and brought on board, and away went the procession in tow of the whale, the three boats hanging astern! It must have been a beautiful sight! The whale towed them along at a good rate, and rockets were fired into it whenever there was a chance, but it only showed its nether end above water, so their effect was only to make it go faster. After fourteen hours' play the engines were reversed and the lines broke, and the whale went away 'with half Jock Tod's smithy shop in its tail.' This is the account given by the crew of the Diana; possibly the men of the Active would give a more graphic description. We were also told that the whale towed the Active on a sunken rock; but whether this happened actually in the pursuit or after the battle is not clear.

The four masters are on board now, and have come to the conclusion that we must make the best of a bad business, fill up with oil and seal-skins, and call for salt to preserve the skins at Monte Video or some other port, then up stick and away home.

I think that almost every one in the fleet still believes that Sir James Ross could not have been mistaken about seeing right whales here, though, unfortunately, we have not had such luck; and I think every one feels that it would have been as well to stop at home as to come out here and potter about in one spot waiting for the whales to come alongside. Of course the masters of the vessels are not responsible for the half measures. They would undoubtedly hunt far and wide if the instructions from home did not bind them down to one quarter.

I must jump over some days in my journal, as my daily notes seem all so much alike that the reading of them must be tedious. Not that any two days here are alike —far from it. Each has its own strange effects: solemn, heavy, misty days,—bright days when the sun blazes down on us, tanning us red-brick, quite a different colour from the mahogany-brown of the tropical tan—cold, windy days, with the wind humming through the frozen shrouds, when we hug the lee of a pack or iceberg and think of home, and fires, and warm rooms. The changes come very rapidly. Whenever the wind goes to the north it brings down thick fog and wet snow. We seem to be just south of a belt of stormy cloud and mist which we can see hanging over the ice-edge to the north, ready to sweep down on us. The wind that comes from the south brings clear, bracing weather, cold, but pleasant and invigorating, with very little snow, and that fine and dust-like. I feel sure that if we were farther into the ice we should find the climate healthier.

We have had a good deal of sickness on board lately, partly owing to the sudden changes of temperature, and partly to the constant exposure and hard work. I think

Lost in the Fog.

every one on board has been knocked up. The common complaint is an extremely painful griping in the stomach, coming on very suddenly—a sort of dysentery; some of the men have been very much pulled down with it.

Saturday, 21st January.—This was a day full of particularly fine effects, with mist hanging over the ice like a muslin veil, the sun shining through, lighting the blue feet of the bergs and the packed ice with many tints. The Jason and our barque pushed their way through the pack, sometimes within a few hundred yards of each other, their boats skirmishing on either flank. From the boats the effects of the dark ships coming looming out of the mist with their tall spars and rigging lost in the thickness aloft, and the vague figures of the men appearing and disappearing in the fog on the ice islands was beautiful in the extreme.

In the evening, when the seals had gone off the ice, we lay at rest, with wonderfully beautiful pack-ice stretching round us as far as the eye could reach; islands all shapes and all pale colours, white, blue and creamy, hollowed with green caves and fringed with icicles, jammed together into the most lovely disorder. The Jason lay a quarter of a mile off. After tea they began making a tremendous uproar on board her, firing harpoon-guns, blowing fog-horns, and shouting altogether at times. We thought one of her boats had not returned, had got jammed in the ice, perhaps, and the row was intended to give the crew an idea where the ship was. So the pipes were ordered up to help the din and wailed into the white silence. By and bye a boat came off from the Jason, and the first mate came up over our side and asked us to come aboard. It was their king's birthday they were celebrating, and there was no boat lost. We were invited to join in the celebration, and were not long before we had our best rags on and the rough of the blood off our faces and hands. Then we jumped into a boat, well pleased with the prospect of our 'evening out.' As we rowed across to the Norwegian, the whale-guns rigged round her bulwarks were going off merrily, and the oakum wads smoked on the still water.

Captain Larsen received us on the poop with Norwegian welcome, and we got down into the cabin to the tune of "Way down the Swanee River,' played on an organ on deck. They really do things well on a Norwegian whaler, and it seemed by the variety of provision below as if the Jason had just left port the day before. There was milk, just like fresh milk, rusks and liqueurs and all

sorts of good things, and such coffee—nothing to speak of in Norway, but what a contrast to our noxious mixture on the Balæna !

Captain Larsen is a good royalist, and we drank a great skald to the king of Gammel Norge, and another to our own crowned head, and then we drank success to Nansen and his bold adventure. . . .

Once before I joined in a toast to Royalty in circumstances even more peculiar than these—in Paris, in Les Invalides.

Rather a sudden leap this from the Antarctic to Paris, but please allow me a little change of scene; it is so tedious always writing about snow, and mist, and bleeding seals.

C., an artist, and I were at the above School of Depravity on a Sunday in February. We had been trying very hard and very long to learn to draw, and were tired in spirit, and did not know what to do. 'Let's go to Les Invalides,' said C., and I also said 'Let's go,' for it was a splendid idea—nobody having been there before that we knew of.

The dome of Les Invalides looks pretty in the distance, especially when you see the gold against a grey wintry sky, with a few brown leaves dangling on the button-wood branches in the foreground; but inside it is a sepulchre, a deserted barrack, as chilling and wet as a sea fog.

We mooned round it for an hour or two, and interested ourselves slightly in the armour room, and then asked an old man who the statue of the little man with the cocked hat in the courtyard was supposed to be; when he said Napoleon, we feebly asked him who that was, and if he was dead, and the old man seemed to be as depressed with the antiquity of our joke as we were ourselves with the dismal surroundings. Just as we were going out, however, we lighted on something really interesting, that brought up the past with a jerk. It was the Invalides themselves. Some twenty of them seated in groups at tables down a low-roofed room with the winter sun slanting into it through a line of low windows. The men were all very old, and all dressed alike in long black coats and stock collars. Some were smoking thoughtfully, and some had little glasses of cognac before them. I suppose it was a sort of bar, and this was the men's weekly treat. They looked so drowsy and harmless that C. and I ventured in and

sat down at a table beside one of the oldest. He was a grim old ruin, and sat by himself, bolt upright, looking straight before him, with his skinny hands resting on his stick. I do not think he knew we were there till we spoke to him, and asked an attendant to bring three *petits verres* of cognac. At first he only answered us shortly in a hollow, deep voice, like the wind in a cannon's mouth; but after a while his memory wakened and his voice rose, and he told us of battles by land and sea, of fighting, of cutting of throats, and of bodies thrown over ships' sides. It was not easy to understand more than the drift of what he said, for his words were mumbled and his *patois* was unfamiliar. But we let him go on, listening intently till his voice died away and he sat silent and grim. We waited for him to begin again, but he had gone too far back in memories of the past to speak to us. Then C. leant towards him and asked him in his gentle, rather weak voice, 'Aimez-vous la République?' and you should have seen how he wakened up! It was not a sudden awakening, but a sort of thaw; a light kindled in his grey eyes; the wrinkles twitched; three times he spat on the floor; and then his square mouth opened, a hole in a death's-head, and a great hoarse voice came out, 'A BAS LA REPUBLIQUE—VIVE LE ROI!—VIVE NAPOLEON!'

The other old men stirred a little when they heard the call, and a slight murmur went round and fell, and the room was quiet again. Then we three—the two *nouveaux* and the old soldier—raised our *petits verres* to the fame of the hero.

The old fellow's hand trembled as he raised his, and he seemed to be looking so intently into the past that I do not think he noticed that his glass was already empty.

... Now—I feel better—after this little change from the ice to Paris, and come back to my log-writing with renewed patience.

We had heard of Nansen and of his proposed venture

at the Falklands. Naturally, whalers are greatly interested in his adventure, and as this Jason, which we were on board, was the barque in which he made his first acquaintance with the Arctic ice, the occasion warranted a toast to his success.

The consensus of the opinion of this Whaling Society is that he will be able to pull through all right, and in much less than five years—that is, if his vessel is to be trusted; but from the description of its build given in a Norwegian paper there are doubts about its suitability.

The Jason in the Arctic ice.   From Nansen's *Crossing of Greenland*.

On deck the Norwegian crew, whether royalists or not, were making the most of the occasion. Unlike our men, they are treated to grog on great occasions, and a very wise plan it seems to me. The amount of discontent on our vessel arising from there being a supply of drink aft and none for the crew cannot be here described. If the vessel was teetotal fore and aft none of the crew would object.

The bo'sun of the Jason had been appointed to serve out the schnaps and the beer. He was a tall man with a wild, black beard and a canvas apron tied from his shoulders and waist. He poured out the grog into tumblers on the head of a cask with tremendous ceremony, and between every glass took a pull at the bottle himself, so he had difficulty in keeping his post.

Some of the men got themselves up as Christy minstrels

and sang negro songs, accompanied by a melodeon; others danced waltzes on deck, but with the oil and ice the floor was too slippery. Some of our party tried a reel, that was positively dangerous.

Some of these Norwegian sailors were superior sort of men, and I was surprised to find myself discussing books and music with one of the focsle hands. He took me down to the men's quarters, and handed me quite a number of books that he had read on the voyage out, for which I agreed to send him others in exchange. Then he brewed coffee, and insisted on my smoking a magnificent Dutch pipe that he took from his chest. His friend [1] was laid up with inflammation of the lungs, brought on by the exposure; so we sat beside him and talked and smoked all the evening. Fancy talking of art, music, and literature in a focsle! and these men knew what they were talking about. I felt very sorry for the invalid: of all places in which to be laid up, a focsle must be the worst. As we sat there we could scarcely hear our own voices—a man was cooking on the stove close to this man's bunk; another was playing on a melodeon; some were singing, and all smoking and talking—a pandemonium of sound, and the whole place reeked with wet clothes, and the smell of seal-skins, cooking, and tobacco. They said their only really happy time was when they pulled-to the sliding-doors of their bunks and read by the light of a small lamp. Imagine shutting yourself up in a frousty box six feet by three, with a book and an oil lamp, and calling it happiness!

Sunday, 22nd.—A long day of hard grinding at the oars, killing and flinching seals. A day full of sunlight and quiet beauty. Lunch of ship-biscuit and snow; returned to the ship late at night, and dog-tired.

---

[1] Sailors often go for years to sea in the company of the same friend. Sometimes three men hang together, and always try to sail on the same vessel.

Monday, 23rd.—Got away from the ship early. Fog came down in the afternoon, and we took our bearings by compass. Then the fog came down very thick, with wind and snow, and we had a long row hunting for the ship, and when at last we picked her up by good luck, we could see the signal for our return flying apeak! The other boats were still out, but they all found the ship by half-past six.

Sunday, 29th.—Same position as on 1st January. We have now on board 4800 seals, killed in twenty-eight days. Our decks are piled with their skins and blubber, high above the rail—a gory heap weighing more than 100 tons. There is fear lest the decks strain and the hatches burst.

Last night the sky cleared up for a blow, and this morning the wind has risen to a strong gale from the south. All five ships are in sight steering full speed amongst the loose pack, against the gale, and scarcely making steering-way. We have reached the shelter of the pack edge and three large bergs, so the sea is smooth, fortunately for us in our present state.

There will be no more sealing for some days, till we get all these skins on deck 'made off.' We are heartily glad that we have nearly got a full ship, for every one is dead-tired. As for myself, I feel as if I had been flayed. The first week brought me into good training, but the after work has run us all down. The sudden changes of temperature are trying. In the morning we go out thickly clad and get steaming hot with working in the strong sunlight, and by evening we are stamping our wet feet in the boats, with a cutting south wind driving the snow dust through our clothes. The crew are all buoyed up with the prospect of what is now almost a certainty, a good pay day when they get home. They receive the principal part of their share of the profits from the blubber-money.

On Thursday last we had quite an exciting day's sealing. In the morning we found ourselves almost outside the last of the streams of loose ice with a lumpy sea running in from the open.

The first four boats were lowered in the smooth water before we came out of the pack. Then the Balæna held on, and dropped us near a small stream of ice in the open water, on which were a great number of seals.

It was a pleasant change rowing in a tumbling sea after the monotony of calm inside the ice, pleasant and exhilarating to see the blue waves surge up behind the white reefs and come pouring over the ice tongues, green as emerald, or burst high into the sunny air, to fall in glittering showers. The ice islands were rolling and grinding against each other with a slow, deep sound, and the small pieces rattled together and filled the air with a clashing as of countless plates and knives. The harpooneer jumped on to the island, and two of us had to blaze away as fast as we could load and fire, for the seals on this piece of ice seemed to believe in flight. We picked off those that were more distant and those that were moving away, the rest gained confidence when they saw their companions lie down, and waited quietly till each had a bullet in the fatal spot at the back of their lovely heads.

After we had got nearly a boat-load of skins off the one stream, we pulled alongside, the skins were hauled on board, and we dropped under the Balæna's stern, and went in tow. This towing behind a ship is bad at any time, and when there is a sea on, with lumps of ice swinging into the ship's wake in addition, it is anything but pleasant.

The event of the day was our getting a number of seals off the side of an iceberg. This, I am told, is unprecedented in the annals of sealing. It is certainly the first time I have seen seals out here on anything but pack ice. They lay scattered over the steeply sloping side of a berg in such numbers that we felt we were bound to get them somehow or other. The difficulty was to get on to the berg, for the ice broke away abruptly at the foot of the slope, and the sea had undercut the edge with green caves, so we had to be pretty cautious about landing, so as to prevent our bows getting under the ledge. Very slowly we approached, waiting for a roller to lift us up to the level of the slope. As we rose, three of us jumped from the boat and clung on to the ice with our picks, whilst those in the boat backed off. I think we were as astonished at finding ourselves on the side of the berg as the seals were at seeing us there. The ice was flinty hard, so after we had flinched them all there was none of the usual grind of dragging the skins, we merely slid them down the slope like toboggans.

While we were flinching, the boat had pulled back to the ship and got some more men to keep her in hand when taking us off. They brought a line with them, and when within a few yards of the berg they threw it up to us and we ran it through the flipper-holes in the skins; then the boat backed off, and the skins slipped down over the ice-edge with a flop into the water and were pulled over the boat's side.

We nearly came to grief getting into the boat. She was backed in very gingerly, bow first, and just as we were jumping the surge drove her in too close, the bow caught under a ledge, and the stern went up in the air, and tumbled us all in a heap, half-drowned in a smother of foam. An ordinary boat would have been smashed in pieces, but these whale boats we use for sealing are very strong.

As the next seals in sight were a long way off, we for once had time to get dinner on board. The moment it was swallowed we were lowered away again to get them. They were the big black seals this time, and lay scattered over a stream of ice a long way out from the main pack.

We never see these large seals in great numbers, generally in couples, or singly. In this case they lay well into the centre of the stream, and though we could push our way through the ice ruins to within a few yards of them, we could not always manage to get them into the boat. All the afternoon we spent shoving and pulling in and out amongst the blocks. At times the boat was jammed out of water, and do what we would we could make no progress. For hours we only made a few yards, and once free became immediately entangled again in another white labyrinth in our attempts to get to some big seal that lay sleeping, perhaps within a boat's length, and yet was as safe as if under water. All the afternoon and evening we tugged and shoved till we were dead-beat, and as tired and hungry as could be, with not a sign of the ship above the horizon. Then it got dusk, and as there was a small sea on, and our boat was down to the thwarts with seals'-skins, we pulled into the shelter of a small berg in the open, and patiently waited for the Balæna to come and pick us up.

As we could not have stowed another seal's tail in the boat, we took our ease behind the ice with minds at rest, pulled on our mitts, buttoned up every button

that would help to keep the cold wind out, lit our pipes, and made the best of it, resting on our oars, and only giving an occasional stroke or two to keep up to our shelter. We had a jolly crew, so the time passed merrily. Willy Watson, *alias* Dee Dong, the steersman, sat on the skins in the stern and made us laugh all over with his funny sayings. Harry Kiddy, the harpooneer, a jolly, chubby little man, sang to us with stentorian voice. He sang the songs that sailors like, of home and the comforts of a fireside, songs of the simplest and most powerful sentiment, with no drawing-room tra-la-las. Jack likes something warm and stirring, 'Steady, Black Watch, Steady,' is one of our great favourites on board. How

the men thunder out the chorus, 'Die we *may*, all do. Fly we will *never*. Steady, Black Watch,' etc. But Kiddy's best song is 'The Light in the Window'—a long, tremendously sobby song. He put his quid on the thwart and gives it to us with such a strong, true voice, that you could hear him through half a mile of iceberg. The hero of this song repeats after every verse: 'There's-a light, in-the win-dow, burns bright-ly for me,' placed there by his mother to welcome him 'home from the sea.' The boy comes home and finds the light burns brightly, but his mother has gone—a sort of song to start the salt in the eyes of the very tarriest old shell back. Then Tailor gives us 'The Banks of my native Australia,' a lovely air, but, with Jack's own words, scarcely proper. Odd, is it not, how sailors must have their songs either deeply pathetic or vividly cerulean? Each man had to do something for the general entertainment, and a youth who couldn't do anything, and had

foolishly let the men know the name of the girl he left
behind him, was chaffed for pastime. It amused them,
and he did not mind; of course he must have been of
Saxon extraction, from Fife or Forfar. Catch a canny
Shetlander or John Highlandman letting out his heart's
secret in a focsle!

About ten we began to think we were going to spend
the night on the ice, and kept an anxious look-out for the
Balæna, and at last to our great relief her spars appeared
over the ice horizon. As we could not go into the small
sea outside our shelter for fear of swamping, we lay
snug, lit another pipe, cut another chew, and waited for
her to come down to us. Some of those who read this
may remark on this objectionable habit of chewing tobacco.
My opinion on the matter is that on occasions, say after
long exposure it is remarkably soothing and sustaining:
and for men working as our crew work from morning
till night in the boats, one hour hot and the next freezing
cold, with boots full of snow-broo and blood, and waist-
belts pulled in to the last hole, anything that dulls the
senses without paralysing them is welcome.

At eleven we were on board tucking into penguin stew
—at least I was. My companions have to do any cooking
for themselves when they come in like this at night, and
of course they were too fagged to cook anything, but ate
their cold tinned meat and biscuit, lit their pipes, looked
to their cut hands, damned a little, and lay down as they
were on their chest-lids for forty winks before turning
out to their morning watch. A man who would work a
hired dog on the 12th as these poor beggars are worked

every day ought to go and hang himself. A dog's food is sumptuous compared with their tasteless, monotonous diet.

And so sailors have been treated for ages, and may be treated to-day. No wonder they have growled a good deal and get the name of growlers; but it is only with their lot at sea that they growl. We all know that there is no one more contented than Jack when he takes to life on shore.

Now they are going to better their lot, and I wish good success to the endeavours of the men who unite their efforts to free themselves from the unutterable evils of the seaman's life. From my little experience of the 'ways of men of the sea,' I know what a hell life can be made for a seaman who has not some confederacy on shore that he can trust to back him against the tyranny of evil and irresponsible men at sea.

There can hardly, in my opinion, be a finer lot than that of a sailor's on a well-found ship, none more evil than his lot on such a vessel as he may find himself aboard any day—badly found, with incompetent men and officers.

A propos of unionism—unions are what the men trust will minimise the evil—I remember once listening to a sailor man of about forty telling his experiences of sea life. He was a small, active man, but too light a weight to hold his own in a rough and tumble, and the bullying he had gone through would scarcely be believed but that it comes within the experience of thousands of seamen. His opinion on the difference between sailing since the unions and before, stated with the light in his eye, was, 'It's the difference between Heaven and Hell.'

On Friday our programme was the same as Thursday,—turned out stiff as a board, rowed, and killed seals all day. *C'est le premier coup qui coûte*, and in this work it is the first few hundred yards rowing that we feel most, then the soreness goes out of our bones, we warm to the work, and the beauty of our surroundings again appeals to us.

Saturday.—We all turned out with our spirits buoyed up with the hope that this would be the last day's sealing, for the tanks are nearly full, and the decks are so piled up with skins that the enormous weight must make something give way.

There was an incident in this Saturday's sealing that made a beautiful subject for an ice-picture. We had found a few scattered seals lying on the end of a stream of ice and the men had landed to kill them, whilst I stayed in the boat to keep her clear of some ice-blocks that threatened to close us in. Happening to look up over the floe in the direction of the men, I was astonished to find a berg was sailing down on the top of us, or rather that the pack on which we were was driving on to it, which came to much the same thing, so I shouted to the men to look out, and they stood up from their work and looked up at the blue mystery stealing over us.

The berg was shaped like the bows of two ironclads side by side, and the great deep cleft between the ice walls seemed brimful of a dazzling glory of liquid blue, changed by infinite gradations to a sparkling emerald green where the ice foot shone through the dark indigo

water. The sun's rays sloped over the snowy top of the berg and fell on the white floe and the splashes of scarlet, and drew golden lines round the dark forms of the men. A marvellously beautiful picture, with just enough of human interest and dramatic suspense to enforce the beauty of the colouring.

For a moment the men stood, knives in hand, looking up at the ponderous cliff, then came helter-skelter over the snow, which happened to be hard, left the skins behind them, and tumbled into the boat. Then we all pulled and shoved out of the stream as hard as we were fit.

At a safe distance we lay on our oars and watched the berg that looked so beautiful and dreamlike cut through the pack. It went from end to end, turning up the huge ice islands twenty feet thick, as a ploughshare turns turf; but the pieces on which our seals lay were fortunately not much disturbed, and we dropped down behind the berg and picked them up in its wake.

Sunday Evening.—The main-hatch has burst at last with the weight of the skins. Fortunately the wind, which is increasing, is from the south, and we have smooth water. Should it veer to the north either the skins must go overboard, or all hands take a deep-sea sounding. Every one is hard at work 'making off,' getting as many skins cleared away as possible in case of emergency.

Monday, 30th Jan.—Wind almost a hurricane—S. and S. by W. with snow. The nights are getting dark, and it seems as if the winter weather is coming on us.

All night it blew furiously, driving us from shelter to shelter. For some hours we sheltered in the lee of a friendly berg, but we drifted a little too far from it, and the wind caught us and hustled us out of the shelter. For five hours we kept struggling to regain the position, steaming our best against the wind; but it was no use, and we finally swept to leeward for a mile or two and dodged in behind another berg. The loose ice drove down on us, and crashed into us with such tremendous force that we marvelled how our timbers stood the strain. All through the night we expected to see their white teeth let in black night through our sides, or at least to have the screw carried away ; but when the morning came we were all right, and got into the lee of some driving streams of ice, and the men set about their work as usual. Cold work it is 'making off' on deck,— standing in freezing slush, with the wind yelling through the cordage, driving blinding snow almost through us.

Tuesday.—Still blowing hard ; but we are in splendid shelter behind a long ridge of pack ice that was piled up last night. It is some thirty feet high—the highest pack that we have seen. The currents and wind have collected it between them ; they have piled block upon block, and the new snow has rounded off the points and angles with a smooth white sheet so that it does not look as if it had only been formed last night.

It is amusing to watch the row of penguins standing on the slope. The wind is driving the falling snow past them, now and then blotting them out of sight. They do not seem to mind the least, but preen their thin, wiry feathers, apparently in perfect comfort. Possibly this

snowy wind is to them pleasantly refreshing, after the hot summer days they have had lately, when the thermometer went up to 30° Fahrenheit, in the shade.

A number of nellies or giant petrels come circling over us as we slowly drift from our shelter to leeward. They gorge themselves with the cran[1] that is constantly being thrown over our sides, then fly back to the snow and sit down beside their penguin friends. Strange, ugly birds they are, the apparent coarseness of their build and their grey-green clumsy beaks and rough brown feathers give the impression that nature has turned them out in a very wholesale fashion. Some of them are partly white, and a few, of the same kind of bird I believe, perhaps one in twenty, are pure white all but one or two brown feathers. The different stages of colouring are rather like those of the gannet, we call them Scavengers. They appear to be on a friendly footing with

---

[1] Scraps of seals' flesh cut off the blubber. This name is also given to the carcass of the seal when its skin and blubber has been stripped off.

the living penguins, and when one of the latter dies the nellie swallows it, and the relations of the deceased do not seem to mind. Two penguins that were shot the other day were gobbled up before there was time to row the boat round a piece of ice to pick them up.

Friday, 3rd February.—Light wind S.S.E. Barometer as usual, between 28 and 29 inches. Danger Islands again in sight. We have been swinging about in much the same

fairly open water for the last three days. The loose ice seems to be filling up Bransfield Straits with this S. and S.E. gale. To the north and east it also seems to be collecting, and it looks as if we are going to be beset than which nothing could be less wished for. A winter in this country is what only a few of us would like to experience.

Monday, 6th February.—In the afternoon we steamed

down to the N.E. of Joinville Land, where the Active met us. Almost any land would be interesting to us now, but we fail to enthuse over this flat, snow-covered, uninteresting country. The only features are a few dark rocks that show above the glacier covering.

We hailed our friend Dr. Donald on the Active and photographed him, and he took us. The doctor took his photographic apparatus up to the crow's-nest and photographed the ice-scape with the Active in the foreground. It ought to make a very old-world-looking picture. The hull of the Active reminds one of the ships of the time of James VI.—low in the bow and high in the stern, but comfortable and homely-looking. The crew on deck seemed anxious about the doctor's bodily safety, not to speak of the camera, and speculated as to what would happen to their blanked heads if the blanked camera was to drop on them.

At night the wind went into the N.W. and blew like blazes.

. . . *Tuesday.*—A still, warm day of subdued sunlight of exquisite beauty—the sky a greeny blue, striped with grey white ribbons—on all sides white silky bergs, in the distance faintly tinted with lilac—sea smooth as glass, with a surface of bronze—black tashes, the five vessels steaming through the white labyrinth of bergs, and some whales trailing fan-shaped wakes of dark purple across the calm reflections. The smoke from the other vessels is almost beautiful to-night; it hangs in level whisps of rusty brown in the middle of the sheen of the bergs and reflections without the least movement, for the air is breathlessly still. Later in the evening a mirage strangely affected the appearance of the bergs. Round the horizon they divided into a circle of pale druidical pillars with yellow light shining between them, and seemed to support the canopy of faintly grey sky. Then a soft white fog fell, and they disappeared, and the ships began calling to one another like partridges in the evening when the mist lies low on the winter field. . . .

Wednesday.—Blowing a gale—*always* gales! We are dismally tired of the meaningless soughing through the icy shrouds, and the clack-clacking of the slack ropes. For half an hour at a time we drift broadside to leeward with the helm lashed, then steam up again into the smooth water on the friendly side of a berg. If we fail to gain the shelter of a berg we drift right down the wind and dodge in behind the next. One berg is as good as another, so be that you get on the right side of it.

Saturday, 11th February.—Another day's sealing, with a jovial boat's crew, and I hope our last day. There was Marshall, the bo'sun of the Eira, harpooneer, and Braidy, cox—two as merry and kind-hearted sailors as you could wish; little Terry M'Mahon, one of the stowaways—a born blue-jacket; and Kant, a fisher-boy, and a juvenile shellback, nicknamed Coiler, as his father had been before him —for what reason I cannot say. Coiler stands to me for handiness and good-nature.

How we did enjoy getting clear of the ship! and how we slaved too, racing with the other boats to get first at a patch of seals, slashing and cutting their coats off, each man vying with his neighbour! Then there was the long row home, chatting and singing as we rowed; that was pleasant, though there are more pleasant ways of rowing than on a sliding seat of seal-skins. We had the story of the loss of the *Chieftain's* men on the way—a grisly tale, that made a stir in the north two years ago. It had a particular and immediate interest to us, as the boat we were rowing in was one of those which had belonged to the Chieftain, and was supposed to be that in which the tragedy took place.

The mist fell one day up in the north, and two of the Chieftain's boats that were out were lost. One was never seen again, but the other was found seventeen days after, off the coast of Iceland, with only one man in it.

The other five had drunk sea-water, and had gone mad and jumped overboard. The man that was found in the boat had eaten his hat and the signal-flag and some other trifles. Both his legs were frost-bitten, and had to come off. Now he sits in a little wooden house in Dundee, where he opens a gate on the N.B. Railway. I daresay he will tell his tale to any one who cares to listen. There was a very grim humour about the last chapter of the story. When the poor castaway was landed at Dundee, the wives of his late companions met him, and made pointed inquiries as to their husbands, about the manner of whose decease there were wild rumours. When he lay in bed recovering, the same ladies continued their visits, to his annoyance, till he hit on the plan of talking in his sleep, as if he recalled the time in the boats. 'Noo, Jock,' he would groan, when Mrs. Jock was at his bedside, 'it's your turn noo, ma man. No' but that I'm sorry for ye, laddie, but ye maun dee, man—I'm fair faumished.' My informant did not linger over the story. Sailors seem to avoid the horrible in their yarns, perhaps because they know that they themselves may at any time have like experiences.

We got back to the ship at 4.15, and were off again at 5.10—sent off with many kindly directions to find seals where there were no seals. They were 'just lyin' a' ower the sea,' so we were told—seals of the *papillons noirs* species, I expect. We were dropped in the middle of a floe of blocks, varying in size from a cottage to a palace, to pick up these phantoms, but in the boats we were not sufficiently elevated to see them, and the pack was so jammed that it was impossible to move more than two or three boat-lengths, so we pulled under a green ice grotto, prettily fringed with icicles, and smoked our pipes peacefully. It was a ridiculous chase. Later the ship came up, and with great difficulty drove her way through the jam to us, and we and two other boats got in tow under the stern of the Mjolnar, and went hunting the snark through the pack at five knots. My word! the Mjolnar was Thor's hammer with a vengeance that night; we had a memorable time astern, with the ice swirling against us and the boats colliding with each other as we raced along. We only got five seals after all.

At 11 o'clock the Balæna was hopelessly jammed in the pack, driving goodness knows where in thick fog, with bergs all round. Sometimes the pressure on her timbers seemed more than they could bear, as if the ice was pressing so that another pound of pressure would burst the ship into splinters. Then as it eased off a little, George on the bridge would bang the bell, and the other George and his mate below turn on full speed ahead, and make a desperate effort to break loose, to gain perhaps twenty yards, just to get jammed again amongst the grey ice-rocks that grinned out of the darkness over the bulwarks at our helplessness.

Sunday.—This morning the wind fell a little, and we breathed with less weight on our chests; but to-night, as I write up my log, it is rising almost to a gale again. The night is dark; but the ice gives a white glimmer which would help us to see where the bergs are, but for the fog and driving snow.

X

... What a pandemonium of sounds—the wind howling and the timbers creaking and cracking as the ice pounds against our sides. What the men say is true, 'it's time we're oot o' this, an' awa' hame.' It is a trifle too dangerous for the philosophic contemplation of life. 'Tis a time for those to pray who can't act, for the rest to stand by, as Callum Bouie put it, only in different words, to the wee Dr. M'G. and the big Dr. M'C. when they were caught in a squall coming over from Jura, ' If ta wee meenister will say a praayer,' he said, ' he will say a praayer; but ta pig meenister will take an oare whatefer'; and it was then, and on no other occasion, believe me—no matter what William Black or anybody else may say to the contrary—that he told the minister, who continued to pray amongst the wet ballast after the squall had blown over, ' You may stop praaying, Dr. M'G., for we will pe peholden to no man.'

Sacré! another shock—enough to dislocate one's vertebræ. It is certainly not time to stop praying yet.

The question before the House is, Which is the strongest, the ship or the ice?—It's the Balæna this time, and we go crushing through the press head-first into the next block, the swell angrily crunching the ice islands against our sides as we jam through.

What a terrible row! The wind is still rising, and the bell keeps ringing intermittently. Once—twice,—the engines are reversed, and we go slowly astern. One! a single clang, and she stops; then immediately come four bells very hurriedly rung into one peal, and we go full speed ahead for a second, and pound into the block in front of us. The screw goes on revolving, but we make no way, and we feel the ice creeping along our sides and round our stern ; another clang of the bell, but too late— the propeller strikes the ice, and the engines are stopped, with an alarming shock—all is quiet but for the howling of the wind outside; then come feet thumping overhead as men hurry aft to see to the rudder. We are fairly caught now, fore and aft, and the Balæna rolls a little, uneasily, in the ice grip.

It was difficult to go to sleep whilst these various shocks and sounds continued ; so I put by my log, blew out my candle, and went on deck to look at the grey ice ghosts that were trying to crush in our bulwarks. . . .

It was comfortable enough in the focsle, so at least I found it when I went to the galley for our evening brew of coffee. Half a dozen of the watch below sat before the fire puffing at their pipes and staring at the red coals. It was comfortable, by contrast at least, but the conversation was doleful and intermittent, and one man was praying beside his sea-chest for our preservation. No wonder the men were depressed : Mark Tapley would have groaned on such a night;[1] and some of the most lugubrious spoke of putting on their best clothes—to be neat and tidy, I suppose, when all hands should be piped aloft. I am afraid that on this occasion my friends brocaded their

---

[1] Dr. Donald, of the Active, tells me they were also in a very tight place on this night, and all their men had packed their chests. The idea with whalers in case of their ship being nipped is to get on to the ice with their belongings and anything of any value they can lay hands on in the ship— rifles, copper pipes, etc., and then get another whaler to take them home. They are quite accustomed to this.

talk with just as many profanities as usual. In safety or in danger, sailors swear, but they mean no harm, and they don't swear nearly so much as their fathers did before them.—

Once upon a time there was a parson on board a sailing vessel in the Mediterranean. On passing by the focsle one day, he heard oaths thick as shot come rattling up the hatch. Surely, he thought, our good ship must be in imminent danger ; I must ask our captain. So he went aft to the skipper, who was lounging in the shade on the poop with a lemonade at his elbow. 'Captain,' he said, 'I have just come from the other end of the ship, where I overheard the men in their cabin using such terrible language that I greatly fear our ship must be in some great danger.'

'I greatly regret,' replied the skipper, with the courtesy of his class, 'that the language of my men should have been such as to cause you the least pain. Rest assured, my dear sir, that there is really no danger just now; and believe me when I tell you, sir, that it is only on occasions such as the present, when the sky is clear and the sea is smooth and all danger far removed, that in his rash confidence the sailor so far forgets the Ever-listening Ear, the Ever-recording Pen.' . . .

In the Bay the barometer went up with a jump and they caught a nor'-wester that brought the mizzen over by the board, blew the fore topmast over the side, shifted the cargo, and laid them over with a two-foot list to starboard.

Down came the skipper to the cabin, blasting and blanking right and left, shouting to the steward for lemonade, cursing the ship and his luck and the day he went to sea.

'Captain,' said the parson, very white and holding on to the table, 'it grieves me to see you thus give way to passion. I have been on deck, and it is all very terrible and incomprehensible to me, and I am all wet. But I feel sure, captain, there is no danger to our lives, for, thank God, captain, the men are swearing—*worse than ever!*'

I think this is the very oldest junk in the merchant service—Reader, I apologise.

Tuesday.—It was quite a pleasant surprise to turn out yesterday and find ourselves still above water. The wind eased off a little in the forenoon, and the ice opened and we struggled out like a fly from a bowl of loaf-sugar and steamed away to the eastward, where the Jason and the Active had found a comfortable shelter behind a berg and some stream ice. The wind was still strong on our starboard bow and made a small sea that burst over our bows in white icy showers. We could take a little spray without harm, but anything in the way of green sea would have given us trouble ; for the main-hatch is still open, the scuppers are all choked with seal-skins, and the bunkers are open with heaps of coal piled on deck to leave room for blubber below.

This afternoon the boats that were out came back to the ship filled to the gunwale with black seal-skins. As they arrived each boat sent up lusty cheers, for the mizzen rigging was adorned with flags to signify our sealing is over. There ought properly to have been great celebrations on this occasion, but for circumstances over which the crew have no control. However, the intensity of the unexpressed joy we all felt could scarcely have been greater. All that has to be done now, before we leave, is to make off the skins on deck, haul the Jack apeak, and turn the Balæna's head for home and the North Countrie.

Just to make my experiences as an Antarctic sealer complete, I was seized in the grey of the morning with the illness that most of our men have been knocked up with, so I am now able to speak from personal experience. The sensation of this perhaps uncatalogued malady is as if you had been shot at with an express rifle and the expansive bullet had caught you fair and true where the little girl explained her doll was sore, 'just where the wax meets the sawdust.' The pain was so acute that for quite a time I wished I had never been born, and kicked horribly against the boards that divide my bunk from the doctor's, till he got up and ministered to me.

Thursday, 16th February.—We are lying gently rolling in the short, smooth swell. Scattered pieces of ice and hollow mist round, the oppressive stillness only broken by the grinding on our sides of a piece of ice against which the ship is resting. Now that our thoughts are set on the home-going, the feeling of being cut off from the world comes over us more than ever. Even the birds that have kept us faithful company have left us, as if they knew that we were wearied with their noiseless flight and the sad grey world they live in. Yet it was well to come here, to this quiet chamber of the south, where nature lies entranced in a death-like sleep; now that we have touched her cold face and marvelled at her white beauty we long to go back to the living world we come from, where the breast of mother earth is kindly and warm, and the air is full of colour and perfume and pleasant sounds.

. . . The very last skins are being made off. The snow is falling and dusting the men's worn clothes, hanging on their shaggy beards and caps till they look like models of old father Christmas. Those who are not making off are busied clearing up the decks and making all fast in the 'tween-decks before we take to the high seas again. The Jason is alongside. She will not leave the ice for several days yet; though she has more seals on board her than we have, yet she still has room for more. We are indebted to her master for supplying us with salt to preserve our seal-skins. The Balæna had only been provided with a small quantity, the owners not expecting, I suppose, that we should get a full ship of seal-skins. I am told that this act of kindness on the part of

Norwegian captains has never had its equal in whaling records. Mr. Adams has just gone on board her to partake of Captain Larsen's hospitality, and all on board down to the stowaways wish him a pleasant evening, for he has not been a day off duty, or an hour on shore, since the day we left Dundee—the 6th of last September.

Friday, 17th February.—Last night the thermometer dropped suddenly, falling five degrees in five minutes. A round bank of mist like a dark boulder formed in the west, with a sort of low rainbow arch of grey light above it, and the wind, that had been in the north, went round suddenly to the west, and blew hard and bitingly cold, giving us a taste of the Antarctic winter which will soon freeze us up here if we are not up and away before long. Every one is delighted with the prospect of leaving this cold country, with, I think, the exception of the doctor and myself. He busies himself with plans for spending a winter here. The crew have their homes and families and their pay waiting for them; possibly new pledges to rejoice their paternal feelings. They have been and seen and got all they wanted—perhaps not so much as if they had got whalebone, but still more than they had expected in the event of there being no whales—whilst Bruce and I have been and seen only a fraction of what we wished to see, and have nothing to speak of in the way of collections either scientific or artistic. However, we try to content ourselves with the hope that this expedition may add to the interest taken in this end of the world, and that another expedition may be sent out, on which the scientist will not be hindered in making his observations, or the artist—I pray I may be he—in making drawings.

The four black barques are here together, collected like crows on a field in the evening before taking flight. The Polar Star has flown already; these gales must have blown her clean out of the ice and away north, or, as some say, sunk her. She was far too small and fragile for this work, with engines far too weak to contend with the buffeting of the gales and ice, though I am told she can

lick us off our feet in the open sea; but that is no great matter to make her owners gay.

All the boats are being brought inboard and turned upside down on the skids, and soon we hope to be swinging under them again, in our hammocks, in the heat of the tropics.

We are lying in Bransfield Straits this afternoon between Joinville Land to the south, and the South Shetlands on the north; to-morrow we shall see them on our way north.

Joinville Land lies S. by E., distant about forty

miles. We can just make it out—a land entirely covered with snow, faintly yellow in the sunlight, with the clouds lying low, hiding its profile outlines. A large black mass, like a great cliff with a white sheet of snow down its middle, is the only feature.

There is very little ice about, only small streams at considerable distances apart, and a few low icebergs twenty or thirty feet above water. On the streams are numbers of black seals lying singly and in couples, owing their safety to the want of space in our tanks for their blubber. They have fully twice as much fat on their skins now as those we found when we first came. Nature in her infinite wisdom has thus provided them with a thick, warm covering to enable them to withstand the rigour of the approaching winter; and in her simple, blundering way she has given us the same sort of coats, and we do not feel particularly grateful—we have the tropics before us. Circumstances were against the crew being treated in the same way, so they are perhaps in better trim for hot weather than we are aft the mainmast; they have had abundant work and a poor diet, but we in the cabin have had the work plus unlimited penguin stew,—the natural food of the country, and the most suitable, I suppose, for a permanent resident.

The doctor found an opportunity of making some scientific research this afternoon. He brought out the empty greybeards and soda-water bottles that we brought from Dundee, which were so tantalising in the tropics, and we fastened lines to them and fished for Antarctic water over the stern. We (the reader and I), being of scientific tastes, both understand what the doctor was taking this cold water all the way home for; but the crew did not. They believe firmly that it is for some patent medicines or a hair-wash that he intends to advertise at home as The Great Antarctic Hair-restorer. In this particular line the doctor has very justly earned great repute on board by inventing a mixture which, I believe, with proper application, would raise down on a billiard-ball.

There is a certain seaman forward, a regular old weather-beaten salt, with a face wrinkled up like a peach-stone with fever and frost. Of all the complaints this elderly man of the sea had picked up in the odd corners of the world, what he suffered from most was his baldness. So he came aft and asked the doctor if he could do anything, and the doctor said 'Yes,' with perfect confidence; for a young practitioner, our doctor has a fair amount of nerve, I consider. But in practice at sea 'you soon gain confidence,' as he has often told me, referring, of course, to surgeons at sea, not their patients.

"You see, doctor,' said the man, 'I ain't got werry much 'air on the top of my 'ead.' There was none at all on the top, and only a little round the sides. 'And before I left my 'ome I married a werry prutty young wife, and it wouldn't be werry nice to go 'ome without any 'air on my 'ead.'

The doctor said nothing, but he took a phial and poured something into it from another bottle, and poured into that some oil of penguins, and added some other ingredients, the names and proportions of which I may not here divulge; then he shook the liquid and gave it to the man

Filling our Water-tanks.

with that calm, Jove-like air of all-knowingness that so few physicians succeed in acquiring even after years of practice, an expression of calm confidence that springs, I suppose, from the absolute knowledge of the complete ignorance of the patient. All he said was, '*Rub this vigorously on your head three times a day.*' And he did rub it—you can trust a sailor to do a thing well when he does do it. The crew tell me he sat for days afterwards holystoning his head in his watch below. The result is astonishing—the good man is as vain as can be of his second crop. Whether it was the mixture, or a faith cure, or massage that made the hair grow, I cannot say; possibly the shocks and frights of this Antarctic life have the opposite effect from that which they have at the other end of the world, possibly all these causes effected the cure. At any rate, it is certain that hair now is where there was none before.

We tried some ourselves, more as a preventive measure, we may say, than as a cure; but the perfume in our small cabin was such that we were obliged to discontinue its use. As assistant-surgeon I have naturally taken considerable interest in my superior's work, and some of the cures I have seen him effect were really interesting; being behind the scenes, as it were, I have had opportunities which I trust have not been neglected.

One case in particular gave me great interest, and our doctor's diagnosis and treatment filled me with admiration. The patient was a youth who suffered from various painful and alarming symptoms, that on different days affected him in different parts of his system; so many and varied were these that I felt anxious as to whether

the lad would ever see his home again. In three days he was completely cured, by taking the pills prescribed for him; he took them three times a day, two at each time. I watched the preparation of the pills used in this case, and the doctor showed me that the ingredients were bread and impure water.

The surgeon or doctor, as he is commonly called on board ship, has often to prescribe for cases of intermittent or continuous attacks of laziness. In former years the cure for this complaint was of a rough and ready nature, and only effective to a slight degree. With the advance of the science, a certain oil has been discovered, a few drops of which administered to the patient are warranted to keep him on the hop for a week. But on this ship there have been absolutely none of these patients, but quite the reverse. Men really ill, have kept struggling out of bed to work in the frost and cold even when dangerously ill, going in the boats in the snow and cold when they ought to have been lying wrapped up in their bunks, slaving at oars and flinching diseased skins with cut and festering hands, standing for days on the slushy deck in the wind and snow, 'making off' with every muscle cramped with rheumatism. All this work they do, and suffer all this pain and unspeakable discomfort, not altogether because they are driven to it, but because they share an infinitesimal proportion of the profits of the voyage.—So much for co-operation.

I think it can be seen that the surgeon's duties on board a sealer are no sinecure. He has to work like the rest of the crew in the boats or at the wheel, for a long day of perhaps twelve hours hard manual labour, and at night has to patch up fingers, to dispense medicine and make scientific notes if he can steal a spare moment. In this case he has besides to turn out two or three times in the night to attend the principal patient, with the certainty of having to listen to endless growling about there being 'too much —— science on board; there's never nobody seeck whan thar's no dooctur:' to the like and worse.

CHAPTER XVIII

SATURDAY, 18th Feb.—Home! Home! Hurrah! we are off to the North again. To and fro we swing into

the sea-way, already out of the still ice-sea, plunging along over 'the rough highway to Freedom and to Peace.' It is as if we had broken from the woof of an eerie, beautiful dream, and wakened in the broad day.

The men are whistling, and talking in an interested way now. How the old ship enjoys the freedom, plunging her nose into the soft sea, tossing the white spray over her bows, swishing the salt sparkling water to and fro, across her deck with a silky rustling, till the least speck of flesh or blood is cleansed out of nook and cranny, and swept through the flowing scuppers.

Only five hours ago we were still in the loose pack-ice, steaming up to each of our consorts in turn, dipping our ensign in farewell, and answering their cheers. In two or three more days they will follow us on the same road. We left them some thirty miles N. by E. of Joinville

Land, all close together. Some of the crews were busy shooting more seals, and the rest were on board, slashing away at the blubber and skins on deck, making off against time, and I have no doubt envying us with their whole hearts. The last farewell cheer we gave to the Antarctic before we turned the broad of our backs on it, and our faces towards home, was a little to the north of the vessels, when we came on one of the Diana's boats out sealing. The crew had just jumped on to the ice to kill a seal, when we passed. The harpooneer fired three shots before he killed it, in such haste was he to wave a farewell. He and his mates and a couple of penguins scrambled up a hummock; the men gave a cheer, and the penguins waved their flippers, and toddled down the snow again and popped under water.

And so we turned from the mystery of the Antarctic, with all its white-bound secrets still unread, as if we had stood before ancient volumes that told of the past and the beginning of all things, and had not opened them to read. Now we go home to the world that is worn down with the feet of many people, to gnaw in our discontent the memory of what we could have done, but did not do.

Saturday Night.—We have had just a glimpse of land to the northward before the night fell—Clarence Island, the most easterly of the South Shetlands. The pack-ice is out of sight now, only a few scattered bergs and broken pieces of sea-worn berg ice remain. The wind is pleasant and warm, N. by W., so we are steaming with only fore and aft sails set. In the engine-room, our social centre aft the mainmast, the conversation is quite animated. Of late the meetings there have been becoming more and more melancholy as the weather became worse and the longing to be off home increased. It was enough to crawl down and sit in the hottest place and doze and let the stiffness grow out of our bones in the warmth, and perhaps revive to the extent of playing a game of dominoes before turning in. But to-night every one had something to say, and the First Mate was in more than usually good form with his songs and character sketches.

We threshed out the subject of matrimony from the sailor's point of view. The opinion of the meeting was decidedly in favour of married life; but the members were almost all married, so their opinion was not unbiassed. A seaman's life is so restless and uncomfortable that it is not worth living if he has not a home somewhere—if he can only see it for one week in the year. I think the common idea that Jack is unfaithful to the wife of his bosom is not quite true. 'Absence makes the heart grow fonder' applies in his case as in others. 'And they're no aye sae verra faithfu' at hame whiles,' as one of the party remarked in apology for his fellows.

'There was Liz ——, ye ken, wha auld Sandy —— marrit,—ye'll mind?' Some of the party did mind, and others did not, so for the benefit of the latter the speaker unrolled his yarn.

'Sandy had long lived a gay bachelor, then married a young wife, whose appearance was not prepossessing, and whose manners were not those of a lady; all the same Sandy doated on her, and through a two-years' voyage kept as true to her as the needle to the Pole, and when he came into port went straight "up the toon," with heart pumping under his jacket, and his pockets full of banknotes, refusing even to have a "sma yin" with his drouthie cronies on Dock Street.

'There was no one to let him in when he knocked at his door on the fifth flat in High Street, but he was not surprised. Liz would be working out-bye, he thought, for a sailor's half-pay is none too much for the wife at home. So, to put in the time and slacken rather a dry throat, he went down the long stair again and turned into the Tay bar —a great sailors' howf in Dundee—when who should he see but his Liz clinking glasses with another sailor man.'

'"Weel, Liz," he said, "I've come hame." The East Scotch are an undemonstrative people.

'"An dod, man," she said, "but it's fell glad I am to see ye, laddie. Wullie, this is my guidman; and Sandy, this is Wullie Lindsay, ma cousin, ye ken, just ca frae th' Wast Ice wi' a full ship."

'So Sandy was introduced to Wullie, and ordered a gill of the special, to celebrate his home-coming, and Liz went "over the way to fettle up the house a wee," taking with her Sandy's two years' earnings, for, as every one knows, a sailor fresh from the sea is not to be trusted with money. . . . Old Sandy was treading on air when he left cousin Lindsay a little later, and went over the way to see his wife; but his throat grew dry again when he found his door still shut. Then he went back to the Tay bar and heard Liz had "been, and gaed awa wi' Meester Lindsay." Some other local gossip he heard too, which gave him a thirst that lasted out a month's advanced pay, and instead of settling down to domestic happiness, Sandy was carried on board ship a week later—very drunk and shameless, an old grey-haired sailor, bound for Hell and Hong Kong.'

'Daumned auld fule!'—remarked the fireman at the end of the story as he got up to rake out the furnace. And so he was, no doubt, but one felt sorry for the old wreck.

Almost all our crew, old and young, are married. They apparently marry in Dundee between the ages of fifteen and twenty, on £1 a week and a childlike faith that their bread and butter will be provided daily. At twenty-five they have large families, and at forty they have grandchildren. Whilst we sat there, leaning against the timbers of the ship in the light of a smoky flare-lamp, talking of these matters of high import I drew the engineer, who was on my right hand. It was by way of a funny caricature. I thought he was unmarried from his youth and generally happy-go-lucky air, and I drew an ideal picture of him as he might appear in years to come, walking out with a damsel, a perambulator, and two and a half brace of kids. To my astonishment, he criticised the drawing by finding fault with the number of kids. There ought to have been two more, possibly three, he said.

The needs of this class of men are simple, merely food and covering. These they can obtain by grinding industry, and consequently repeat themselves *ad lib.* When they are taught, or come to realise that they have cravings for higher things—Nature, and Art, and Music—as well as for mere work and food, and when they learn how they can satisfy these wholesome appetites, then they will breed fewer and bigger, and less like rabbits in a protected warren.

Sunday, 19th February.—Last night we lay close-hauled, for it was dark and misty, and there would have been a risk of running into some of the small, scattered bergs.

This morning we steamed again with fore-and-aft canvas, steering N. by W. The air was warm to-day, and we had rain for the first time since we made the ice. In the middle of the day we were under the lee of Clarence Island, the most easterly of the South Shetland Islands. We passed it distant about twenty miles, I should think.

We cannot help thinking with a shudder that there may be some poor fellows on those wild, snow-covered mountains watching the ship sail past. Every year ships are wrecked or disabled going round the Horn, and their wreck or boats might very possibly have drifted on to these unvisited islands. Only last year two large ships were lost. They were last spoken south of the Horn, and it is supposed they struck ice and foundered, or were disabled and drifted south-east in a north-west gale. It would be a humane plan for our Government to send a vessel to look up these islands occasionally, on the chance of picking up castaways. We could see other islands of the group stretching to the westward. Clarence Island appears to be the highest; the view we had reminded me of the peaks of Arran, only they were as high again and covered with snow, except where black rocks showed through long, steep slopes of snow. It would be a lovely country for Alpine club men, or for tobogganing—splendid slopes at an angle of 45°, two or three thousand feet high, with a clear jump at the bottom of, say, five hundred feet into the soft sea.

We have the molly mawks with us again, and Mother Carey's chickens in considerable numbers. A few of these last have white breasts.

Monday.—Sun and breeze. We feel completely out of the Polar world. The albatross have joined us again. On our way out, those we saw were old white birds in full plumage, and the rest were in the stage immediately preceding full plumage. Now we see pairs of old birds taking charge of young birds whose plumage is entirely brown.

Saturday.—A bad sea. Wind, N.W. to W. We are

very much down by the head by reason of the coal being all stowed forward, so we are taking the sea heavily over our bows.

Friday.—A head wind under reefed topsails, staysails, reefed foresail. A heavy cross sea still running, making us roll tremendously, decks always awash, everything loose, banging about. In the dog watch the wind fell and we got up steam, then it came fair and we sailed.

We have had nothing but contrary winds for some days, so the change was very welcome. Both watches were on deck, and so the two crowds each hauled at a topsail halyard at the same time. What a clang of voices there was, each watch shouting down the other! What a wild fresh picture to remember in the foul streets in towns,—the sea plunging from bulwark to bulwark seething white, the men singing and laughing; up to the tops of their boots in glittering foam, and a fair yellow light filling the sky, making the dark, lumpy waves look soft and delicate, shining through the jets of glittering broken water thrown up by the cross sea.

Thursday.—Heavy Cape Horn sea. Bright, clear weather. We smelt land to-day; I could swear to it. When I came out of the cabin there was a pleasant aromatic perfume of burning wood in the air, but on looking forward there was no smoke to be seen, and the wind was right across our deck.

So it dawned on me that it must be from land, and standing right up to windward the smell was the same. Two hundred miles seems rather a long way for the scent of land to carry. The wind was blowing straight from the islands on our port bow. Perhaps being so long in absolutely pure air makes one unusually alive to the least change in its quality.

I made a jotting of Harvey this afternoon as he was laying it off to Peter beside the galley stove that is still kept in the focsle. How I wish I could give Harvey's yarns, with his mixture of Cornish and Scotch and good Queen's

English, patched with quaint nautical terms from all seas. He told of their forty days' voyage in the open boats from Franz Joseph Land, in the spring of the year, to Spitzbergen, where Sir Allan Young met them and took them home on board the Hope, and how the food on board the Hope made their hands and feet swell because they had eaten nothing but meat of walrus and bear for a twelvemonth. And he described their landing in Peterhead; and how the people, when they heard of the return

of the Eira crew, came to the docks to welcome those they
had long thought dead. Their feet were so sore with the
pavements that they had to stop at the first shop and buy
canvas shoes. After the triumph in Peterhead, and the day
spent in festivities, Harvey took the night train to Dundee
and set off to the far end of the town to his home. Half
way up the town his feet became so sore, and he was so
tired with the day's excitement, and nervous with prospect of meeting his wife and children, that he sat down
on a doorstep to pull himself together. As he sat there a
policeman came by and flashed his lantern on the dejected-
looking figure, gave him a shove and told him to move
on. But Harvey felt at that moment he had as much
right to his share of native soil as the policeman, and told
him so, and a little more besides. And the policeman,
an ordinary individual, with more sense of duty than
common sense, collared our friend and marched him up
to the police station.

'What's your charge?' said the superintendent.

'Drunk and disorderly, sir,' said policeman M'Crae.

Then weather-beaten Harvey was questioned, and
answered with his fine-weather, childlike smile, both hands
across his waistcoat.

'Now, my man, what's your name?'

'Jock Harvey, sir.'

'What trade?'

'Sailor, sir.'

'Ship?'

'The Eira, sir.'

'Tuts, man, the Eira's been lost this year back.'

'Yes, sir, but her crew have come home in the Hope, sir.'
'Allan Young's ship?'
'Yes, sir.'

Then there were explanations, and M'Crae saw the glint of a five-shilling bit in Mr. Harvey's fist when he showed him into a cab.

Monday, 27th.—In the dog watch we made out the hills of the Malvinas or Falkland Islands, which name you please, a low, broken line of purple on the horizon against a yellow sunset sky, flecked and striped with ridges of lavender cloudlets each fringed with rosy red. It was like our West Highland sunsets, with a glow in the air that gave our dark hull and the men's faces, looking over the bulwarks, a warm, rusty tint, and made our masts shine like bars of gold. Gradually the hills grew larger, the afterglow grew colder, and the welcome spark of light on Cape Pembroke became keener as the darkness crept over us from the east.

It was too late to make our way into the roadstead, so we lay off and on through the night. As I write, we are gently rolling in the lee of the land; the easy rolling motion that makes one feel so drowsy.

Tuesday broke clear as crystal, a caller morning with a fresh breeze blowing off shore, bringing down the peat smoke from the burning moors.

There was as before no pilot to be seen, so we followed our own lead up Port William and through the Narrows into Stanley harbour. I heard afterwards that the pilot was laid up. Two policemen, however, came off, to

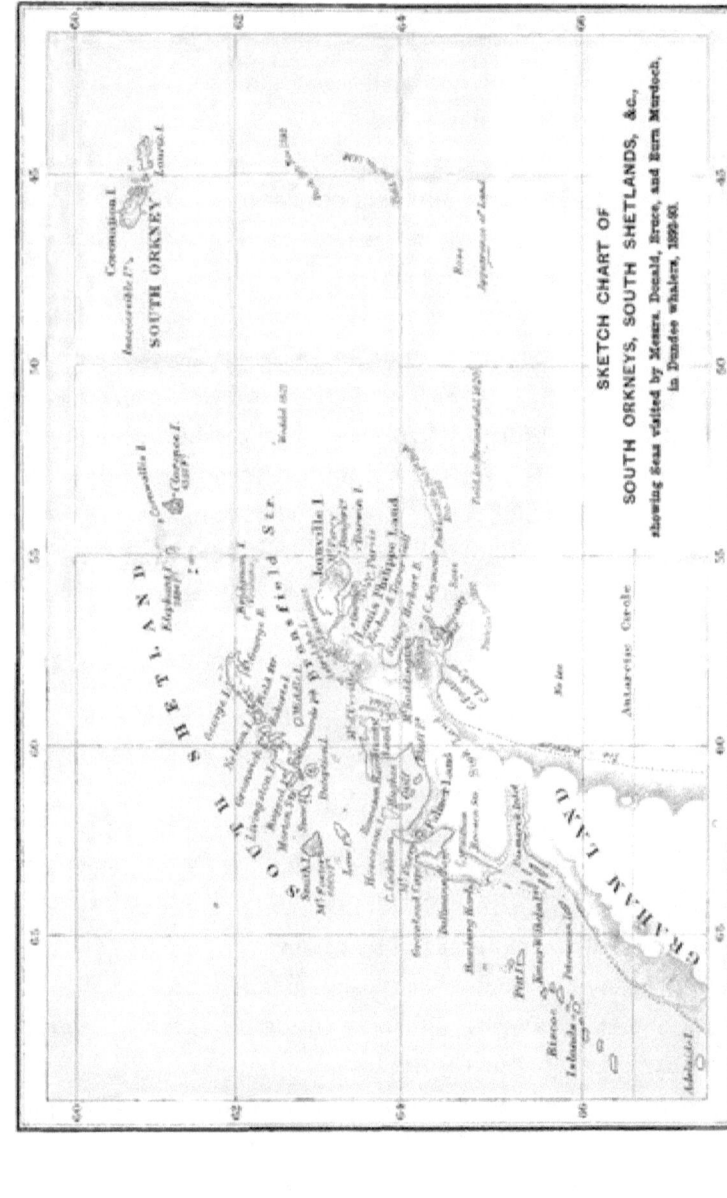

CHAPTER XIX

BY WILLIAM S. BRUCE, NATURALIST TO S.S. BALÆNA

WITH the exception of a flying visit made in 1874 by H.M.S. Challenger, the Antarctic regions have been entirely neglected since Ross's Expedition of 1839-43, and have been well nigh forgotten. An accident of commerce led in the autumn of 1892 to a slight revival of scientific interest. A fleet of whalers set out in September from Dundee to search the Antarctic seas for the Bowhead (*Balæna mysticetus*), or some similar whale. The fleet consisted of the Balæna, in which Mr. Burn-Murdoch and myself sailed, the Active, the Diana, and the Polar Star. Our vessels, after a voyage which was prolonged to thirty or forty days beyond the calculated time, met at the southern ice in Erebus and Terror Gulf. There we found an earlier arrival, the Norwegian sealing vessel Jason (Captain Larsen)—the ship in which Nansen set out from Iceland for his famous crossing of Greenland. The Jason was strictly on commerce bound, though the spirit of the great explorer, who had sailed in her, had in some measure descended on Captain Larsen, for, without any special resources, he showed a zeal for extending our knowledge of these regions that would not have been unworthy of the leader of a purely scientific expedition. But the four Dundee whalers had an element of interest unusual in such a fleet. A scientific and artistic department had been attached to them. The Royal Geographical Society and the Meteorological Office equipped the fleet with instruments, and appointed officers to undertake the work of observation and research. Mr. Leigh Smith, Dr. H. R. Mill, and Professor Haddon also added handsomely to the scientific outfit of the Balæna.

The Balæna first saw ice on the afternoon of December 16th, in about 60° S., just to the N.E. of the South Shetlands. The same night we sighted our second berg. The weather was fine and bright in the earlier part of the day, becoming overcast and rainy in the afternoon and evening. All day we were surrounded by myriads of birds, mostly Cape pigeons (*Procellaria capensis*); among them being thousands of blue petrel, and smaller numbers of molly mawk (*Diomedia culminata*). On the surface of the water, from near the ship to far on the horizon, we could see hundreds of the Finner Whale blowing fountainlike spouts, and filling the air with their characteristic note of booming resonance. The next day, the 17th December, the weather was foggy and the temperature fell from 34° F. to 30° F. We met with drift ice and a few bergs, both great and small. On this day we saw and shot our first seal, a sea-leopard (*Leptonyx stenorhyncus*), one of the largest kinds, as it drifted past us asleep.

The same weather continued until the 23rd of December. Fog, sleet, rain, squalls, bergs! We scarcely made any headway: it was with difficulty we saw our jibboom: we were in almost unknown seas. Suddenly the fog lifted; we were completely surrounded with bergs, the resounding murmur of which had been reaching us through it.

Bergs.—Antarctic bergs are quite different from those of the North. In the Arctic regions they are tall, irregular, and pinnacled; in the South they are flat-topped. They may be of any length. We saw many three or four miles long, one twelve miles long, and one, a floating island of ice, thirty miles long. Their usual height above the water is about 150 feet, and their depth beneath the surface must be seven or eight times as great as this. Those bergs that are not tabular are weather-worn varieties of the tabular. We came across several more varied in shape than usual. One was beautifully conical, and some had very well marked stratification; we saw a castellated berg looking like part of some strange fortification; one was hewn into beautiful Doric pillars, others were in the form of grand arches, others still had great caves hollowed out of them, which, in some cases, were connected with vertical holes piercing their upper surface. Through these holes, when a heavy swell beat up the caverns, columns of water and spray were ejected, often to a great height. Other bergs overhung their water-worn bases. Strange cracks and fissures abounded. Although these bergs are brilliant with whiteness, yet they glow with colour. It is beyond my power to describe them. I have counted from the deck as many as sixty-five at one time. The field-, floe-, and pack-ice is similar to that of the North. In parts we found it very closely packed; in parts it was more open and easy to penetrate.

Sea.—The colour of the sea varies very much. Now it is blue and clear; now olive-brown, and opaque. Between these two colours there is a series of shades from greenish blue, dark green, and olive green, and from clearness to opacity. The browner water appears to be in the neighbourhood of a great body of ice. This colour is due to a diatom, which swarms in the water, and which colours the pack-ice and the base of bergs with a rusty brown.

In the bluest water it was most profitable to hunt for seals. Ross and other navigators experienced the most terrific swells in the pack, but we escaped them even after the heaviest gales. In the neighbourhood of the Danger Islets the currents were very strong—at times it was difficult for our vessel to make headway against them. In the neighbourhood of bergs they were also impetuous. I was in one of two boats one day, in the neighbourhood of a berg, and so strong was the current that, although we pulled steadily for about four hours, we were only just able to hold our own against it. Near bergs the drift-ice moves very fast—now onward, now swaying round caught in a whirlpool, and boats have to keep a sharp look-out to prevent being nipped. Surface and deep-sea temperatures were recorded, and it is of interest to note that for the first time in Antarctic Seas the reversing thermometer was used. On two or three occasions we saw ice forming on the water, but never to any great extent. Besides temperatures, salinities were recorded, and several soundings were made with Lord Kelvin's patent sounding machine, and bottom specimens secured. Floats were also thrown out to test the direction and speed of the surface currents.

Weather.—All the observations that have been made in the Antarctic have been in the height of summer—that is, during the months of December, January, and February; and an account of our experiences during these months will give you a very fair idea of what Cook, Weddell, D'Urville, Wilkes, and Ross experienced before us.

Like our predecessors, we found it to be a region of gales and calms—gales from the north, with wet fog; gales from the south, with fine blinding snow; calms with fog, and calms with brilliant sunshine. Towards the middle of December, when we were approaching the icy regions, we lay-to in squally weather and thick fogs. Gradually we pushed southward, and soon entered latitudes where flat-topped icebergs surrounded us on every side, and where pack-ice floated on the water. Squally weather continued till the 24th of December, when, in the vicinity of the Danger Islets, we met with a great number of bergs. Long shall I remember this Christmas Eve, when we were fast anchored to a floe. There was a perfect calm; the sky, except at the horizon, had a dense canopy of cumulus clouds, which rested on the summits of the hills of Louis Philippe Land to the west; and when the sun was just below the horizon, the soft greys and blues of the clouds, and the spotless whiteness of the ice as it floated in the black and glassy sea, were tinted with the most delicate of colours—faint purples and rosy hues, blues, and greens, passing into translucent yellows. At midnight the solitude was grand and impressive, perhaps the more so since we had for well-nigh a week been drifting among bergs, with dense fog and very squally weather. No sound disturbed the silence; at times a flock of the beautiful sheath-bills would hover round the vessel, fanning the air with their soundless wings. All was in such unison, all in such perfect harmony; but it was a passing charm. Soon we had to think of more prosaic things, and reluctantly we turned our thoughts to the cargo we were to seek.

This is the picture of a calm midnight in mid-summer, different, indeed, from the heavy weather we experienced at other times, when for days we sheltered behind bergs and streams of pack, during black nights thick with fog or snow. One of the gales we encountered, the skipper described as the hardest that ever blew in the Arctic or Antarctic; and, indeed, it was stiff. For ten hours we steamed as hard as we could against it, and at the end had only made one knot. Picture to yourselves a sailing-vessel: what a different agency we have now! Where Cook, Ross, Weddell, and others would have been in the greatest peril, we with steam were comparatively safe.

The records of air temperature are very remarkable; our lowest temperature was $20.8°$ Fahr., our highest $37.6°$ Fahr.—only a difference of $16.8°$ Fahr. in the total range for a period extending slightly over two months. Compare this with our climate, where in a single day and night there may be a variation of more than twice that amount.

During the five months since our return, I have experienced in London temperatures ten degrees higher than on either of our crossings of the Equator, and five degrees lower than our lowest recorded temperature in the Antarctic.

The average temperatures show a still more remarkable uniformity. December averaged $31.14°$ Fahr. for one hundred and fifteen readings; January, $31.10°$ Fahr. for one hundred and ninety-eight readings; February, $29.65°$ for one hundred and sixteen readings—a range of less than $1.5°$ Fahr. This seems worthy of the special attention of future Antarctic explorers, for may it not indicate a similar uniformity of temperature throughout the year? Antarctic cold has been much dreaded by some; the four hundred and twenty-nine readings I took during December, January, and February, show an average temperature of only $30.76°$ Fahr. This was in the very height of summer, in latitudes corresponding to that of the Faröe Islands in the North, but I believe the temperature of winter does not vary so much from that of the summer as in the North.

Land.—What land we saw was entirely snow-clad, except in the steepest slopes, where the snow was unable to lie. These uncovered parts appeared quite black. On the 12th of January 1893, the Balæna discovered a tract of mountainous land lying to the S.W. of Erebus and Terror Gulf; this land has been more fully described by Captain Larsen, who later in the year traced it out in about 60° W. from 65° S. to 68° S., whence the land seemed to trend eastwards. It is high, rocky land, and entirely snow-clad. In about 65° S. and 58½° W. he discovered two active volcanoes which he has named Jason and Sarsee. Captain Larsen landed on the South Orkneys and Seymour Island, and in the latter he found some fossils which had fallen from a decomposing cliff. These are the first fossils ever brought from Antarctica. There are specimens among them of *Cucullæa*, *Cytherea*, and *Natæa*, and pieces of a coniferous tree. They are probably of the Tertiary age, and indicate a warmer climate than now prevails in these high southern latitudes. Dr. Donald had the advantage of landing in the region of Erebus and Terror Bay, and the Active, the vessel in which he sailed, passed through an unknown strait in Joinville Land.

Biology.—Whales were the object of our voyage, and we saw many, but none that were worth the catching. Whilst in the ice we met with three kinds—Finners (probably *Physalus Australis*), called 'Blue Whales' by Captain Larsen of the Norwegian vessel 'Jason,' others strongly resembling the Pacific Hunchback Whale, and Bottle-nose Whale, two of which he captured. Besides these, there was present in considerable numbers the grampus or sword-fish (*Orca*), conspicuous by its long dorsal fin. Ross says that in Erebus and Terror Gulf, on New Year's Day 1843, 'great numbers of the largest-sized black whales were lying upon the water in all directions: their enormous breadth quite astonished us.' At that time he was within a mile of the position held by us on Christmas Eve 1892 (viz., in 64° S. 55° 28′ W.). Elsewhere also, he talks of a whale 'greatly resembling, but said to be distinct from, the Greenland Whale.'[1] It was chiefly upon the authority of these two statements, in addition to some others made by Ross, that the Dundee and Norwegian whaling-fleet ventured to the south last year. None of the vessels saw any sign of a whale in the least resembling the Greenland or Bowhead Whale (*Balæna mysticetus*), although they were in the ice for a period extending over two months. Are we to conclude that Ross was mistaken, or that he has made a misleading statement? I think not. All we can say is that we failed to confirm Ross's statement, and that, on further search, the whale 'greatly resembling the Greenland Whale' may yet be found. Indeed the vessels of Captain Larsen's fleet, during their subsequent voyage in 1893-94, gave chase to a whale which seemed to resemble the Bowhead, but failed to capture it. We shall see whether the plucky little Norwegian vessel Antarctic, that is pushing to 78° S., in the region of Victoria Land, has better luck this season.

Ross says that the whales he saw were '*lying*' on the water, and this is one great characteristic of *Balæna mysticetus*. Contrary to the habits of the Finner Whales in the north, on more than one occasion we saw the southern Finners also *lying* on the water, and sometimes the dorsal fin seemed to have been almost entirely torn away, perhaps

---

[1] Ross's *Voyage*, vol. i. p. 109.

by the ice. But it is hardly possible that Ross could have been thus deceived after thirteen years' experience in Arctic Seas. Besides, he also adds, 'their enormous breadth quite astonished us.' This is a second great characteristic. The Bowhead Whale has a great, broad, flat back, with a head one-third the total length of its body. The finners which we saw had a bony vertebral ridge, and very much smaller heads.

On the 16th of December, when we first made ice, we passed among thousands of finner whales. Many came quite close to the ship, and, as far as the eye could reach in all directions, one could see their curved backs, and see and hear their resounding 'blasts.' *Euphasia* swarmed in the water. Many blue petrels, and myriads of Cape pigeons were flying around, and settling on the surface.

On the 26th of January, while out in a boat, I saw what at first appeared to be a rolling piece of ice, but what was in reality a white finner whale.

The whale which I have said strongly resembled the Pacific Hunchback Whale (*Megaptera versabilis*), I have seen going 'tail up,' a characteristic of the Bowhead Whale. It has a broader and flatter back than the finner whale mentioned, but can scarcely be said to resemble *Balæna mysticetus*.

On the outward and homeward voyage, we constantly met with great schools of dolphins and porpoises, as well as, on several occasions, with whales, but I must confess that I found identification very difficult. At Port Stanley I secured a ground porpoise, the skeleton of which is now in University College Museum, Dundee. It was a curious fact that in almost every case the schools of dolphins and porpoises were going, more or less, in the direction of the vessel, and one wonders if there were any particular reason for this. Was it migration? Were those we met with in October and November migrating southward at the approach of the northern winter, and those we saw south of the line in November and December moving southward with the southern summer? Similarly, were those seen by us in southern latitudes in March and April fleeing from the southern winter, and those that passed us in April and May going northward with the approach of the northern summer?

We met with only four species of seals, all of them being true seals, and belonging to the genus *Stenorhynchus* (Allen). The Sea Elephant seal was not seen, nor were any of the Otariidæ. The four were—the Sea Leopard (*Stenorhynchus leptonyx*), Weddell's False Sea Leopard (*Stenorhynchus Weddellii*), a creamy white seal with a darker dorsal stripe, the so-called Crab-Eating Seal or White Antarctic Seal (*Stenorhynchus carcinophaga*), and Ross's Large-Eyed Seal (*Stenorhynchus Rossii*). Besides these there was another, which I think was certainly a younger form of the Sea Leopard.

The creamy white seals, the so-called Crab-Eating Seals, and the mottled grey seals (Ross's Seal), were in greatest abundance; these lay four, five, or even ten on a single piece of pack-ice; the greatest number I saw on one piece of ice at a time was forty-seven. On one occasion we found some seals on a tilted berg, and so high was the ledge above the level of the water that our men clambered up with difficulty and secured their prey. This illustrates their great power of jumping out of the water. I have seen them rising eight or ten feet above the sea, and cover distances of fully twenty feet in length.

The mode of progression of true seals is well known: but although on *terra firma* man can easily outrun them, yet on the pack they glide onward while their pursuer sinks deeply in the snow.

The present generation had never seen man, and at his approach they did not attempt to flee, but surveyed him open-mouthed and fearful, while he laid them low with club or bullet. Sometimes they were so lazy with sleep that I have several times seen a man strike one in the ribs with the muzzle of his gun, till, wondering what was disturbing its slumbers, it raised its head, only too quickly to fall pierced by a bullet. Seldom did they escape—one bullet meant one seal. On the last day of sealing we were among a great host of the large Sea Leopards, and as we were returning to the ship they were moaning loudly. This was said to be a sign that they were about to start on a long journey; but was it not rather a sigh of relief on seeing their slaughterers' craft run up her bunting, and announce to all that she was a full ship, and that her thirst for blood was quenched?

While we continue to require sacks, while we persist in wearing patent-leather shoes, and while we satisfy our fancies with certain purses and card-cases, the slaughter of these seals will continue. But I would protest against the *indiscriminate* massacre which takes place in order to supply blubber, as well as hides, for the purposes indicated. Old and young, females with young, are slaughtered alike, and should this continue, these seals, like the Antarctic Fur Seals at the beginning of the century, will undoubtedly be quickly exterminated.

In December all the seals were in bad condition, thinly blubbered, and grievously scarred, and it is noteworthy that the females appeared to be as freely scarred as the males. During January their condition improved, and by February they were heavily blubbered and free of scars. The males were apparently as numerous as the females, but I made no definite statistics. Loving the sun, they lie on the pack all day digesting their meal of the previous night, which had consisted of fish or small crustaceans, or both; the penguin is also occasionally the victim of the Sea Leopard, and I have found stones in their stomachs. These stones are likely part of the geological collection which the penguins are accustomed to carry about with them. Nematode worms were almost invariably present in the stomachs.

All the seals were obtained from the pack-ice, in the bluest and clearest water; the Sea Leopard was on the outermost streams of the ice, and was most frequently found singly, but sometimes in pairs or threes on one piece of ice. Of Weddell's False Sea Leopards, we on board the Balæna only saw about four altogether, and these singly; Dr. Donald, however, met with greater numbers. Two were quite young, and one of these we attempted to bring on board alive, but failed.

2 A

Of birds we saw in all some twenty species, the most remarkable being the gregarious penguin. The first I saw of these birds was off the shores of the Falkland Islands, over two hundred miles from the nearest land. The vessel was making little headway through the water, the wind having fallen, and, on my coming on deck at mid-day, my attention was called to 'some small seals,' which where playing round the stern of the vessel. They were swimming calmly about in the water, now immersing themselves entirely, now lifting their heads only above the water much as one sees seals doing in the evening, or on a bleak day, when they prefer to remain in the water rather than come out and lie on the ice, as they do when the sun shines brightly. What the sailors took for seals were, however, really macaroni penguins (*Eudyptes chrysolophus*), with their silky hair-like feathers looking like wet fur. The sailors quite refused to recognise feathers in this close-fitting fleece, black on the back and white on the breast. Penguins also move through the water like shoals of very active, very small porpoises. On the ice they move swiftly, gliding upon their breasts, and using their fore limbs as well as their hind limbs to help them along. Sometimes also they may be seen walking in an erect position. After this they were our daily companions, and we saw in all four or five different species. We captured some very fine Emperor penguins; very monarchs, clothed in silken robes of white and black, and decked with gold and purple.

In the vicinity of the Danger Islands we first saw the sheath-bill (*Chionis alba*). We saw, too, the Snowy Petrel, the greedy Giant Petrel, and the Blue Petrel. Mother Carey's chickens are also to be found here, as in all other parts of the oceanic world. There are no land plants known to be within the Antarctic Circle.

All these observations were made, and these specimens procured, between December 16, 1892, and February 18, 1893. On the latter date we had glutted our ship with seals, and turned her head homewards. The following afternoon we passed Clarence Islands, the most easterly of the South Shetland group, its three bold ridges looming through mist and scud. The land was wild and majestic, towering over the adjacent icebergs. Like other land we had seen, it was entirely snow-clad, except on the most precipitous slopes, which were short and abrupt to the south, but long and easy to the north. On February 20 at 9 A.M. we passed our last berg in about 60° 27′ S. and 53° 40′ W., or about forty miles north of Clarence Island. Port Stanley was reached on the morning of 28th February; Portland on 24th May; and finally, on 30th May, we came to rest at Dundee.

It is to be hoped that before long we shall see another expedition sailing to Antarctic Seas, but one in which scientific research will be the primary object. A rush to the South Pole is not what we urge; but a systematic exploration of the whole South Polar regions. The outline of Antarctica has to be definitely mapped out; we must sound, dredge, and trawl; make temperature and salinity observations throughout the breadth and depth of the ocean, and study the direction, force, and nature of oceanic currents. We can study the problems of the Ice Age, which are there alone to be seen in active operation, and we must investigate the nature and distribution of the rocks, which contain for the palæontologist an entirely new fossil fauna and flora. For the botanist, unfortunately, we cannot hold out any hopes, but for the zoologist there awaits a most interesting and extensive fauna. Pendulum observations ought also to be made; and above all we must take systematic magnetic observations both on land and at sea, and make meteorological observations at several points throughout the entire year. Much can, and we hope much will, be done by private enterprise; but can we not make a national effort, as we did in the days of Cook, Weddell, Ross, and the Challenger, and show that the Britain of to-day is not behind the Britain of our fathers?

Printed by T. and A. Constable, Printers to Her Majesty
at the Edinburgh University Press

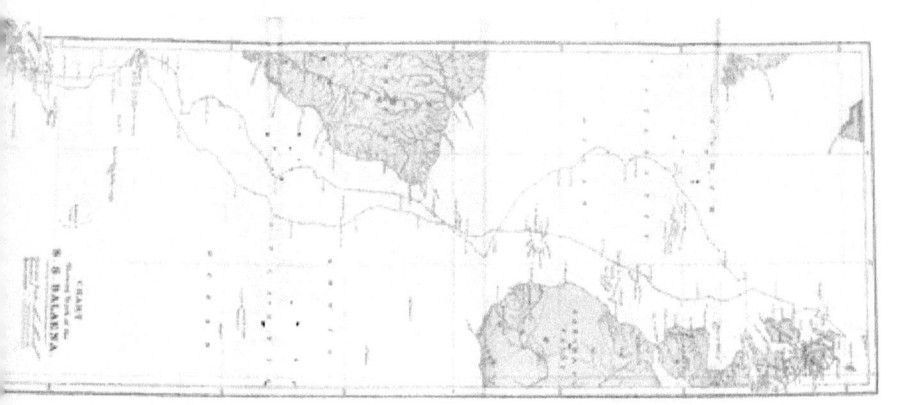

A Classified Catalogue

OF WORKS IN

GENERAL LITERATURE

PUBLISHED BY

LONGMANS, GREEN, & CO.

39 PATERNOSTER ROW, LONDON, E.C.

91 AND 93 FIFTH AVENUE, NEW YORK, AND 32 HORNBY ROAD, BOMBAY.

CONTENTS.

	PAGE		PAGE
BADMINTON LIBRARY (THE)	10	MANUALS OF CATHOLIC PHILOSOPHY	16
BIOGRAPHY, PERSONAL MEMOIRS, &c.	7	MENTAL, MORAL, AND POLITICAL PHILOSOPHY	14
CHILDREN'S BOOKS	26		
CLASSICAL LITERATURE TRANSLATIONS, ETC.	18	MISCELLANEOUS AND CRITICAL WORKS	29
COOKERY, DOMESTIC MANAGEMENT, &c.	28	MISCELLANEOUS THEOLOGICAL WORKS	31
EVOLUTION, ANTHROPOLOGY, &c.	17	POETRY AND THE DRAMA	18
FICTION, HUMOUR, &c.	21	POLITICAL ECONOMY AND ECONOMICS	16
FUR AND FEATHER SERIES	12	POPULAR SCIENCE	24
HISTORY, POLITICS, POLITY, POLITICAL MEMOIRS, &c.	3	SILVER LIBRARY (THE)	27
		SPORT AND PASTIME	10
LANGUAGE, HISTORY AND SCIENCE OF	16	TRAVEL AND ADVENTURE, THE COLONIES, &c.	8
LONGMANS' SERIES OF BOOKS FOR GIRLS	26	VETERINARY MEDICINE, &c.	9
		WORKS OF REFERENCE	25

INDEX OF AUTHORS AND EDITORS.

	Page		Page		Page		Page
Abbott (Evelyn)	3, 18	Bacon	7, 11	Boedder (B.)	16	Cholmondeley-Pennell (H.)	11
—— (T. K.)	14, 15	Baden-Powell (B. H.)	3	Bolland (W. E.)	14	Christie (Nimmo)	19
—— (E. A.)	14	Bagehot (W.)	7, 16, 29	Bosanquet (B.)	14	Cicero	18
Acland (A. H. D.)	3	Bagwell (R.)	3	Boyd (Rev. A. K. H.)	17, 29, 31	Clarke (Rev. R. F.)	16
Acton (Eliza)	28	Bain (Alexander)	14	Brassey (Lady)	8, 9	Clodd (Edward)	17
Acworth (H. A.)	18	Baker (James)	21	—— (Lord)	3, 8, 12, 16	Clutterbuck (W. J.)	9
Adeane (J. H.)	7	—— (Sir S. W.)	8	Bray (C. and Mrs.)	14	Cochrane (A.)	19
Æschylus	18	Balfour (A. J.)	11, 31	Bright (J. F.)	3	Comyn (L. N.)	26
Ainger (A. C.)	12	Ball (J. T.)	3	Broadfoot (Major W.)	10	Conington (John)	18
Albemarle (Earl of)	11	Baring-Gould (Rev. S.)	27, 29	Brögger (W. C.)	7	Conybeare (Rev. W. J.) & Howson (Dean)	27
Alden (W. L.)	21	Barnett (Rev. S. A. & Mrs.)	16	Brown (J. Moray)	11	Coventry (A.)	11
Allen (Grant)	24	Baynes (T. S.)	29	Browning (H. Ellen)	9	Cox (Harding)	10
Allingham (W.)	18, 29	Beaconsfield (Earl of)	21	Buck (H. A.)	12	Crake (Rev. A. D.)	26
Anstey (F.)	21	Beaufort (Duke of)	10, 11	Buckle (H. T.)	3	Creighton (Bishop)	4
Aristophanes	18	Becker (Prof.)	18	Bull (T.)	28	Cuningham (G. C.)	3
Aristotle	14, 18	Beesly (A. H.)	19	Burke (U. R.)	3	Curzon (Hon. G. N.)	3
Armstrong (G. F. Savage)	19	Bell (Mrs. Hugh)	19	Burrows (Montagu)	18	Cutts (Rev. E. L.)	4
—— (E. J.)	7, 19, 29	Bent (J. Theodore)	8	Butler (E. A.)	24		
Arnold (Sir Edwin)	8, 19	Besant (Sir Walter)	3	—— (Samuel)	29	Davidson (W. L.)	14, 16
—— (Dr. T.)	3	Bickerdyke (J.)	11, 12			Davies (J. F.)	18
Ashley (W. J.)	16	Bicknell (A. C.)	8	Cameron of Lochiel	12	De la Saussaye (C.)	32
Astor (J. J.)	21	Bird (R.)	31	Cannan (E.)	17	Deland (Mrs.)	26
Atelier du Lys (Author of)	26	Black (Clementina)	21	—— (F. Laura)	13	Dent (C. T.)	11
		Blackwell (Elizabeth)	7	Carmichael (J.)	19	Deploige	17
Babington (W. D.)	17	Boase (Rev. C. W.)	4	Chesney (Sir G.)	3	De Salis (Mrs.)	28, 29
				Chisholm (G. G.)	25		

INDEX OF AUTHORS AND EDITORS—continued.

Name	Page
De Tocqueville (A.)	3
Devas (C. S.)	16
Dickinson (G. L.)	4
Dougall (L.)	21
Dowell (S.)	16
Doyle (A. Conan)	21
Dreyfus (Irma)	30
Du Bois (W. E. B.)	4
Dufferin (Marquis of)	4
Dunbar (Mary F.)	20
Ebrington (Viscount)	12
Egbert (J. C.)	18
Ellis (J. H.)	13
Ewald (H.)	1
Falkner (E.)	13
Farnell (G. S.)	18
Farrar (Dean)	16, 21
Fitzwygram (Sir F.)	10
Florian	19
Follett (M. P.)	4
Ford (I.)	13
Fowler (Edith H.)	21
Francis (Francis)	13
Freeman (Edward A.)	1
Frothingham (A. L.)	30
Froude (James A.)	4, 7, 9, 21
Furneaux (W.)	24
Galton (W. F.)	19
Gardiner (Samuel R.)	4
Gerard (D.)	26
Gibbons (J. S.)	11, 12
Gilson (Hon. H.)	13
Gill (H. J.)	22
Gleig (Rev. G. R.)	8
Goethe	19
Graham (P. A.)	13, 21
—— (G. F.)	16
Grant (Sir A.)	14
Graves (R. P.)	7
Green (T. Hill)	14
Greville (C. C. F.)	4
Grey (Maria)	26
Grose (T. H.)	14
Grove (F. C.)	8
—— (Mrs. Lilly)	11
Gurney (Rev. A.)	19
Gwilt (J.)	30
Haggard (H. Rider)	21
Hake (O.)	12
Halliwell-Phillipps (J.)	8
Hamlin (A. D. F.)	30
Harding (S. B.)	4
Hart (Albert B.)	2
Harte (Bret)	22
Hartwig (G.)	24
Hassall (A.)	6
Haweis (Rev. H. R.)	7, 30
Hayward (Jane M.)	24
Hearn (W. E.)	4
Heathcote (J. M. and C. G.)	12
Helmholtz (Hermann von)	24
Henry (W.)	12
Herbert (Col. Kenney)	12
Hewins (W. A. S.)	17
Hillier (G. Lacy)	10
Hodgson (Shadworth H.)	14
Holroyd (Maria J.)	7
Hope (Anthony)	22
Hornung (E. W.)	22
Houston (D. F.)	4
Howell (G.)	16
Howitt (W.)	9
Hudson (W. H.)	24
Hueffer (F. M.)	7
Hume (David)	14
Hunt (Rev. W.)	4
Hutchinson (Horace G.)	11
Ingelow (Jean)	19, 26
Jefferies (Richard)	30
Jones (H. Bence)	25
Johnson (J. & J. H.)	30
Jordan (W. L.)	16
Jowett (Dr. B.)	17
Joyce (P. W.)	4
Justinian	14
Kalisch (M. M.)	32
Kant (I.)	14, 15
Kaye (Sir J. W.)	5
Kerr (Rev. J.)	12
Killick (Rev. A. H.)	15
Kitchin (Dr. G. W.)	4
Knight (E. F.)	5, 9, 22
Köstlin (J.)	7
Ladd (G. T.)	25
Lang (Andrew)	5, 10, 11, 13, 14, 17, 18, 19, 20, 22, 26, 30
Lascelles (Hon. G.)	10, 11
Laurie (S. S.)	5
Leaf (Walter)	13
Lear (H. L. Sidney)	29
Lecky (W. E. H.)	5, 19
Lees (J. A.)	9
Lester (L. V.)	7
Lewes (G. H.)	15
Lindley (J.)	25
Lindsay (Lady)	19
Lodge (H. C.)	4
Loftie (Rev. W. J.)	1
Longman (C. J.)	10, 13, 30
—— (F. W.)	13
—— (G. H.)	11, 12
Lowell (A. L.)	5
Lubbock (Sir John)	17
Lucan	18
Lyall (Edna)	22
Lyttelton (Hon. R. H.)	10
Lytton (Earl of)	19
MacArthur (Miss E. A.)	17
Macaulay (Lord)	5, 6, 20
MacColl (Canon)	6
Macdonald (George)	20, 32
Macfarren (Sir G. A.)	30
Magruder (Julia)	22
Mackail (J. W.)	18
Mackinnon (J.)	6
Macleod (H. D.)	16
Macpherson (Rev. H. A.)	12
Maher (M.)	16
Malleson (Col. G. B.)	5
Mandello (J.)	17
Marbot (Baron de)	7
Marquand (A.)	30
Marshman (J. C.)	7
Martineau (Dr. James)	32
Maskelyne (J. N.)	13
Matthews (Brander)	22
Maunder (S.)	25
Max Müller (F.)	15, 16, 30, 32
May (Sir T. Erskine)	6
Meade (L. T.)	26
Melville (G. J. Whyte)	22
Merivale (Dean)	6
Merriman (H. S.)	22
Mill (James)	15
—— (John Stuart)	15, 16
Milner (G.)	30
Miss Molly (Author of)	26
Molesworth (Mrs.)	26
Montague (F. C.)	6
Moore (T.)	25
—— (Rev. Edward)	25
Morris (W.)	20, 22, 31
—— (Mowbray)	11
Mosso (A.)	15
Mulhall (M. G.)	17
Munk (W.)	7
Murray (R. F.)	20
Nansen (F.)	7
Nesbit (E.)	20
Newman (Cardinal)	22
O'Brien (W.)	6
Ogle (W.)	18
Oliphant (Mrs.)	22
Oliver (W. D.)	9
Onslow (Earl of)	12
Orchard (T. N.)	31
Osbourne (L.)	23
Palmer (A. H.)	8
Park (W.)	13
Parr (Mrs. Louisa)	26
Payne-Gallwey (Sir R.)	11, 13
Peary (Mrs. Josephine)	9
Peek (H.)	11
Pembroke (Earl of)	12
Perring (Sir P.)	19
Phillips (M.)	32
Phillipps-Wolley (C.)	10, 22
Piatt (S. & J. J.)	20
Pleydell-Bouverie (E. O.)	12
Pole (W.)	13
Pollock (W. H.)	11
Poole (W. H. and Mrs.)	29
Poore (G. V.)	31
Potter (J.)	16
Prevost (C.)	11
Pritchett (R. T.)	12
Proctor (R. A.)	13, 24, 31
Quill (A. W.)	18
Quillinan (Mrs.)	9
Quintana (A.)	22
Raine (Rev. James)	4
Ransome (Cyril)	3
Rhoades (J.)	18, 20
Rhoscomyl (O.)	23
Rich (A.)	18
Richardson (Sir B. W.)	31
—— (C.)	12
Rickman (I. B.)	6
Rickaby (John)	16
—— (Joseph)	16
Ridley (Annie E.)	7
—— (E.)	18
Riley (J. W.)	20
Rocer (Peter M.)	16, 25
Rokeby (C.)	23
Rolfsen (N.)	7
Romanes (G. J.)	8, 15, 17, 20, 32
—— (Mrs.)	8
Ronalds (A.)	13
Roosevelt (T.)	4
Rossetti (M. F.)	31
Russell (Bertrand)	17
Saintsbury (G.)	12
Sandars (T. C.)	14
Seebohm (F.)	6, 8
Selous (F. C.)	10
Selss (A. M.)	19
Sewell (Elizabeth M.)	23
Shakespeare	20
Shand (A. I.)	12
Sharpe (R. R.)	6
Shearman (M.)	10
Sheppard (Rev. Edgar)	8
Sinclair (A.)	12
Smith (R. Bosworth)	6
—— (W. P. Haskett)	9
Soderini (Count E.)	17
Solovyoff (V. S.)	31
Sophocles	18
Soulsby (Lucy H.)	26
Spedding (J.)	7, 14
Stanley (Bishop)	24
Steel (A. G.)	10
—— (J. H.)	10
Stephen (Sir Jas.)	6
—— (Leslie)	9
Stephens (H. Morse)	6
—— (W. W.)	8
Stevens (R. W.)	8
Stevenson (R. L.)	23, 26
Stock (St. George)	15
'Stonehenge'	10
Storr (F.)	11
Stuart-Wortley (A. J.)	11, 12
Stubbs (J. W.)	6
Sturdy (E. T.)	30
Sturgis (J.)	20
Suffolk & Berkshire (Earl of)	11
Sullivan (Sir E.)	12
Sully (James)	15
Supernatural Religion (Author of)	32
Sutherland (A. and G.)	6
Suttner (B. von)	23
Swinburne (A. J.)	15
Symes (J. E.)	17
Tacitus	18
Taylor (Meadows)	17
Tebbutt (C. G.)	12
Thompson (N. G.)	13
Thornhill (W. J.)	18
Todd (A.)	6
Toynbee (A.)	17
Trevelyan (Sir G. O.)	7
—— (G. P.)	17
Trollope (Anthony)	23
Tyndall (J.)	9
Tyrrell (R. Y.)	18
Upton (F. K. and Bertha)	26
Verney (Frances P. and Margaret M.)	8
Vincent (J. E.)	17
Virgil	18
Vivekananda (Swami)	32
Wakeman (H. O.)	6
Walford (Mrs.)	23
Walker (Jane H.)	29
Walpole (Spencer)	6
Walrond (Col. L.)	10
Walsingham (Lord)	11
Walter (J.)	8
Watson (A. E. T.)	1, 12
Waylen (H. S. H.)	30
Webb (Mr. and Mrs. Sidney)	17
—— (T. E.)	19
Weber (A.)	15
Weir (Capt. R.)	11
West (B. B.)	23, 31
Weyman (Stanley)	23
Whately (Archbishop)	14, 15
—— (E. Jane)	16
Whishaw (F. J.)	9, 23
Whitelaw (R.)	18
Wilcocks (J. C.)	13
Willich (C. M.)	25
Witham (T. M.)	12
Wolff (H. W.)	6
Wood (Rev. J. G.)	25
Woodgate (W. B.)	10
Wood-Martin (W. G.)	8
Wordsworth (Elizabeth)	26
Wylie (J. H.)	6
Youatt (W.)	10
Zeller (E.)	15

MESSRS. LONGMANS & CO.'S STANDARD AND GENERAL WORKS. 3

History, Politics, Polity, Political Memoirs, &c.

Abbott.—*A History of Greece.*
By EVELYN ABBOTT, M.A., LL.D.
Part I.—From the Earliest Times to the Ionian Revolt. Crown 8vo., 10s. 6d.
Part II.—500-445 B.C. Crown 8vo., 10s. 6d.

Acland and Ransome.—*A Handbook in Outline of the Political History of England to 1894.* Chronologically Arranged. By A. H. DYKE ACLAND, M.P., and CYRIL RANSOME, M.A. Crown 8vo., 6s.

ANNUAL REGISTER (THE). A Review of Public Events at Home and Abroad, for the year 1895. 8vo., 18s.
Volumes of the *ANNUAL REGISTER* for the years 1863-1894 can still be had. 18s. each.

Arnold (THOMAS, D.D.), formerly Head Master of Rugby School.
INTRODUCTORY LECTURES ON MODERN HISTORY. 8vo., 7s. 6d.
MISCELLANEOUS WORKS. 8vo., 7s. 6d.

Baden-Powell.—*The Indian Village Community.* Examined with Reference to the Physical, Ethnographic, and Historical Conditions of the Provinces; chiefly on the Basis of the Revenue-Settlement Records and District Manuals. By B. H. BADEN-POWELL, M.A., C.I.E. With Map. 8vo., 16s.

Bagwell.—*Ireland under the Tudors.* By RICHARD BAGWELL, LL.D. (3 vols.) Vols. I. and II. From the first invasion of the Northmen to the year 1578. 8vo., 32s. Vol. III. 1578-1603. 8vo. 18s.

Ball.—*Historical Review of the Legislative Systems operative in Ireland,* from the Invasion of Henry the Second to the Union (1172-1800). By the Rt. Hon. J. T. BALL. 8vo., 6s.

Besant.—*The History of London.* By Sir WALTER BESANT. With 74 Illustrations. Crown 8vo., 1s. 9d. Or bound as a School Prize Book, 2s. 6d.

Brassey (LORD).—PAPERS AND ADDRESSES.
NAVAL AND MARITIME. 1872-1893. 2 vols. Crown 8vo., 10s.

Brassey (LORD) PAPERS AND ADDRESSES—*continued.*
MERCANTILE MARINE AND NAVIGATION, from 1871-1894. Crown 8vo., 5s.
IMPERIAL FEDERATION AND COLONISATION FROM 1880 to 1894. Cr. 8vo., 5s.
POLITICAL AND MISCELLANEOUS. 1861-1894. Crown 8vo 5s.

Bright.—*A History of England.* By the Rev. J. FRANCK BRIGHT, D.D.
Period I. *MEDIEVAL MONARCHY:* A.D. 449 to 1485. Crown 8vo., 4s. 6d.
Period II. *PERSONAL MONARCHY.* 1485 to 1688. Crown 8vo., 5s.
Period III. *CONSTITUTIONAL MONARCHY.* 1689 to 1837. Crown 8vo., 7s. 6d.
Period IV. *THE GROWTH OF DEMOCRACY.* 1837 to 1880 Crown 8vo., 6s.

Buckle.—*History of Civilisation in England and France, Spain and Scotland.* By HENRY THOMAS BUCKLE. 3 vols. Crown 8vo., 24s.

Burke.—*A History of Spain* from the Earliest Times to the Death of Ferdinand the Catholic. By ULICK RALPH BURKE, M.A. 2 vols. 8vo., 32s.

Chesney.—*Indian Polity:* a View of the System of Administration in India. By General Sir GEORGE CHESNEY, K.C.B., With Map showing all the Administrative Divisions of British India. 8vo., 21s.

Cuningham.—*A Scheme for Imperial Federation:* a Senate for the Empire. By GRANVILLE C. CUNINGHAM, of Montreal, Canada. Crown 8vo., 3s. 6d.

Curzon.—*Persia and the Persian Question.* By the Right Hon. GEORGE N. CURZON, M.P. With 9 Maps, 96 Illustrations, Appendices, and an Index. 2 vols. 8vo., 42s.

De Tocqueville.—*Democracy in America.* By ALEXIS DE TOCQUEVILLE. 2 vols. Crown 8vo., 16s.

History, Politics, Polity, Political Memoirs, &c.—*continued.*

Dickinson.—THE DEVELOPMENT OF PARLIAMENT DURING THE NINETEENTH CENTURY. By G. LOWES DICKINSON, M.A. 8vo, 7s. 6d.

Ewald.—THE HISTORY OF ISRAEL. By HEINRICH EWALD. 8 vols., 8vo, £5 18s.

Follett.—THE SPEAKER OF THE HOUSE OF REPRESENTATIVES. By M. P. FOLLETT. With an Introduction by ALBERT BUSHNELL HART, Ph.D., of Harvard University. Crown 8vo, 6s.

Froude (JAMES A.).

THE HISTORY OF ENGLAND, from the Fall of Wolsey to the Defeat of the Spanish Armada.
  Popular Edition. 12 vols. Crown 8vo. 3s. 6d. each.
  'Silver Library' *Edition.* 12 vols. Crown 8vo., 3s. 6d. each.

THE DIVORCE OF CATHERINE OF ARAGON. Crown 8vo., 6s.

THE SPANISH STORY OF THE ARMADA, and other Essays. Cr. 8vo., 3s. 6d.

THE ENGLISH IN IRELAND IN THE EIGHTEENTH CENTURY.
  Cabinet Edition. 3 vols. Cr. 8vo., 18s.
  'Silver Library' Edition. 3 vols. Cr. 8vo., 10s. 6d.

ENGLISH SEAMEN IN THE SIXTEENTH CENTURY. Cr. 8vo., 6s.

THE COUNCIL OF TRENT. Crown 8vo., 6s.

SHORT STUDIES ON GREAT SUBJECTS. 4 vols. Cr. 8vo., 3s. 6d. each.

CÆSAR: a Sketch. Cr. 8vo, 3s. 6d.

Gardiner (SAMUEL RAWSON, D.C.L., LL.D.).

HISTORY OF ENGLAND, from the Accession of James I. to the Outbreak of the Civil War, 1603-1642. 10 vols. Crown 8vo., 6s. each.

A HISTORY OF THE GREAT CIVIL WAR, 1642-1649. 4 vols. Cr. 8vo., 6s. each.

A HISTORY OF THE COMMONWEALTH AND THE PROTECTORATE. 1649-1660. Vol. I. 1649-1651. With 14 Maps. 8vo., 21s.

Gardiner (SAMUEL RAWSON, D.C.L., LL.D.)—*continued.*

THE STUDENT'S HISTORY OF ENGLAND. With 378 Illustrations. Crown 8vo., 12s.
  Also in Three Volumes, price 4s. each.
  Vol. I. B.C. 55—A.D. 1509. 173 Illustrations.
  Vol. II. 1509-1689. 96 Illustrations.
  Vol. III. 1689-1885. 109 Illustrations.

Greville.—A JOURNAL OF THE REIGNS OF KING GEORGE IV., KING WILLIAM IV., AND QUEEN VICTORIA. By CHARLES C. F. GREVILLE, formerly Clerk of the Council.
  Cabinet Edition. 8 vols. Crown 8vo., 6s. each.
  'Silver Library' *Edition.* 8 vols. Crown 8vo., 3s. 6d. each.

HARVARD HISTORICAL STUDIES.

THE SUPPRESSION OF THE AFRICAN SLAVE TRADE TO THE UNITED STATES OF AMERICA, 1638-1870. By W. E. B. DU BOIS, Ph.D. 8vo., 7s. 6d.

THE CONTEST OVER THE RATIFICATION OF THE FEDERAL CONSTITUTION IN MASSACHUSETTS. By S. B. HARDING, A.M. 8vo., 6s.

A CRITICAL STUDY OF NULLIFICATION IN SOUTH CAROLINA. By D. F. HOUSTON, A.M. 8vo., 6s.

*** Other Volumes are in preparation.

Hearn.—THE GOVERNMENT OF ENGLAND: its Structure and its Development. By W. EDWARD HEARN. 8vo., 16s.

Historic Towns.—Edited by E. A. FREEMAN, D.C.L., and Rev. WILLIAM HUNT, M.A. With Maps and Plans. Crown 8vo., 3s. 6d. each.

Bristol. By Rev. W. Hunt.	Oxford. By Rev. C. W. Boase.
Carlisle. By Mandell Creighton, D.D.	Winchester. By G. W. Kitchin, D.D.
Cinque Ports. By Montague Burrows.	York. By Rev. James Raine.
Colchester. By Rev. E. L. Cutts.	New York. By Theodore Roosevelt.
Exeter. By E. A. Freeman.	Boston (U.S.) By Henry Cabot Lodge.
London. By Rev. W. J. Loftie.	

Joyce.—A SHORT HISTORY OF IRELAND, from the Earliest Times to 1608. By P. W. JOYCE, LL.D. Crown 8vo., 10s. 6d.

MESSRS. LONGMANS & CO.'S STANDARD AND GENERAL WORKS.　5

History, Politics, Polity, Political Memoirs, &c.—*continued*.

Kaye and Malleson.—*History of the Indian Mutiny*, 1857-1858'. By Sir John W. Kaye and Colonel G. B. Malleson. With Analytical Index and Maps and Plans. Cabinet Edition. 6 vols. Crown 8vo., 6s. each.

Knight.—*Madagascar in War Time: The Experiences of 'The Times' Special Correspondent with the Hovas during the French Invasion of* 1895. By E. F. Knight. With 16 Illustrations and a Map. 8vo., 12s. 6d.

Lang (Andrew).

Pickle the Spy: or, The Incognito of Prince Charles. With 6 Portraits. 8vo., 18s.

St. Andrews. With 8 Plates and 24 Illustrations in the Text by T. Hodge. 8vo., 15s. net.

Laurie.—*Historical Survey of Pre-Christian Education.* By S. S. Laurie, A.M., LL.D. Crown 8vo., 12s.

Lecky (William Edward Hartpole).
History of England in the Eighteenth Century.
　Library Edition. 8 vols. 8vo., £7 4s.
　Cabinet Edition. England. 7 vols. Crown 8vo., 6s. each. Ireland. 5 vols. Crown 8vo., 6s. each.

History of European Morals from Augustus to Charlemagne. 2 vols. Crown 8vo., 16s.

History of the Rise and Influence of the Spirit of Rationalism in Europe. 2 vols. Crown 8vo., 16s.

Democracy and Liberty. 2 vols. 8vo., 36s.

The Empire: its value and its Growth. An Inaugural Address delivered at the Imperial Institute, November 20, 1893. Cr. 8vo., 1s. 6d.

Lowell.—*Governments and Parties in Continental Europe.* By A. Lawrence Lowell. 2 vols. 8vo., 21s.

Macaulay (Lord).

The Life and Works of Lord Macaulay. 'Edinburgh' Edition. 10 vols. 8vo., 6s. each.
　Vols. I.-IV. *History of England.*
　Vols. V.-VII. *Essays; Biographies; Indian Penal Code; Contributions to Knight's 'Quarterly Magazine'.*
　Vol. VIII. *Speeches; Lays of Ancient Rome; Miscellaneous Poems.*
　Vols. IX. and X. *The Life and Letters of Lord Macaulay.* By the Right Hon. Sir G. O. Trevelyan, Bart., M.P.

This Edition is a cheaper reprint of the Library Edition of Lord Macaulay's *Life and Works*.

Complete Works.
　Cabinet Edition. 16 vols. Post 8vo., £4 16s.
　Library Edition. 8 vols. 8vo., £5 5s.
　'Edinburgh' Edition. 8 vols. 8vo., 6s. each.

History of England from the Accession of James the Second.
　Popular Edition. 2 vols. Cr. 8vo., 5s.
　Student's Edition. 2 vols. Cr. 8vo., 12s.
　People's Edition. 4 vols. Cr. 8vo., 16s.
　Cabinet Edition. 8 vols. Post 8vo., 48s.
　'Edinburgh' Edition. 4 vols. 8vo., 6s. each.
　Library Edition. 5 vols. 8vo., £4.

Critical and Historical Essays, with Lays of Ancient Rome, in 1 volume.
　Popular Edition. Crown 8vo., 2s. 6d.
　Authorised Edition. Crown 8vo., 2s. 6d., or 3s. 6d., gilt edges.
　Silver Library Edition. Cr. 8vo., 3s. 6d.

Critical and Historical Essays.
　Student's Edition. 1 vol. Cr. 8vo., 6s.
　People's Edition. 2 vols. Cr. 8vo., 8s.
　'Trevelyan' Edition. 2 vols. Cr. 8vo., 9s.
　Cabinet Edition. 4 vols. Post 8vo., 24s.
　'Edinburgh' Edition. 4 vols. 8vo., 6s. each.
　Library Edition. 3 vols. 8vo., 36s.

Essays which may be had separately price 6d. each sewed, 1s. each cloth.
Addison and Walpole.　Ranke and Gladstone.
Croker's Boswell's Johnson.　Milton and Machiavelli.
Hallam's Constitutional History.　Lord Byron.
Warren Hastings.　Lord Clive.
The Earl of Chatham (Two Essays).　Lord Byron, and The Comic Dramatists of the Restoration.
Frederick the Great.

Miscellaneous Writings.
　People's Edition. 1 vol. Cr. 8vo., 4s. 6d.
　Library Edition. 2 vols. 8vo., 21s.

History, Politics, Polity, Political Memoirs, &c.—*continued*.

Macaulay (LORD)—*continued*.
  MISCELLANEOUS WRITINGS AND SPEECHES.
  Popular Edition. Crown 8vo., 2s. 6d.
  Cabinet Edition. Including Indian Penal Code, Lays of Ancient Rome, and Miscellaneous Poems. 4 vols. Post 8vo., 24s.
  SELECTIONS FROM THE WRITINGS OF LORD MACAULAY. Edited, with Occasional Notes, by the Right Hon. Sir G. O. Trevelyan, Bart. Crown 8vo., 6s.

MacColl.—THE SULTAN AND THE POWERS. By the Rev. MALCOLM MACCOLL, M.A., Canon of Ripon. 8vo., 10s. 6d.

Mackinnon.—THE UNION OF ENGLAND AND SCOTLAND: A STUDY OF INTERNATIONAL HISTORY. By JAMES MACKINNON, Ph.D. Examiner in History to the University of Edinburgh. 8vo., 16s.

May.—THE CONSTITUTIONAL HISTORY OF ENGLAND since the Accession of George III. 1760-1870. By Sir THOMAS ERSKINE MAY, K.C.B. (Lord Farnborough). 3 vols. Cr. 8vo., 18s.

Merivale (THE LATE DEAN).
  HISTORY OF THE ROMANS UNDER THE EMPIRE. 8 vols. Crown 8vo., 3s. 6d. each.
  THE FALL OF THE ROMAN REPUBLIC: a Short History of the Last Century of the Commonwealth. 12mo., 7s. 6d.

Montague.—THE ELEMENTS OF ENGLISH CONSTITUTIONAL HISTORY. By F. C. MONTAGUE, M.A. Crown 8vo., 3s. 6d.

O'Brien.—IRISH IDEAS. REPRINTED ADDRESSES. By WILLIAM O'BRIEN. Cr. 8vo. 2s. 6d.

Richman. APPENZELL: PURE DEMOCRACY AND PASTORAL LIFE IN INNER-RHODEN. A Swiss Study. By IRVING B. RICHMAN, Consul-General of the United States to Switzerland. With Maps. Crown 8vo., 5s.

Seebohm (FREDERICK).
  THE ENGLISH VILLAGE COMMUNITY Examined in its Relations to the Manorial and Tribal Systems, &c. With 13 Maps and Plates. 8vo., 16s.
  THE TRIBAL SYSTEM IN WALES: Being Part of an Inquiry into the Structure and Methods of Tribal Society. With 3 Maps. 8vo., 12s.

Sharpe.—LONDON AND THE KINGDOM: a History derived mainly from the Archives at Guildhall in the custody of the Corporation of the City of London. By REGINALD R. SHARPE, D.C.L., Records Clerk in the Office of the Town Clerk of the City of London. 3 vols. 8vo., 10s. 6d. each.

Sheppard.—MEMORIALS OF ST. JAMES'S PALACE. By the Rev. EDGAR SHEPPARD, M.A., Sub-Dean of H.M. Chapels Royal. With 41 Full-page Plates (8 Photo-Intaglio) and 32 Illustrations in the Text. 2 vols. 8vo., 36s. net.

Smith.—CARTHAGE AND THE CARTHAGINIANS. By R. BOSWORTH SMITH, M.A., With Maps, Plans, &c. Cr. 8vo., 3s. 6d.

Stephens.—A HISTORY OF THE FRENCH REVOLUTION. By H. MORSE STEPHENS. 3 vols. 8vo. Vols. I. and II. 18s. each.

Stubbs.—HISTORY OF THE UNIVERSITY OF DUBLIN, from its Foundation to the End of the Eighteenth Century. By J. W. STUBBS. 8vo., 12s. 6d.

Sutherland.—THE HISTORY OF AUSTRALIA AND NEW ZEALAND, from 1606 to 1890. By ALEXANDER SUTHERLAND, M.A., and GEORGE SUTHERLAND, M.A. Crown 8vo., 2s. 6d.

Taylor.—A STUDENT'S MANUAL OF THE HISTORY OF INDIA. By Colonel MEADOWS TAYLOR, C.S.I., &c. Cr. 8vo., 7s. 6d.

Todd.—PARLIAMENTARY GOVERNMENT IN THE BRITISH COLONIES. By ALPHEUS TODD, LL.D. 8vo., 30s. net.

Wakeman and Hassall.—ESSAYS INTRODUCTORY TO THE STUDY OF ENGLISH CONSTITUTIONAL HISTORY. By Resident Members of the University of Oxford. Edited by HENRY OFFLEY WAKEMAN, M.A., and ARTHUR HASSALL, M.A. Crown 8vo., 6s.

Walpole.—HISTORY OF ENGLAND FROM THE CONCLUSION OF THE GREAT WAR IN 1815 TO 1858. By SPENCER WALPOLE. 6 vols. Crown 8vo., 6s. each.

Wolff.—ODD BITS OF HISTORY: being Short Chapters intended to Fill Some Blanks. By HENRY W. WOLFF. 8vo., 8s. 6d.

Wood-Martin.—PAGAN IRELAND: AN ARCHÆOLOGICAL SKETCH. A Handbook of Irish Pre-Christian Antiquities. By W. G. WOOD-MARTIN, M.R.I.A. With 512 Illustrations. Crown 8vo., 15s.

Wylie.—HISTORY OF ENGLAND UNDER HENRY IV. By JAMES HAMILTON WYLIE, M.A., one of H. M. Inspectors of Schools. 3 vols. Crown 8vo. Vol. I., 1399-1404. 10s. 6d. Vol. II., 15s. Vol. III., 15s.
[Vol. IV. *In the press*.

Biography, Personal Memoirs, &c.

Armstrong.—THE LIFE AND LETTERS OF EDMUND J. ARMSTRONG. Edited by G. F. ARMSTRONG. Fcp. 8vo., 7s. 6d.

Bacon.—THE LETTERS AND LIFE OF FRANCIS BACON, INCLUDING ALL HIS OCCASIONAL WORKS. Edited by JAMES SPEDDING. 7 vols. 8vo., £4 4s.

Bagehot. BIOGRAPHICAL STUDIES. By WALTER BAGEHOT. Crown 8vo., 3s. 6d.

Blackwell.— PIONEER WORK IN OPENING THE MEDICAL PROFESSION TO WOMEN: Autobiographical Sketches. By Dr. ELIZABETH BLACKWELL. Cr. 8vo., 6s.

Boyd (A. K. H.) ('A.K.H.B.').
TWENTY-FIVE YEARS OF ST. ANDREWS. 1865-1890. 2 vols. 8vo. Vol. I. 12s. Vol. II. 15s.
ST. ANDREWS AND ELSEWHERE: Glimpses of Some Gone and of Things Left. 8vo., 15s.
THE LAST YEARS OF ST. ANDREWS: SEPTEMBER 1890 TO SEPTEMBER 1895. 8vo., 15s.

Brown.—FORD MADOX BROWN: A Record of his Life and Works. By FORD M. HUEFFER. With 45 Full-page Plates (44 Autotypes) and 7 Illustrations in the Text. 8vo., 42s.

Buss.—FRANCES MARY BUSS AND HER WORK FOR EDUCATION. By ANNIE E. RIDLEY. With 5 Portraits and 4 Illustrations. Crown 8vo, 7s. 6d.

Carlyle.—THOMAS CARLYLE: A History of his Life. By JAMES ANTHONY FROUDE.
1795-1835. 2 vols. Crown 8vo., 7s.
1834-1881. 2 vols. Crown 8vo., 7s.

Digby.—THE LIFE OF SIR KENELM DIGBY, by one of his Descendants, the Author of 'The Life of a Conspirator,' 'A Life of Archbishop Laud,' etc. With 7 Illustrations. 8vo., 16s.

Erasmus. LIFE AND LETTERS OF ERASMUS. By JAMES ANTHONY FROUDE. Crown 8vo.

Fox.—THE EARLY HISTORY OF CHARLES JAMES FOX. By the Right Hon. Sir G. O. TREVELYAN, Bart.
Library Edition. 8vo., 18s.
Cabinet Edition. Crown 8vo., 6s.

Halford.—THE LIFE OF SIR HENRY HALFORD, BART., G.C.H., M.D., F.R.S., By WILLIAM MUNK, M.D., F.S.A. 8vo., 12s. 6d.

Hamilton.—LIFE OF SIR WILLIAM HAMILTON. By R. P. GRAVES. 8vo. 3 vols. 15s. each. ADDENDUM. 8vo., 6d. sewed.

Harper.—A MEMOIR OF HUGO DANIEL HARPER, D.D., late Principal of Jesus College, Oxford, and for many years Head Master of Sherborne School. By L. V. LESTER, M.A. Crown 8vo., 5s.

Havelock.—MEMOIRS OF SIR HENRY HAVELOCK, K.C.B. By JOHN CLARK MARSHMAN. Crown 8vo., 3s. 6d.

Haweis.—MY MUSICAL LIFE. By the Rev. H. R. HAWEIS. With Portrait of Richard Wagner and 3 Illustrations. Crown 8vo., 7s. 6d.

Holroyd.—THE GIRLHOOD OF MARIA JOSEPHA HOLROYD (Lady Stanley of Alderley). Recorded in Letters of a Hundred Years Ago, from 1776 to 1796. Edited by J. H. ADEANE. With 6 Portraits. 8vo., 18s.

Luther.—LIFE OF LUTHER. By JULIUS KOSTLIN. With Illustrations from Authentic Sources. Translated from the German. Crown 8vo., 7s. 6d.

Macaulay.—THE LIFE AND LETTERS OF LORD MACAULAY. By the Right Hon. Sir G. O. TREVELYAN, Bart., M.P.
Popular Edition. 1 vol. Cr. 8vo., 2s. 6d.
Student's Edition. 1 vol. Cr. 8vo., 6s.
Cabinet Edition. 2 vols. Post 8vo., 12s.
Library Edition. 2 vols. 8vo., 36s.
'Edinburgh' Edition. 2 vols. 8vo., 6s. each.

Marbot.—THE MEMOIRS OF THE BARON DE MARBOT. Translated from the French. Crown 8vo., 7s. 6d.

Nansen.—FRIDTJOF NANSEN, 1861-1893. By W. C. BRÖGGER and NORDAHL ROLFSEN. Translated by WILLIAM ARCHER. With 8 Plates, 48 Illustrations in the Text, and 3 Maps. 8vo., 12s. 6d.

Biography, Personal Memoirs, &c.—*continued.*

Romanes.—THE LIFE AND LETTERS OF GEORGE JOHN ROMANES, M.A., LL.D., F.R.S. Written and Edited by his WIFE. With Portrait and 2 Illustrations. Crown 8vo., 6s.

Seebohm.—THE OXFORD REFORMERS—JOHN COLET, ERASMUS AND THOMAS MORE: a History of their Fellow-Work. By FREDERIC SEEBOHM. 8vo., 14s.

Shakespeare.— OUTLINES OF THE LIFE OF SHAKESPEARE. By J. O. HALLIWELL-PHILLIPPS. With Illustrations and Fac-similes. 2 vols. Royal 8vo., £1 1s.

Shakespeare's TRUE LIFE. By JAMES WALTER. With 500 Illustrations by GERALD E. MOIRA. Imp. 8vo., 21s.

Stephen.— ESSAYS IN ECCLESIASTICAL BIOGRAPHY. By Sir JAMES STEPHEN. Crown 8vo., 7s. 6d.

Turgot.—THE LIFE AND WRITINGS OF TURGOT. Comptroller-General of France, 1774-1776. Edited for English Readers by W. WALKER STEPHENS. 8vo., 12s. 6d.

Verney.—MEMOIRS OF THE VERNEY FAMILY.
Vols. I. & II., DURING THE CIVIL WAR. By FRANCES PARTHENOPE VERNEY. With 38 Portraits, Woodcuts and Fac-simile. Royal 8vo., 42s.
Vol. III., DURING THE COMMONWEALTH. 1650-1660. By MARGARET M. VERNEY. With 10 Portraits, &c. Royal 8vo., 21s.

Wellington.—LIFE OF THE DUKE OF WELLINGTON. By the Rev. G. R. GLEIG, M.A. Crown 8vo., 3s. 6d.

Wolf.—THE LIFE OF JOSEPH WOLF, ANIMAL PAINTER. By A. H. PALMER. With 53 Plates and 14 Illustrations in the Text. 8vo., 21s.

Travel and Adventure, the Colonies, &c.

Arnold (SIR EDWIN).
SEAS AND LANDS. With 71 Illustrations. Cr. 8vo., 3s. 6d.
WANDERING WORDS. With 45 Illustrations. 8vo., 18s.
EAST AND WEST: With 14 Illustrations by R. T. PRITCHETT. 8vo., 18s.

AUSTRALIA AS IT IS, or Facts and Features, Sketches, and Incidents of Australia and Australian Life with Notices of New Zealand. By A CLERGYMAN, thirteen years resident in the interior of New South Wales. Crown 8vo., 5s.

Baker (SIR S. W.).
EIGHT YEARS IN CEYLON. With 6 Illustrations. Crown 8vo., 3s. 6d.
THE RIFLE AND THE HOUND IN CEYLON. With 6 Illustrations. Crown 8vo., 3s. 6d.

Bent (J. THEODORE).
THE RUINED CITIES OF MASHONALAND: being a Record of Excavation and Exploration in 1891. With 117 Illustrations. Crown 8vo., 3s. 6d.

Bent (J. THEODORE)—*continued.*
THE SACRED CITY OF THE ETHIOPIANS: being a Record of Travel and Research in Abyssinia in 1893. With 8 Plates and 65 Illustrations in the Text. 8vo., 10s. 6d.

Bicknell.—TRAVEL AND ADVENTURE IN NORTHERN QUEENSLAND. By ARTHUR C. BICKNELL. With 24 Plates and 22 Illustrations in the Text. 8vo., 15s.

Brassey.—VOYAGES AND TRAVELS OF LORD BRASSEY, K.C.B., D.C.L., 1862-1894. Arranged and Edited by Captain S. EARDLEY-WILMOT. 2 vols. Cr. 8vo., 10s.

Brassey (THE LATE LADY).
A VOYAGE IN THE 'SUNBEAM;' OUR HOME ON THE OCEAN FOR ELEVEN MONTHS.
Library Edition. With 8 Maps and Charts, and 118 Illustrations. 8vo. 21s.
Cabinet Edition. With Map and 66 Illustrations. Crown 8vo., 7s. 6d.
Silver Library Edition. With 66 Illustrations. Crown 8vo., 3s. 6d.
Popular Edition. With 60 Illustrations. 4to., 6d. sewed, 1s. cloth.
School Edition. With 37 Illustrations. Fcp., 2s. cloth, or 3s. white parchment.

Travel and Adventure, the Colonies, &c.—*continued.*

Brassey (THE LATE LADY)—*continued.*

SUNSHINE AND STORM IN THE EAST.
  Library Edition. With 2 Maps and 141 Illustrations. 8vo., 21s.
  Cabinet Edition. With 2 Maps and 114 Illustrations. Crown 8vo., 7s. 6d.
  Popular Edition. With 103 Illustrations. 4to., 6d. sewed, 1s. cloth.

IN THE TRADES, THE TROPICS, AND THE 'ROARING FORTIES.'
  Cabinet Edition. With Map and 220 Illustrations. Crown 8vo., 7s. 6d.
  Popular Edition. With 183 Illustrations. 4to., 6d. sewed, 1s. cloth.

THREE VOYAGES IN THE 'SUNBEAM'.
  Popular Ed. With 346 Illust. 4to., 2s. 6d.

Browning.—*A GIRL'S WANDERINGS IN HUNGARY.* By H. ELLEN BROWNING. With Map and 20 Illustrations. Crown 8vo., 7s. 6d.

Froude (JAMES A.).

OCEANA: or England and her Colonies. With 9 Illustrations. Crown 8vo., 2s. boards, 2s. 6d. cloth.

THE ENGLISH IN THE WEST INDIES: or, the Bow of Ulysses. With 9 Illustrations. Crown 8vo., 2s. boards, 2s. 6d. cloth.

Howitt.—*VISITS TO REMARKABLE PLACES.* Old Halls, Battle-Fields, Scenes, illustrative of Striking Passages in English History and Poetry. By WILLIAM HOWITT. With 80 Illustrations. Crown 8vo., 3s. 6d.

Knight (E. F.).

THE CRUISE OF THE 'ALERTE': the Narrative of a Search for Treasure on the Desert Island of Trinidad. With 2 Maps and 23 Illustrations. Crown 8vo., 3s. 6d.

WHERE THREE EMPIRES MEET: a Narrative of Recent Travel in Kashmir, Western Tibet, Baltistan, Ladak, Gilgit, and the adjoining Countries. With a Map and 54 Illustrations. Cr. 8vo., 3s. 6d.

THE 'FALCON' ON THE BALTIC: a Voyage from London to Copenhagen in a Three-Tonner. With 10 Full-page Illustrations. Crown 8vo., 3s. 6d.

Lees and Clutterbuck.—B.C. 1887: *A RAMBLE IN BRITISH COLUMBIA.* By J. A. LEES and W. J. CLUTTERBUCK. With Map and 75 Illustrations. Crown 8vo., 3s. 6d.

Nansen (FRIDTJOF).

THE FIRST CROSSING OF GREENLAND. With numerous Illustrations and a Map. Crown 8vo., 3s. 6d.

ESKIMO LIFE. With 31 Illustrations. 8vo., 16s.

Oliver.—*CRAGS AND CRATERS:* Rambles in the Island of Réunion. By WILLIAM DUDLEY OLIVER, M.A. With 27 Illustrations and a Map. Cr. 8vo., 6s.

Peary.—*MY ARCTIC JOURNAL:* a year among Ice-Fields and Eskimos. By JOSEPHINE DIEBITSCH-PEARY. With 19 Plates, 3 Sketch Maps, and 44 Illustrations in the Text. 8vo., 12s.

Quillinan. *JOURNAL OF A FEW MONTHS' RESIDENCE IN PORTUGAL,* and Glimpses of the South of Spain. By Mrs. QUILLINAN (Dora Wordsworth). New Edition. Edited, with Memoir, by EDMUND LEE, Author of 'Dorothy Wordsworth,' &c. Crown 8vo., 6s.

Smith.—*CLIMBING IN THE BRITISH ISLES.* By W. P. HASKETT SMITH. With Illustrations by ELLIS CARR, and Numerous Plans.
  Part I. *ENGLAND.* 16mo., 3s. 6d.
  Part II. *WALES AND IRELAND.* 16mo., 3s. 6d.
  Part III. *SCOTLAND.* [*In preparation.*

Stephen.—*THE PLAY-GROUND OF EUROPE.* By LESLIE STEPHEN. New Edition, with Additions and 4 Illustrations. Crown 8vo., 6s. net.

THREE IN NORWAY. By Two of Them. With a Map and 59 Illustrations. Crown 8vo., 2s. boards, 2s. 6d. cloth.

Tyndall.—*THE GLACIERS OF THE ALPS:* being a Narrative of Excursions and Ascents. An Account of the Origin and Phenomena of Glaciers, and an Exposition of the Physical Principles to which they are related. By JOHN TYNDALL, F.R.S. With numerous Illustrations. Crown 8vo., 6s. 6d. net.

Whishaw.—*THE ROMANCE OF THE WOODS:* Reprinted Articles and Sketches. By FRED. J. WHISHAW. Crown 8vo., 6s.

Veterinary Medicine, &c.

Steel (JOHN HENRY).

A TREATISE ON THE DISEASES OF THE DOG. With 88 Illustrations. 8vo., 10s. 6d.

A TREATISE ON THE DISEASES OF THE OX. With 119 Illustrations. 8vo., 15s.

A TREATISE ON THE DISEASES OF THE SHEEP. With 100 Illustrations. 8vo., 12s.

OUTLINES OF EQUINE ANATOMY: a Manual for the use of Veterinary Students in the Dissecting Room. Cr. 8vo., 7s. 6d.

Fitzwygram.—HORSES AND STABLES. By Major-General Sir F. FITZWYGRAM, Bart. With 56 pages of Illustrations. 8vo., 2s. 6d. net.

'Stonehenge.'—THE DOG IN HEALTH AND DISEASE. By 'STONEHENGE'. With 78 Wood Engravings. 8vo., 7s. 6d.

Youatt (WILLIAM).

THE HORSE. Revised and Enlarged by W. WATSON, M.R.C.V.S. With 52 Wood Engravings. 8vo., 7s. 6d.

THE DOG. Revised and Enlarged. With 33 Wood Engravings. 8vo., 6s.

Sport and Pastime.

THE BADMINTON LIBRARY.

Edited by HIS GRACE THE DUKE OF BEAUFORT, K.G.; Assisted by ALFRED E. T. WATSON.

Complete in 28 Volumes. Crown 8vo., Price 10s. 6d. each Volume, Cloth.

*** *The Volumes are also issued half-bound in Leather, with gilt top. The price can be had from all Booksellers.*

ARCHERY. By C. J. LONGMAN and Col. H. WALROND. With Contributions by Miss LEGH, Viscount DILLON, Major C. HAWKINS FISHER, &c. With 2 Maps, 23 Plates and 172 Illustrations in the Text. Crown 8vo., 10s. 6d.

ATHLETICS AND FOOTBALL. By MONTAGUE SHEARMAN. With 6 Plates and 52 Illustrations in the Text. Crown 8vo., 10s. 6d.

BIG GAME SHOOTING. By CLIVE PHILLIPPS-WOLLEY.

Vol. I. AFRICA AND AMERICA. With Contributions by Sir SAMUEL W. BAKER, W. C. OSWELL, F. J. JACKSON, WARBURTON PIKE, and F. C. SELOUS. With 20 Plates and 57 Illustrations in the Text. Crown 8vo., 10s. 6d.

Vol. II. EUROPE, ASIA, AND THE ARCTIC REGIONS. With Contributions by Lieut.-Colonel R. HEBER PERCY, ARNOLD PIKE, Major ALGERNON C. HEBER PERCY, &c. With 17 Plates and 56 Illustrations in the Text. Crown 8vo., 10s. 6d.

BILLIARDS. By Major W. BROADFOOT, R.E. With Contributions by A. H. BOYD, SYDENHAM DIXON, W. J. FORD, DUDLEY D. PONTIFEX, &c. With 11 Plates, 19 Illustrations in the Text, and numerous Diagrams and Figures. Crown 8vo., 10s. 6d.

BOATING. By W. B. WOODGATE. With 10 Plates, 39 Illustrations in the Text, and from Instantaneous Photographs, and 4 Maps of the Rowing Courses at Oxford, Cambridge, Henley, and Putney. Crown 8vo., 10s. 6d.

COURSING AND FALCONRY. By HARDING COX and the Hon. GERALD LASCELLES. With 20 Plates and 56 Illustrations in the Text. Crown 8vo., 10s. 6d.

CRICKET. By A. G. STEEL and the Hon. R. H. LYTTELTON. With Contributions by ANDREW LANG, W. G. GRACE, F. GALE, &c. With 12 Plates and 52 Illustrations in the Text. Crown 8vo., 10s. 6d.

Sport and Pastime—*continued*.

THE BADMINTON LIBRARY—*continued*.

CYCLING. By the EARL OF ALBEMARLE and G. LACY HILLIER. With 19 Plates and 44 Illustrations in the Text. Crown 8vo., 10s. 6d.

DANCING. By Mrs. LILLY GROVE, F.R.G.S. With Contributions by Miss MIDDLETON, The Hon. MRS. ARMYTAGE, &c. With Musical Examples, and 38 Full-page Plates and 93 Illustrations in the Text. Crown 8vo., 10s. 6d.

DRIVING. By His Grace the DUKE of BEAUFORT, K.G. With Contributions by other Authorities. With Photogravure Intaglio Portrait of His Grace the DUKE OF BEAUFORT, and 11 Plates and 54 Illustrations in the Text. Crown 8vo., 10s. 6d.

FENCING, BOXING, AND WRESTLING. By WALTER H. POLLOCK, F. C. GROVE, C. PREVOST, E. B. MITCHELL, and WALTER ARMSTRONG. With 18 Intaglio Plates and 24 Illustrations in the Text. Crown 8vo., 10s. 6d.

FISHING. By H. CHOLMONDELEY-PENNELL, Late Her Majesty's Inspector of Sea Fisheries.

* Vol. I. SALMON AND TROUT. With Contributions by H. R. FRANCIS, Major JOHN P. TRAHERNE, &c. With Frontispiece, 8 Full-page Illustrations of Fishing Subjects, and numerous Illustrations of Tackle, &c. Crown 8vo., 10s. 6d.

* Vol. II. PIKE AND OTHER COARSE FISH. With Contributions by the MARQUIS OF EXETER, WILLIAM SENIOR, G., CHRISTOPHER DAVIS, &c. With Frontispiece, 6 Full-page Illustrations of Fishing Subjects, and numerous Illustrations of Tackle, &c. Crown 8vo., 10s. 6d.

GOLF. By HORACE G. HUTCHINSON. With Contributions by the Rt. Hon. A. J. BALFOUR, M.P., Sir WALTER SIMPSON, Bart., ANDREW LANG, &c. With 25 Plates and 65 Illustrations in the Text. Crown 8vo., 10s. 6d.

HUNTING. By His Grace the DUKE of BEAUFORT, K.G., and MOWBRAY MORRIS. With Contributions by the EARL OF SUFFOLK AND BERKSHIRE, Rev. E. W. L. DAVIES, J. S. GIBBONS, G. H. LONGMAN, &c. With 5 Plates and 54 Illustrations in the Text. Crown 8vo., 10s. 6d.

MOUNTAINEERING. By C. T. DENT. With Contributions by Sir W. M. CONWAY, D. W. FRESHFIELD, C. E. MATTHEWS, &c. With 13 Plates and 95 Illustrations in the Text. Cr. 8vo., 10s. 6d.

POETRY OF SPORT (THE).—Selected by HEDLEY PEEK. With a Chapter on Classical Allusions to Sport by ANDREW LANG, and a Special Preface to the Badminton Library by A. E. T. WATSON. With 32 Plates and 74 Illustrations in the Text. Crown 8vo., 10s. 6d.

RACING AND STEEPLE-CHASING. By the EARL OF SUFFOLK AND BERKSHIRE, W. G. CRAVEN, the Hon. F. LAWLEY, ARTHUR COVENTRY, and ALFRED E. T. WATSON. With Coloured Frontispiece and 56 Illustrations in the Text. Crown 8vo., 10s. 6d.

RIDING AND POLO.

RIDING. By Captain ROBERT WEIR, the DUKE OF BEAUFORT, the EARL OF SUFFOLK AND BERKSHIRE, the EARL OF ONSLOW, J. MURRAY BROWN, &c. With 18 Plates and 41 Illustrations in the Text. Crown 8vo., 10s. 6d.

SEA FISHING. By JOHN BICKERDYKE, Sir H. W. GORE-BOOTH, ALFRED C. HARMSWORTH, and W. SENIOR. With 22 Full-page Plates and 175 Illustrations in the Text. Crown 8vo., 10s. 6d.

SHOOTING.

Vol. I. FIELD AND COVERT. By LORD WALSINGHAM and Sir RALPH PAYNE-GALLWEY, Bart. With Contributions by the Hon. GERALD LASCELLES and A. J. STUART-WORTLEY. With 11 Full-page Illustrations and 94 Illustrations in the Text. Crown 8vo., 10s. 6d.

Vol. II. MOOR AND MARSH. By LORD WALSINGHAM and Sir RALPH PAYNE-GALLWEY, Bart. With Contributions by LORD LOVAT and Lord CHARLES LENNOX KERR. With 8 Full-page Illustrations and 57 Illustrations in the Text. Crown 8vo., 10s. 6d.

Sport and Pastime—*continued.*
THE BADMINTON LIBRARY—*continued.*

SKATING, CURLING, TOBOG-GANING. By J. M. HEATHCOTE, C. G. TEBBUTT, T. MAXWELL WITHAM, Rev. JOHN KERR, ORMOND HAKE, HENRY A. BUCK, &c. With 12 Plates and 272 Illustrations and Diagrams in the Text. Crown 8vo., 10s. 6d.

SWIMMING. By ARCHIBALD SINCLAIR and WILLIAM HENRY, Hon. Secs. of the Life-Saving Society. With 13 Plates and 106 Illustrations in the Text. Crown 8vo., 10s. 6d.

TENNIS, LAWN TENNIS, RACKETS AND FIVES. By J. M. and C. G. HEATHCOTE, E. O. PLEYDELL-BOUVERIE, and A.C. AINGER. With Contributions by the Hon. A. LYTTELTON, W. C. MARSHALL, Miss L. DOD, &c. With 12 Plates and 67 Illustrations in the Text. Crown 8vo., 10s. 6d.

YACHTING.

Vol. I. CRUISING, CONSTRUCTION OF YACHTS, YACHT RACING RULES, FITTING-OUT, &c. By Sir EDWARD SULLIVAN, Bart., THE EARL OF PEMBROKE, LORD BRASSEY, K.C.B., C. E. SETH-SMITH, C.B., G. L. WATSON, R. T. PRITCHETT, E. F. KNIGHT, &c. With 21 Plates and 93 Illustrations in the Text, and from Photographs. Crown 8vo., 10s. 6d.

Vol. II. YACHT CLUBS, YACHTING IN AMERICA AND THE COLONIES, YACHT RACING, &c. By R. T. PRITCHETT, THE MARQUIS OF DUFFERIN AND AVA, K.P., THE EARL OF ONSLOW, JAMES MCFERRAN, &c. With 35 Plates and 160 Illustrations in the Text. Crown 8vo., 10s. 6d.

FUR AND FEATHER SERIES.
Edited by A. E. T. WATSON.
Crown 8vo., price 5s. each Volume, cloth.

*** *The Volumes are also issued half-bound in Leather, with gilt top. The price can be had from all Booksellers.*

THE PARTRIDGE. Natural History by the Rev. H. A. MACPHERSON; Shooting, by A. J. STUART-WORTLEY; Cookery, by GEORGE SAINTSBURY. With 11 Illustrations and various Diagrams in the Text. Crown 8vo., 5s.

THE GROUSE. Natural History by the Rev. H. A. MACPHERSON; Shooting, by A. J. STUART-WORTLEY; Cookery, by GEORGE SAINTSBURY. With 13 Illustrations and various Diagrams in the Text. Crown 8vo., 5s.

THE PHEASANT. Natural History by the Rev. H. A. MACPHERSON; Shooting, by A. J. STUART-WORTLEY; Cookery, by ALEXANDER INNES SHAND. With 10 Illustrations and various Diagrams. Crown 8vo., 5s.

THE HARE. Natural History by the Rev. H. A. MACPHERSON; Shooting, by the Hon. GERALD LASCELLES; Coursing, by CHARLES RICHARDSON; Hunting, by J. S. GIBBONS and G. H. LONGMAN; Cookery, by Col. KENNEY HERBERT. With 9 Illustrations. Crown 8vo, 5s.

RED DEER.—Natural History. By the Rev. H. A. MACPHERSON. Deer Stalking. By CAMERON OF LOCHIEL.—Stag Hunting. By Viscount EBRINGTON.—Cookery. By ALEXANDER INNES SHAND. With 10 Illustrations by J. CHARLTON and A. THORBURN. Crown 8vo., 5s.

*** *Other Volumes are in preparation.*

BADMINTON MAGAZINE (THE) OF SPORTS AND PASTIMES. Edited by ALFRED E. T. WATSON ("Rapier"). With numerous Illustrations. Price 1s. monthly.
Vols. I.-III. 6s. each.

Bickerdyke.—*DAYS OF MY LIFE ON WATERS FRESH AND SALT*; and other Papers. By JOHN BICKERDYKE. With Photo-Etched Frontispiece and 8 Full-page Illustrations. Crown 8vo., 6s.

Sport and Pastime—*continued.*

DEAD SHOT (THE): or, Sportsman's Complete Guide. Being a Treatise on the Use of the Gun, with Rudimentary and Finishing Lessons on the Art of Shooting Game of all kinds. Also Game-driving, Wildfowl and Pigeon-shooting, Dog-breaking, etc. By MARKSMAN. Illustrated. Cr. 8vo., 10s. 6d.

Ellis.—*CHESS SPARKS*; or, Short and Bright Games of Chess. Collected and Arranged by J. H. ELLIS, M.A. 8vo., 4s. 6d.

Falkener.—*GAMES, ANCIENT AND ORIENTAL, AND HOW TO PLAY THEM.* By EDWARD FALKENER. With numerous Photographs, Diagrams, &c. 8vo., 21s.

Ford.—*THE THEORY AND PRACTICE OF ARCHERY.* By HORACE FORD. New Edition, thoroughly Revised and Re-written by W. BUTT, M.A. With a Preface by C. J. LONGMAN, M.A. 8vo., 14s.

Francis.—*A BOOK ON ANGLING:* or, Treatise on the Art of Fishing in every Branch; including full Illustrated List of Salmon Flies. By FRANCIS FRANCIS. With Portrait and Coloured Plates. Crown 8vo., 15s.

Gibson.—*TOBOGGANING ON CROOKED RUNS.* By the Hon. HARRY GIBSON. With Contributions by F. DE B. STRICKLAND and 'LADY-TOBOGANNER'. With 40 Illustrations. Crown 8vo., 6s.

Graham.—*COUNTRY PASTIMES FOR BOYS.* By P. ANDERSON GRAHAM. With 252 Illustrations from Drawings and Photographs. Crown 8vo. 6s.

Lang.—*ANGLING SKETCHES.* By ANDREW LANG. With 20 Illustrations. Crown 8vo., 3s. 6d.

Longman.—*CHESS OPENINGS.* By FREDERICK W. LONGMAN. Fcp. 8vo., 2s. 6d.

Maskelyne.—*SHARPS AND FLATS:* a Complete Revelation of the Secrets of Cheating at Games of Chance and Skill. By JOHN NEVIL MASKELYNE, of the Egyptian Hall. With 62 Illustrations. Crown 8vo., 6s.

Park.—*THE GAME OF GOLF.* By WILLIAM PARK, Jun., Champion Golfer, 1887-89. With 17 Plates and 26 Illustrations in the Text. Crown 8vo., 7s. 6d.

Payne-Gallwey (SIR RALPH, Bart.).

LETTERS TO YOUNG SHOOTERS (First Series). On the Choice and use of a Gun. With 41 Illustrations. Crown 8vo., 7s. 6d.

LETTERS TO YOUNG SHOOTERS (Second Series). On the Production, Preservation, and Killing of Game. With Directions in Shooting Wood-Pigeons and Breaking-in Retrievers. With Portrait and 103 Illustrations. Crown 8vo., 12s. 6d.

LETTERS TO YOUNG SHOOTERS. (Third Series.) Comprising a Short Natural History of the Wildfowl that are Rare or Common to the British Islands, with complete directions in Shooting Wildfowl on the Coast and Inland. With 200 Illustrations. Crown 8vo., 18s.

Pole (WILLIAM).

THE THEORY OF THE MODERN SCIENTIFIC GAME OF WHIST. Fcp. 8vo., 2s. 6d.

THE EVOLUTION OF WHIST: a Study of the Progressive Changes which the Game has undergone. Cr. 8vo., 2s. 6d.

Proctor.—*HOW TO PLAY WHIST: WITH THE LAWS AND ETIQUETTE OF WHIST.* By RICHARD A. PROCTOR. Crown 8vo., 3s. 6d.

Ronalds.—*THE FLY-FISHER'S ENTOMOLOGY.* By ALFRED RONALDS. With 20 coloured Plates. 8vo., 14s.

Thompson and Cannan. *HAND-IN-HAND FIGURE SKATING.* By NORCLIFFE G. THOMPSON and F. LAURA CANNAN, Members of the Skating Club. With an Introduction by Captain J. H. THOMSON, R.A. With Illustrations. 16mo., 6s.

Wilcocks.—*THE SEA FISHERMAN:* Comprising the Chief Methods of Hook and Line Fishing in the British and other Seas, and Remarks on Nets, Boats, and Boating. By J. C. WILCOCKS. Illustrated. Cr. 8vo., 6s.

Mental, Moral, and Political Philosophy.
LOGIC, RHETORIC, PSYCHOLOGY, &C.

Abbott.—*The Elements of Logic.*
By T. K. Abbott, B.D. 12mo., 3s.

Aristotle.

The Politics: G. Bekker's Greek Text of Books I., III., IV. (VII.), with an English Translation by W. E. Bolland, M.A.; and short Introductory Essays by A. Lang, M.A. Crown 8vo., 7s. 6d.

The Politics: Introductory Essays. By Andrew Lang (from Bolland and Lang's 'Politics'). Crown 8vo., 2s. 6d.

The Ethics: Greek Text, Illustrated with Essay and Notes. By Sir Alexander Grant, Bart. 2 vols. 8vo., 32s.

An Introduction to Aristotle's Ethics. Books I.-IV. (Book X. c. vi.-ix. in an Appendix). With a continuous Analysis and Notes. By the Rev. Edward Moore, D.D., Cr. 8vo. 10s. 6d.

Bacon (Francis).

Complete Works. Edited by R. L. Ellis, James Spedding and D. D. Heath. 7 vols. 8vo., £3 13s. 6d.

Letters and Life, including all his occasional Works. Edited by James Spedding. 7 vols. 8vo., £4 4s.

The Essays: with Annotations. By Richard Whately, D.D. 8vo., 10s. 6d.

The Essays. Edited, with Notes, by F. Storr and C. H. Gibson. Crown 8vo, 3s. 6d.

The Essays: with Introduction, Notes, and Index. By E. A. Abbott, D.D. 2 Vols. Fcp. 8vo., 6s. The Text and Index only, without Introduction and Notes, in One Volume. Fcp. 8vo., 2s. 6d.

Bain (Alexander).

Mental Science. Cr. 8vo., 6s. 6d.

Moral Science. Cr. 8vo., 4s. 6d.

The two works as above can be had in one volume, price 10s. 6d.

Senses and the Intellect. 8vo., 15s.

Emotions and the Will. 8vo., 15s.

Bain (Alexander)—*continued.*

Logic, Deductive and Inductive. Part I. 4s. Part II. 6s. 6d.

Practical Essays. Cr. 8vo., 2s.

Bray (Charles).

The Philosophy of Necessity: or, Law in Mind as in Matter. Cr. 8vo., 5s.

The Education of the Feelings: a Moral System for Schools. Cr. 8vo., 2s. 6d.

Bray.—*Elements of Morality,* in Easy Lessons for Home and School Teaching. By Mrs. Charles Bray. Crown 8vo., 1s. 6d.

Davidson.—*The Logic of Definition,* Explained and Applied. By William L. Davidson, M.A. Crown 8vo., 6s.

Green (Thomas Hill).—*The Works of.* Edited by R. L. Nettleship.
Vols. I. and II. Philosophical Works. 8vo., 16s. each.
Vol. III. Miscellanies. With Index to the three Volumes, and Memoir. 8vo., 21s.
Lectures on the Principles of Political Obligation. With Preface by Bernard Bosanquet. 8vo., 5s.

Hodgson (Shadworth H.).

Time and Space: A Metaphysical Essay. 8vo., 16s.

The Theory of Practice: an Ethical Inquiry. 2 vols. 8vo., 24s.

The Philosophy of Reflection. 2 vols. 8vo., 21s.

Hume.—*The Philosophical Works of David Hume.* Edited by T. H. Green and T. H. Grose. 4 vols. 8vo., 56s. Or separately, Essays. 2 vols. 28s. Treatise of Human Nature. 2 vols. 28s.

Justinian.—*The Institutes of Justinian:* Latin Text, chiefly that of Huschke, with English Introduction, Translation, Notes, and Summary. By Thomas C. Sandars, M.A. 8vo., 18s.

Kant (Immanuel).

Critique of Practical Reason, and Other Works on the Theory of Ethics.. Translated by T. K. Abbott, B.D. With Memoir. 8vo., 12s. 6d.

Mental, Moral and Political Philosophy—*continued.*

Kant (IMMANUEL)—*continued.*
FUNDAMENTAL PRINCIPLES OF THE METAPHYSIC OF ETHICS. Translated by T. K. ABBOTT, B.D. (Extracted from 'Kant's Critique of Practical Reason and other Works on the Theory of Ethics.') Crown 8vo, 3s.

INTRODUCTION TO LOGIC, AND HIS ESSAY ON THE MISTAKEN SUBTILTY OF THE FOUR FIGURES. Translated by T. K. ABBOTT. 8vo., 6s.

Killick.—*HANDBOOK TO MILL'S SYSTEM OF LOGIC.* By Rev. A. H. KILLICK, M.A. Crown 8vo., 3s. 6d.

Ladd (GEORGE TRUMBULL).
PHILOSOPHY OF MIND: An Essay on the Metaphysics of Psychology. 8vo., 16s.
ELEMENTS OF PHYSIOLOGICAL PSYCHOLOGY. 8vo., 21s.
OUTLINES OF PHYSIOLOGICAL PSYCHOLOGY. A Text-book of Mental Science for Academies and Colleges. 8vo., 12s.
PSYCHOLOGY, DESCRIPTIVE AND EXPLANATORY: a Treatise of the Phenomena, Laws, and Development of Human Mental Life. 8vo., 21s.
PRIMER OF PSYCHOLOGY. Cr. 8vo., 5s. 6d.

Lewes.—*THE HISTORY OF PHILOSOPHY*, from Thales to Comte. By GEORGE HENRY LEWES. 2 vols. 8vo., 32s.

Max Müller (F.).
THE SCIENCE OF THOUGHT. 8vo., 21s.
THREE INTRODUCTORY LECTURES ON THE SCIENCE OF THOUGHT. 8vo., 2s. 6d.

Mill.—*ANALYSIS OF THE PHENOMENA OF THE HUMAN MIND.* By JAMES MILL. 2 vols. 8vo., 28s.

Mill (JOHN STUART).
A SYSTEM OF LOGIC. Cr. 8vo., 3s. 6d.
ON LIBERTY. Crown 8vo., 1s. 4d.
ON REPRESENTATIVE GOVERNMENT. Crown 8vo., 2s.
UTILITARIANISM. 8vo., 2s. 6d.
EXAMINATION OF SIR WILLIAM HAMILTON'S PHILOSOPHY. 8vo., 16s.
NATURE, THE UTILITY OF RELIGION, AND THEISM. Three Essays. 8vo., 5s.

Mosso.—*FEAR.* By ANGELO MOSSO. Translated from the Italian by E. LOUGH and F. KIESOW. With 8 Illustrations. Cr. 8vo., 7s. 6d.

Romanes.—*MIND AND MOTION AND MONISM.* By GEORGE JOHN ROMANES, LL.D., F.R.S. Cr. 8vo., 4s. 6d.

Stock.—*DEDUCTIVE LOGIC.* By ST. GEORGE STOCK. Fcp. 8vo., 3s. 6d.

Sully (JAMES).
THE HUMAN MIND: a Text-book of Psychology. 2 vols. 8vo., 21s.
OUTLINES OF PSYCHOLOGY. 8vo., 9s.
THE TEACHER'S HANDBOOK OF PSYCHOLOGY. Crown 8vo., 5s.
STUDIES OF CHILDHOOD. 8vo, 10s. 6d.

Swinburne.—*PICTURE LOGIC:* an Attempt to Popularise the Science of Reasoning. By ALFRED JAMES SWINBURNE, M.A. With 23 Woodcuts. Crown 8vo., 5s.

Weber.—*HISTORY OF PHILOSOPHY.* By ALFRED WEBER, Professor in the University of Strasburg. Translated by FRANK THILLY, Ph.D. 8vo., 16s.

Whately (ARCHBISHOP).
BACON'S ESSAYS. With Annotations. 8vo., 10s. 6d.
ELEMENTS OF LOGIC. Cr. 8vo., 4s. 6d.
ELEMENTS OF RHETORIC. Cr. 8vo., 4s. 6d.
LESSONS ON REASONING. Fcp. 8vo., 1s. 6d.

Zeller (Dr. EDWARD, Professor in the University of Berlin).
THE STOICS, EPICUREANS, AND SCEPTICS. Translated by the Rev. O. J. REICHEL, M.A. Crown 8vo., 15s.
OUTLINES OF THE HISTORY OF GREEK PHILOSOPHY. Translated by SARAH F. ALLEYNE and EVELYN ABBOTT. Crown 8vo., 10s. 6d.
PLATO AND THE OLDER ACADEMY. Translated by SARAH F. ALLEYNE and ALFRED GOODWIN, B.A. Crown 8vo. 18s.
SOCRATES AND THE SOCRATIC SCHOOLS. Translated by the Rev. O. J. REICHEL, M.A. Crown 8vo., 10s. 6d.

Mental, Moral, and Political Philosophy—*continued*

MANUALS OF CATHOLIC PHILOSOPHY.
(Stonyhurst Series).

A MANUAL OF POLITICAL ECONOMY. By C. S. DEVAS, M.A. Crown 8vo., 6s. 6d.

FIRST PRINCIPLES OF KNOWLEDGE. By JOHN RICKABY, S.J. Crown 8vo., 5s.

GENERAL METAPHYSICS. By JOHN RICKABY, S.J. Crown 8vo., 5s.

LOGIC. By RICHARD F. CLARKE, S.J. Crown 8vo., 5s.

MORAL PHILOSOPHY (ETHICS AND NATURAL LAW). By JOSEPH RICKABY, S.J. Crown 8vo., 5s.

NATURAL THEOLOGY. By BERNARD BOEDDER, S.J. Crown 8vo., 6s. 6d.

PSYCHOLOGY. By MICHAEL MAHER, S.J. Crown 8vo., 6s. 6d.

History and Science of Language, &c.

Davidson.—LEADING AND IMPORTANT ENGLISH WORDS: Explained and Exemplified. By WILLIAM L. DAVIDSON, M.A. Fcp. 8vo., 3s. 6d.

Farrar.—LANGUAGE AND LANGUAGES: By F. W. FARRAR, D.D., F.R.S. Crown 8vo., 6s.

Graham.—ENGLISH SYNONYMS, Classified and Explained: with Practical Exercises. By G. F. GRAHAM. Fcp. 8vo., 6s.

Max Müller (F.).

THE SCIENCE OF LANGUAGE.—Founded on Lectures delivered at the Royal Institution in 1861 and 1863. 2 vols. Crown 8vo., 21s.

Max Müller (F.)—*continued.*

BIOGRAPHIES OF WORDS, AND THE HOME OF THE ARYAS. Crown 8vo., 7s. 6d.

THREE LECTURES ON THE SCIENCE OF LANGUAGE, AND ITS PLACE IN GENERAL EDUCATION, delivered at Oxford, 1889. Crown 8vo., 3s.

Roget.—THESAURUS OF ENGLISH WORDS AND PHRASES. Classified and Arranged so as to Facilitate the Expression of Ideas and assist in Literary Composition. By PETER MARK ROGET, M.D., F.R.S. Recomposed throughout, enlarged and improved, partly from the Author's Notes, and with a full Index, by the Author's Son, JOHN LEWIS ROGET. Crown 8vo. 10s. 6d.

Whately.—ENGLISH SYNONYMS. By E. JANE WHATELY. Fcp. 8vo., 3s.

Political Economy and Economics.

Ashley.—ENGLISH ECONOMIC HISTORY AND THEORY. By W. J. ASHLEY, M.A. Crown 8vo., Part I., 5s. Part II. 10s. 6d.

Bagehot.—ECONOMIC STUDIES. By WALTER BAGEHOT. Crown 8vo., 3s. 6d.

Barnett.—PRACTICABLE SOCIALISM. Essays on Social Reform. By the Rev. S. A. and Mrs. BARNETT. Crown 8vo., 6s.

Brassey.—PAPERS AND ADDRESSES ON WORK AND WAGES. By Lord BRASSEY. Edited by J. POTTER, and with Introduction by GEORGE HOWELL, M.P. Crown 8vo., 5s.

Devas.—A MANUAL OF POLITICAL ECONOMY. By C. S. DEVAS, M.A. Cr. 8vo., 6s. 6d. (Manuals of Catholic Philosophy.)

Dowell.—A HISTORY OF TAXATION AND TAXES IN ENGLAND, from the Earliest Times to the Year 1885. By STEPHEN DOWELL. (4 vols. 8vo). Vols. I. and II. The History of Taxation, 21s. Vols. III. and IV. The History of Taxes, 21s.

Jordan.—THE STANDARD OF VALUE. By WILLIAM LEIGHTON JORDAN, Fellow of the Royal Statistical Society, &c. Crown 8vo., 6s.

Macleod (HENRY DUNNING).

BIMETALISM. 8vo., 5s. net.

THE ELEMENTS OF BANKING. Cr. 8vo., 3s. 6d.

THE THEORY AND PRACTICE OF BANKING. Vol. I. 8vo., 12s. Vol. II. 14s.

THE THEORY OF CREDIT. 8vo. Vol. I., 10s. net. Vol. II., Part I., 10s. net. Vol. II., Part II., 10s. 6d.

A DIGEST OF THE LAW OF BILLS OF EXCHANGE, BANK-NOTES, &c. [*In the press.*

Mill.—POLITICAL ECONOMY. By JOHN STUART MILL.
Popular Edition. Crown 8vo., 3s. 6d.
Library Edition. 2 vols. 8vo., 30s.

Political Economy and Economics—*continued.*

Mulhall.—*INDUSTRIES AND WEALTH OF NATIONS.* By MICHAEL G. MULHALL, F.S.S. With 32 full-page Diagrams. Crown 8vo., 8s. 6d.

Soderini.—*SOCIALISM AND CATHOLICISM.* From the Italian of Count EDWARD SODERINI. By RICHARD JENERY-SHEE. With a Preface by Cardinal VAUGHAN. Crown 8vo., 6s.

Symes.—*POLITICAL ECONOMY:* a Short Text-book of Political Economy. With Problems for Solution, and Hints for Supplementary Reading; also a Supplementary Chapter on Socialism. By Professor J. E. SYMES, M.A., of University College, Nottingham. Crown 8vo., 2s. 6d.

Toynbee.—*LECTURES ON THE INDUSTRIAL REVOLUTION OF THE 18TH CENTURY IN ENGLAND:* Popular Addresses, Notes and other Fragments. By ARNOLD TOYNBEE. With a Memoir of the Author by BENJAMIN JOWETT, D.D. 8vo., 10s. 6d.

Vincent.—*THE LAND QUESTION IN NORTH WALES:* being a Brief Survey of the History, Origin, and Character of the Agrarian Agitation, and of the Nature and Effect of the Proceedings of the Welsh Land Commission. By J. E. VINCENT. 8vo., 5s.

Webb.—*THE HISTORY OF TRADE UNIONISM.* By SIDNEY and BEATRICE WEBB. With Map and full Bibliography of the Subject. 8vo., 18s.

STUDIES IN ECONOMICS AND POLITICAL SCIENCE.
Issued under the auspices of the London School of Economics and Political Science.

THE HISTORY OF LOCAL RATES IN ENGLAND: Five Lectures. By EDWIN CANNAN, M.A. Crown 8vo., 2s. 6d.

GERMAN SOCIAL DEMOCRACY. By BERTRAND RUSSELL, B.A. With an Appendix on Social Democracy and the Woman Question in Germany by ALYS RUSSELL, B.A. Crown 8vo., 3s. 6d.

SELECT DOCUMENTS ILLUSTRATING THE HISTORY OF TRADE UNIONISM.
1. The Tailoring Trade. Edited by W. F. GALTON. With a Preface by SIDNEY WEBB, LL.B. Crown 8vo., 5s.

DEPLOIGE'S REFERENDUM EN SUISSE. Translated, with Introduction and Notes, by C. P. TREVELYAN, M.A. [*In preparation.*

SELECT DOCUMENTS ILLUSTRATING THE STATE REGULATION OF WAGES. Edited, with Introduction and Notes, by W. A. S. HEWINS, M.A. [*In preparation.*

HUNGARIAN GILD RECORDS. Edited by Dr. JULIUS MANDELLO, of Budapest. [*In preparation.*

THE RELATIONS BETWEEN ENGLAND AND THE HANSEATIC LEAGUE. By Miss E. A. MACARTHUR. [*In preparation.*

Evolution, Anthropology, &c.

Babington.—*FALLACIES OF RACE THEORIES AS APPLIED TO NATIONAL CHARACTERISTICS.* Essays by WILLIAM DALTON BABINGTON, M.A. Crown 8vo., 6s.

Clodd (EDWARD).

THE STORY OF CREATION: a Plain Account of Evolution. With 77 Illustrations. Crown 8vo., 3s. 6d.

A PRIMER OF EVOLUTION: being a Popular Abridged Edition of 'The Story of Creation'. With Illustrations. Fcp. 8vo., 1s. 6d.

Lang.—*CUSTOM AND MYTH:* Studies of Early Usage and Belief. By ANDREW LANG. With 15 Illustrations. Crown 8vo., 3s. 6d.

Lubbock.—*THE ORIGIN OF CIVILISATION,* and the Primitive Condition of Man. By Sir J. LUBBOCK, Bart., M.P. With 5 Plates and 20 Illustrations in the Text. 8vo., 18s.

Romanes (GEORGE JOHN).

DARWIN, AND AFTER DARWIN: an Exposition of the Darwinian Theory, and a Discussion on Post-Darwinian Questions.
Part I. THE DARWINIAN THEORY. With Portrait of Darwin and 125 Illustrations. Crown 8vo., 10s. 6d.
Part II. POST-DARWINIAN QUESTIONS: Heredity and Utility. With Portrait of the Author and 5 Illustrations. Cr. 8vo., 10s. 6d.

AN EXAMINATION OF WEISMANNISM. Crown 8vo., 6s.

ESSAYS.—Edited by C. LLOYD MORGAN, Principal of University College, Bristol.

Classical Literature, Translations, &c.

Abbott.—*HELLENICA.* A Collection of Essays on Greek Poetry, Philosophy, History, and Religion. Edited by EVELYN ABBOTT, M.A., LL.D. 8vo., 16s.

Æschylus.—*EUMENIDES OF ÆSCHYLUS.* With Metrical English Translation. By J. F. DAVIES. 8vo., 7s.

Aristophanes.—*THE ACHARNIANS OF ARISTOPHANES*, translated into English Verse. By R. Y. TYRRELL. Crown 8vo., 1s.

Aristotle.—*YOUTH AND OLD AGE, LIFE AND DEATH, AND RESPIRATION.* Translated, with Introduction and Notes, by W. OGLE, M.A., M.D., F.R.C.P., sometime Fellow of Corpus Christi College, Oxford.

Becker (PROFESSOR).

GALLUS: or, Roman Scenes in the Time of Augustus. Illustrated. Post 8vo., 3s. 6d.

CHARICLES: or, Illustrations of the Private Life of the Ancient Greeks. Illustrated. Post 8vo., 3s. 6d.

Cicero.—*CICERO'S CORRESPONDENCE.* By R. Y. TYRRELL. Vols. I., II., III., 8vo., each 12s. Vol. IV., 15s.

Egbert.—*INTRODUCTION TO THE STUDY OF LATIN INSCRIPTIONS.* By JAMES C. EGBERT, Junr., Ph.D. With numerous Illustrations and Facsimiles. Square crown 8vo., 16s.

Farnell.—*GREEK LYRIC POETRY:* a Complete Collection of the Surviving Passages from the Greek Song-Writing. Arranged with Prefatory Articles, Introductory Matter and Commentary. By GEORGE S. FARNELL, M.A. With 5 Plates. 8vo., 16s.

Lang.—*HOMER AND THE EPIC.* By ANDREW LANG. Crown 8vo., 9s. net.

Lucan.—*THE PHARSALIA OF LUCAN.* Translated into Blank Verse. By EDWARD RIDLEY, Q.C. 8vo., 14s.

Mackail.—*SELECT EPIGRAMS FROM THE GREEK ANTHOLOGY.* By J. W. MACKAIL. Edited with a Revised Text, Introduction, Translation, and Notes. 8vo., 16s.

Rich.—*A DICTIONARY OF ROMAN AND GREEK ANTIQUITIES.* By A. RICH, B.A With 2000 Woodcuts. Crown 8vo., 7s. 6d.

Sophocles.—Translated into English Verse. By ROBERT WHITELAW, M.A., Assistant Master in Rugby School. Cr. 8vo., 8s. 6d.

Tacitus.—*THE HISTORY OF P. CORNELIUS TACITUS.* Translated into English, with an Introduction and Notes, Critical and Explanatory, by ALBERT WILLIAM QUILL, M.A., T.C.D. 2 vols. Vol. I. 8vo., 7s. 6d. Vol. II. 8vo., 12s. 6d.

Tyrrell.—*TRANSLATIONS INTO GREEK AND LATIN VERSE.* Edited by R. Y. TYRRELL. 8vo., 6s.

Virgil.

THE ÆNEID OF VIRGIL. Translated into English Verse by JOHN CONINGTON. Crown 8vo., 6s.

THE POEMS OF VIRGIL. Translated into English Prose by JOHN CONINGTON. Crown 8vo., 6s.

THE ÆNEID OF VIRGIL, freely translated into English Blank Verse. By W. J. THORNHILL. Crown 8vo., 7s. 6d.

THE ÆNEID OF VIRGIL. Translated into English Verse by JAMES RHOADES. Books I.-VI. Crown 8vo., 5s. Books VII.-XII. Crown 8vo., 5s.

Poetry and the Drama.

Acworth.—*BALLADS OF THE MARATHAS.* Rendered into English Verse from the Marathi Originals. By HARRY ARBUTHNOT ACWORTH. 8vo., 5s.

Allingham (WILLIAM).

IRISH SONGS AND POEMS. With Frontispiece of the Waterfall of Asaroe. Fcp. 8vo., 6s.

LAURENCE BLOOMFIELD. With Portrait of the Author. Fcp. 8vo., 3s. 6d.

FLOWER PIECES; DAY AND NIGHT SONGS; BALLADS. With 2 Designs by D. G. ROSSETTI. Fcp. 8vo., 6s.; large paper edition, 12s.

Allingham (WILLIAM)—*continued.*

LIFE AND PHANTASY: with Frontispiece by Sir J. E. MILLAIS, Bart., and Design by ARTHUR HUGHES. Fcp. 8vo., 6s.; large paper edition, 12s.

THOUGHT AND WORD, AND ASHBY MANOR: a Play. Fcp. 8vo., 6s.; large paper edition, 12s.

BLACKBERRIES. Imperial 16mo., 6s.

Sets of the above 6 vols. may be had in uniform Half-parchment binding, price 30s.

Poetry and the Drama—*continued*.

Armstrong (G. F. SAVAGE).
POEMS: Lyrical and Dramatic. Fcp. 8vo., 6s.
KING SAUL. (The Tragedy of Israel, Part I.) Fcp. 8vo., 5s.
KING DAVID. (The Tragedy of Israel, Part II.) Fcp. 8vo., 6s.
KING SOLOMON. (The Tragedy of Israel, Part III.) Fcp. 8vo., 6s.
UGONE: a Tragedy. Fcp. 8vo., 6s.
A GARLAND FROM GREECE: Poems. Fcp. 8vo., 7s. 6d.
STORIES OF WICKLOW: Poems. Fcp. 8vo., 7s. 6d.
MEPHISTOPHELES IN BROADCLOTH: a Satire. Fcp. 8vo., 4s.
ONE IN THE INFINITE: a Poem. Crown 8vo., 7s. 6d.

Armstrong.—THE POETICAL WORKS OF EDMUND J. ARMSTRONG. Fcp. 8vo., 5s.

Arnold (Sir EDWIN).
THE LIGHT OF THE WORLD: or the Great Consummation. With 14 Illustrations after HOLMAN HUNT. Cr. 8vo., 6s.
POTIPHAR'S WIFE, and other Poems. Crown 8vo., 5s. net.
ADZUMA: or the Japanese Wife. A Play. Crown 8vo., 6s. 6d. net.
THE TENTH MUSE, and other Poems. Crown 8vo., 5s. net.

Beesly (A. H.).
BALLADS AND OTHER VERSE. Fcp. 8vo., 5s.
DANTON, AND OTHER VERSE. Fcp. 8vo., 4s. 6d.

Bell (MRS. HUGH).
CHAMBER COMEDIES: a Collection of Plays and Monologues for the Drawing Room. Crown 8vo., 6s.
FAIRY TALE PLAYS, AND HOW TO ACT THEM. With 91 Diagrams and 52 Illustrations. Crown 8vo., 6s.

Carmichael.—POEMS. By JENNINGS CARMICHAEL (Mrs. FRANCIS MULLIS). Crown 8vo., 6s. net.

Christie.—LAYS AND VERSES. By NIMMO CHRISTIE. Crown 8vo., 3s. 6d.

Cochrane (ALFRED).
THE KESTREL'S NEST, and other Verses. Fcp. 8vo., 3s. 6d.
LEVIORE PLECTRO: Occasional Verses. Fcap. 8vo., 3s. 6d.

Florian's Fables.—THE FABLES OF FLORIAN. Done into English Verse by Sir PHILIP PERRING, Bart. Cr. 8vo., 3s. 6d.

Goethe.
FAUST, Part I., the German Text, with Introduction and Notes. By ALBERT M. SELSS, Ph.D., M.A. Crown 8vo., 5s.
FAUST. Translated, with Notes. By T. E. WEBB. 8vo., 12s. 6d.

Gurney.—DAY-DREAMS: Poems. By Rev. ALFRED GURNEY, M.A. Crown 8vo., 3s. 6d.

Ingelow (JEAN).
POETICAL WORKS. 2 vols. Fcp. 8vo., 12s.
LYRICAL AND OTHER POEMS. Selected from the Writings of JEAN INGELOW. Fcp. 8vo., 2s. 6d. cloth plain, 3s. cloth gilt.

Lang (ANDREW).
BAN AND ARRIÈRE BAN: a Rally of Fugitive Rhymes. Fcp. 8vo., 5s. net.
GRASS OF PARNASSUS. Fcp. 8vo., 2s. 6d. net.
BALLADS OF BOOKS. Edited by ANDREW LANG. Fcp. 8vo., 6s.
THE BLUE POETRY BOOK. Edited by ANDREW LANG. With 100 Illustrations. Crown 8vo., 6s.

Lecky.—POEMS. By W. E. H. LECKY. Fcp. 8vo., 5s.

Lindsay.—THE FLOWER SELLER, and other Poems. By LADY LINDSAY. Crown 8vo., 5s.

Lytton (THE EARL OF), (OWEN MEREDITH).
MARAH. Fcp. 8vo., 6s. 6d.
KING POPPY: a Fantasia. With 1 Plate and Design on Title-Page by ED. BURNE-JONES, A.R.A. Cr. 8vo., 10s. 6d.
THE WANDERER. Cr. 8vo., 10s. 6d.
LUCILE. Crown 8vo., 10s. 6d.
SELECTED POEMS. Cr. 8vo., 10s. 6d.

Poetry and the Drama—*continued*.

Macaulay.—*Lays of Ancient Rome,
&c.* By Lord Macaulay.
Illustrated by G. Scharf. Fcp. 4to., 10s. 6d.
——— Bijou Edition.
18mo., 2s. 6d. gilt top.
——— Popular Edition.
Fcp. 4to., 6d. sewed, 1s. cloth.
Illustrated by J. R. Weguelin. Crown 8vo., 3s. 6d.
Annotated Edition. Fcp. 8vo., 1s. sewed, 1s. 6d. cloth.

Macdonald (George, LL.D.).
A Book of Strife, in the Form of the Diary of an Old Soul: Poems. 18mo., 6s.
Rampolli; Growths from an Old Root; containing a Book of Translations, old and new; also a Year's Diary of an Old Soul. Crown 8vo., 6s.

Morris (William).
Poetical Works—Library Edition.
Complete in Ten Volumes. Crown 8vo., price 6s. each.
The Earthly Paradise. 4 vols. 6s. each.
The Life and Death of Jason. 6s.
The Defence of Guenevere, and other Poems. 6s.
The Story of Sigurd the Volsung, and The Fall of the Niblungs. 6s.
Love is Enough; or, the Freeing of Pharamond: A Morality; and *Poems by the Way.* 6s.
The Odyssey of Homer. Done into English Verse. 6s.
The Æneids of Virgil. Done into English Verse. 6s.

Certain of the Poetical Works may also be had in the following Editions:—
The Earthly Paradise.
Popular Edition. 5 vols. 12mo., 25s.; or 5s. each, sold separately.
The same in Ten Parts, 25s.; or 2s. 6d. each, sold separately.
Cheap Edition, in 1 vol. Crown 8vo., 7s. 6d.
Love is Enough; or, the Freeing of Pharamond: A Morality. Square crown 8vo., 7s. 6d.
Poems by the Way. Square crown 8vo., 6s.
*** For Mr. William Morris's Prose Works, see pp. 22 and 31.

Murray (Robert F.).—Author of 'The Scarlet Gown'. His Poems, with a Memoir by Andrew Lang. Fcp. 8vo., 5s. net.

Nesbit.—*Lays and Legends.* By E. Nesbit (Mrs. Hubert Bland). First Series. Crown 8vo., 3s. 6d. Second Series. With Portrait. Crown 8vo., 5s.

Peek (Hedley) (Frank Leyton).
Skeleton Leaves: Poems. With a Dedicatory Poem to the late Hon. Roden Noel. Fcp. 8vo., 2s. 6d. net.
The Shadows of the Lake, and other Poems. Fcp. 8vo., 2s. 6d. net.

Piatt (Sarah).
An Enchanted Castle, and Other Poems: Pictures, Portraits, and People in Ireland. Crown 8vo., 3s. 6d.
Poems: With Portrait of the Author. 2 vols. Crown 8vo., 10s.

Piatt (John James).
Idyls and Lyrics of the Ohio Valley. Crown 8vo., 5s.
Little New World Idyls. Cr. 8vo., 5s.

Rhoades.—*Teresa and other Poems.* By James Rhoades. Crown 8vo., 3s. 6d.

Riley (James Whitcomb).
Old Fashioned Roses: Poems, 12mo., 5s.
Poems: Here at Home. Fcp. 8vo 6s. net.
A Child-World: Poems. Fcp. 8vo., 5s.

Romanes.—*A Selection from the Poems of George John Romanes, M.A., LL.D., F.R.S.* With an Introduction by T. Herbert Warren, President of Magdalen College, Oxford. Crown 8vo., 4s. 6d.

Shakespeare.—*Bowdler's Family Shakespeare.* With 36 Woodcuts. 1 vol. 8vo., 14s. Or in 6 vols. Fcp. 8vo., 21s.
The Shakespeare Birthday Book. By Mary F. Dunbar. 32mo., 1s. 6d.

Sturgis.—*A Book of Song.* By Julian Sturgis. 16mo. 5s.

MESSRS. LONGMANS & CO.'S STANDARD AND GENERAL WORKS.   21

Works of Fiction, Humour, &c.

Alden.—AMONG THE FREAKS. By W. L. ALDEN. With 55 Illustrations by J. F. SULLIVAN and FLORENCE K. UPTON. Crown 8vo., 3s. 6d.

Anstey (F., Author of 'Vice Versâ').

VOCES POPULI. Reprinted from 'Punch'. First Series. With 20 Illustrations by J. BERNARD PARTRIDGE. Crown 8vo., 3s. 6d.

THE MAN FROM BLANKLEY'S: a Story in Scenes, and other Sketches. With 24 Illustrations by J. BERNARD PARTRIDGE. Post 4to., 6s.

Astor.—A JOURNEY IN OTHER WORLDS: a Romance of the Future. By JOHN JACOB ASTOR. With 10 Illustrations. Cr. 8vo., 6s.

Baker.—BY THE WESTERN SEA. By JAMES BAKER, Author of 'John Westacott'. Crown 8vo., 3s. 6d.

Beaconsfield (THE EARL OF).

NOVELS AND TALES. Complete in 11 vols. Crown 8vo., 1s. 6d. each.

Vivian Grey.	Sybil.
The Young Duke, &c.	Henrietta Temple.
Alroy, Ixion, &c.	Venetia.
Contarini Fleming, &c.	Coningsby.
	Lothair.
Tancred.	Endymion.

NOVELS AND TALES. The Hughenden Edition. With 2 Portraits and 11 Vignettes. 11 vols. Crown 8vo., 42s.

Black.—THE PRINCESS DÉSIRÉE. By CLEMENTINA BLACK. With 8 Illustrations by JOHN WILLIAMSON. Cr. 8vo., 6s.

Dougall (L.).

BEGGARS ALL. Cr. 8vo., 3s. 6d.

WHAT NECESSITY KNOWS. Crown 8vo., 6s.

Doyle (A. CONAN).

MICAH CLARKE: A Tale of Monmouth's Rebellion. With 10 Illustrations. Cr. 8vo., 3s. 6d.

THE CAPTAIN OF THE POLESTAR, and other Tales. Cr. 8vo., 3s. 6d.

THE REFUGEES: A Tale of Two Continents. With 25 Illustrations. Cr. 8vo., 3s. 6d.

THE STARK MUNRO LETTERS. Cr. 8vo, 6s.

Farrar (F. W., DEAN OF CANTERBURY).

DARKNESS AND DAWN: or, Scenes in the Days of Nero. An Historic Tale. Cr. 8vo., 7s. 6d.

GATHERING CLOUDS: a Tale of the Days of St. Chrysostom. Cr. 8vo., 7s. 6d.

Fowler.—THE YOUNG PRETENDERS. A Story of Child Life. By EDITH H. FOWLER. With 12 Illustrations by PHILIP BURNE-JONES. Crown 8vo., 6s.

Froude.—THE TWO CHIEFS OF DUNBOY: an Irish Romance of the Last Century. By JAMES A. FROUDE. Cr. 8vo., 3s. 6d.

Graham.—THE RED SCAUR: A Novel of Manners. By P. ANDERSON GRAHAM. Crown 8vo., 6s.

Haggard (H. RIDER).

HEART OF THE WORLD. With 15 Illustrations. Crown 8vo., 6s.

JOAN HASTE. With 20 Illustrations. Crown 8vo., 6s.

THE PEOPLE OF THE MIST. With 16 Illustrations. Crown 8vo., 3s. 6d.

MONTEZUMA'S DAUGHTER. With 24 Illustrations. Crown 8vo., 3s. 6d.

SHE. With 32 Illustrations. Crown 8vo., 3s. 6d.

ALLAN QUATERMAIN. With 31 Illustrations. Crown 8vo., 3s. 6d.

MAIWA'S REVENGE: Cr. 8vo., 1s. 6d.

COLONEL QUARITCH, V.C. Cr. 8vo. 3s. 6d.

CLEOPATRA. With 29 Illustrations. Crown 8vo., 3s. 6d.

Works of Fiction, Humour, &c.—*continued.*

Haggard (H. Rider)—*continued.*
  Beatrice. Cr. 8vo., 3s. 6d.
  Eric Brighteyes. With 51 Illustrations. Crown 8vo., 3s. 6d.
  Nada the Lily. With 23 Illustrations. Crown 8vo., 3s. 6d.
  Allan's Wife. With 34 Illustrations. Crown 8vo., 3s. 6d.
  The Witch's Head. With 16 Illustrations. Crown 8vo., 3s. 6d.
  Mr. Meeson's Will. With 16 Illustrations. Crown 8vo., 3s. 6d.
  Dawn. With 16 Illustrations. Cr. 8vo., 3s. 6d.

Haggard and Lang.—*The World's Desire.* By H. Rider Haggard and Andrew Lang. With 27 Illustrations. Crown 8vo., 3s. 6d.

Harte.—*In the Carquinez Woods* and other stories. By Bret Harte. Cr. 8vo., 3s. 6d.

Hope.—*The Heart of Princess Osra.* By Anthony Hope. With 9 Illustrations by John Williamson. Crown 8vo., 6s.

Hornung.—*The Unbidden Guest.* By E. W. Hornung. Crown 8vo., 3s. 6d.

Lang.—*A Monk of Fife:* being the Chronicle written by Norman Leslie of Pitcullo, concerning Marvellous Deeds that befel in the Realm of France, 1429-31. By Andrew Lang. With 13 Illustrations by Selwyn Image. Cr. 8vo., 6s.

Lyall (Edna).
  The Autobiography of a Slander. Fcp. 8vo., 1s., sewed.
    Presentation Edition. With 20 Illustrations by Lancelot Speed. Crown 8vo., 2s. 6d. net.
  The Autobiography of a Truth. Fcp. 8vo., 1s., sewed; 1s. 6d., cloth.
  Doreen. The Story of a Singer. Crown 8vo., 6s.

Magruder.—*The Violet.* By Julia Magruder. With 11 Illustrations by C. D. Gibson. Crown 8vo., 6s.

Matthews.—*His Father's Son:* a Novel of the New York Stock Exchange. By Brander Matthews. With 13 Illustrations. Cr. 8vo., 6s.

Melville (G. J. Whyte).
The Gladiators.	Holmby House.
The Interpreter.	Kate Coventry.
Good for Nothing.	Digby Grand.
The Queen's Maries.	General Bounce.

  Crown 8vo., 1s. 6d. each.

Merriman.—*Flotsam:* The Study of a Life. By Henry Seton Merriman. With Frontispiece and Vignette by H. G. Massey, A.R.E. Crown 8vo., 6s.

Morris (William).
  The Well at the World's End. 2 vols. 8vo., 28s.
  The Story of the Glittering Plain, which has been also called The Land of the Living Men, or The Acre of the Undying. Square post 8vo., 5s. net.
  The Roots of the Mountains, wherein is told somewhat of the Lives of the Men of Burgdale, their Friends, their Neighbours, their Foemen, and their Fellows-in-Arms. Written in Prose and Verse. Square crown 8vo., 8s.
  A Tale of the House of the Wolfings, and all the Kindreds of the Mark. Written in Prose and Verse. Second Edition. Square crown 8vo., 6s.
  A Dream of John Ball, and a King's Lesson. 12mo., 1s. 6d.
  News from Nowhere; or, An Epoch of Rest. Being some Chapters from an Utopian Romance. Post 8vo., 1s. 6d.
  *** For Mr. William Morris's Poetical Works, see p. 20.

Newman (Cardinal).
  Loss and Gain: The Story of a Convert. Crown 8vo. Cabinet Edition, 6s.; Popular Edition, 3s. 6d.
  Callista: A Tale of the Third Century. Crown 8vo. Cabinet Edition, 6s.; Popular Edition, 3s. 6d.

Oliphant.—*Old Mr. Tredgold.* By Mrs. Oliphant. Crown 8vo., 6s.

Phillipps-Wolley.—*Snap:* a Legend of the Lone Mountain. By C. Phillipps-Wolley. With 13 Illustrations. Crown 8vo., 3s. 6d.

Quintana.—*The Cid Campeador:* an Historical Romance. By D. Antonio de Trueba y la Quintana. Translated from the Spanish by Henry J. Gill, M.A., T.C.D. Crown 8vo., 6s.

Works of Fiction, Humour, &c.—*continued.*

Rhoscomyl (OWEN).

THE JEWEL OF YNYS GALON: being a hitherto unprinted Chapter in the History of the Sea Rovers. With 12 Illustrations by LANCELOT SPEED. Cr. 8vo., 3*s*. 6*d*.

BATTLEMENT AND TOWER: a Romance. With Frontispiece by R. CATON WOODVILLE. Crown 8vo., 6*s*.

Rokeby.—*DORCAS HOBDAY.* By CHARLES ROKEBY. Crown 8vo., 6*s*.

Sewell (ELIZABETH M.).

A Glimpse of the World | Amy Herbert
Laneton Parsonage. | Cleve Hall.
Margaret Percival. | Gertrude.
Katharine Ashton. | Home Life.
The Earl's Daughter. | After Life.
The Experience of Life | Ursula. Ivors

Cr. 8vo., 1*s*. 6*d*. each cloth plain. 2*s*. 6*d*. each cloth extra, gilt edges.

Stevenson (ROBERT LOUIS).

THE STRANGE CASE OF DR. JEKYLL AND MR. HYDE. Fcp. 8vo., 1*s*. sewed. 1*s*. 6*d*. cloth.

THE STRANGE CASE OF DR. JEKYLL AND MR. HYDE; WITH OTHER FABLES. Crown 8vo., 3*s*. 6*d*.

MORE NEW ARABIAN NIGHTS—THE DYNAMITER. By ROBERT LOUIS STEVENSON and FANNY VAN DE GRIFT STEVENSON. Crown 8vo., 3*s*. 6*d*.

THE WRONG BOX. By ROBERT LOUIS STEVENSON and LLOYD OSBOURNE. Crown 8vo., 3*s*. 6*d*.

Suttner.—*LAY DOWN YOUR ARMS (Die Waffen Nieder)*: The Autobiography of Martha Tilling. By BERTHA VON SUTTNER. Translated by T. HOLMES. Cr. 8vo., 1*s*. 6*d*.

Trollope (ANTHONY).

THE WARDEN. Cr. 8vo., 1*s*. 6*d*.

BARCHESTER TOWERS. Cr. 8vo., 1*s*. 6*d*.

TRUE (A) RELATION OF THE TRAVELS AND PERILOUS ADVENTURES OF MATHEW DUDGEON, GENTLEMAN: Wherein is truly set down the Manner of his Taking, the Long Time of his Slavery in Algiers, and Means of his Delivery. Written by Himself, and now for the first time printed. Cr. 8vo., 5*s*.

Walford (L. B.).

MR. SMITH: a Part of his Life. Crown 8vo., 2*s*. 6*d*.

THE BABY'S GRANDMOTHER. Cr. 8vo., 2*s*. 6*d*.

COUSINS. Crown 8vo., 2*s*. 6*d*.

TROUBLESOME DAUGHTERS. Cr. 8vo., 2*s*. 6*d*.

PAULINE. Crown. 8vo., 2*s*. 6*d*.

DICK NETHERBY. Cr. 8vo., 2*s*. 6*d*.

THE HISTORY OF A WEEK. Cr. 8vo. 2*s*. 6*d*.

A STIFF-NECKED GENERATION. Cr. 8vo. 2*s*. 6*d*.

NAN, and other Stories. Cr. 8vo., 2*s*. 6*d*.

THE MISCHIEF OF MONICA. Cr. 8vo., 2*s*. 6*d*.

THE ONE GOOD GUEST. Cr. 8vo. 2*s*. 6*d*.

'*PLOUGHED,*' and other Stories. Crown 8vo., 2*s*. 6*d*.

THE MATCHMAKER. Cr. 8vo., 2*s*. 6*d*.

West (B. B.).

HALF-HOURS WITH THE MILLIONAIRES: Showing how much harder it is to spend a million than to make it. Cr. 8vo., 6*s*.

SIR SIMON VANDERPETTER. and *MINDING HIS ANCESTORS.* Cr. 8vo., 5*s*.

A FINANCIAL ATONEMENT. Cr. 8vo., 6*s*.

Weyman (STANLEY).

THE HOUSE OF THE WOLF. Cr. 8vo., 3*s*. 6*d*.

A GENTLEMAN OF FRANCE. Cr. 8vo., 6*s*.

THE RED COCKADE. Cr. 8vo., 6*s*.

Whishaw.—*A BOYAR OF THE TERRIBLE*: a Romance of the Court of Ivan the Cruel, First Tzar of Russia. By FRED. WHISHAW. With 12 Illustrations by H. G. MASSEY, A.R.E. Crown 8vo., 6*s*.

Popular Science (Natural History, &c.).

Butler.—*Our Household Insects.* An Account of the Insect-Pests found in Dwelling-Houses. By Edward A. Butler, B.A., B.Sc. (Lond.). With 113 Illustrations. Crown 8vo., 3s. 6d.

Furneaux (W.).

The Outdoor World: or The Young Collector's Handbook. With 18 Plates 16 of which are coloured, and 549 Illustrations in the Text. Crown 8vo., 7s. 6d.

Butterflies and Moths (British). With 12 coloured Plates and 241 Illustrations in the Text. Crown 8vo., 12s. 6d.

Life in Ponds and Streams. With 8 coloured Plates and 331 Illustrations in the Text. Crown 8vo., 12s. 6d.

Hartwig (Dr. George).

The Sea and its Living Wonders. With 12 Plates and 303 Woodcuts. 8vo., 7s. net.

The Tropical World. With 8 Plates and 172 Woodcuts. 8vo., 7s. net.

The Polar World. With 3 Maps, 8 Plates and 85 Woodcuts. 8vo., 7s. net.

The Subterranean World. With 3 Maps and 80 Woodcuts. 8vo., 7s. net.

The Aerial World. With Map, 8 Plates and 60 Woodcuts. 8vo., 7s. net.

Heroes of the Polar World. 19 Illustrations. Cr. 8vo., 2s.

Wonders of the Tropical Forests. 40 Illustrations. Cr. 8vo., 2s.

Workers under the Ground. 29 Illustrations. Cr. 8vo., 2s.

Marvels Over our Heads. 29 Illustrations. Cr. 8vo., 2s.

Sea Monsters and Sea Birds. 75 Illustrations. Cr. 8vo., 2s. 6d.

Denizens of the Deep. 117 Illustrations. Cr. 8vo., 2s. 6d.

Hartwig (Dr. George)—*continued.*

Volcanoes and Earthquakes. 30 Illustrations. Cr. 8vo., 2s. 6d.

Wild Animals of the Tropics. 66 Illustrations. Cr. 8vo., 3s. 6d.

Hayward.—*Bird Notes.* By the late Jane Mary Hayward. Edited by Emma Hubbard. With Frontispiece and 15 Illustrations by G. E. Lodge. Cr. 8vo., 6s.

Helmholtz.—*Popular Lectures on Scientific Subjects.* By Hermann von Helmholtz. With 68 Woodcuts. 2 vols. Cr. 8vo., 3s. 6d. each.

Hudson.—*British Birds.* By W. H. Hudson, C.M.Z.S. With a Chapter on Structure and Classification by Frank E. Beddard, F.R.S. With 16 Plates (8 of which are Coloured), and over 100 Illustrations in the Text. Crown 8vo., 12s. 6d.

Proctor (Richard A.).

Light Science for Leisure Hours. Familiar Essays on Scientific Subjects. 3 vols. Cr. 8vo., 5s. each.

Rough Ways made Smooth. Familiar Essays on Scientific Subjects. Crown 8vo., 3s. 6d.

Pleasant Ways in Science. Crown 8vo., 3s. 6d.

Nature Studies. By R. A. Proctor, Grant Allen, A. Wilson, T. Foster and E. Clodd. Crown 8vo., 3s. 6d.

Leisure Readings. By R. A. Proctor, E. Clodd, A. Wilson, T. Foster and A. C. Ranyard. Cr. 8vo., 3s. 6d.

⁎⁎ For Mr. Proctor's other books see Messrs. Longmans & Co.'s Catalogue of Scientific Works.

Stanley.—*A Familiar History of Birds.* By E. Stanley, D.D., formerly Bishop of Norwich. With Illustrations. Cr. 8vo., 3s. 6d.

Popular Science (Natural History, &c.)—*continued*.

Wood (Rev. J. G.).

Homes without Hands: A Description of the Habitation of Animals, classed according to the Principle of Construction. With 140 Illustrations. 8vo., 7s., net.

Insects at Home: A Popular Account of British Insects, their Structure, Habits and Transformations. With 700 Illustrations. 8vo., 7s. net.

Insects Abroad: a Popular Account of Foreign Insects, their Structure, Habits and Transformations. With 600 Illustrations. 8vo., 7s. net.

Bible Animals: a Description of every Living Creature mentioned in the Scriptures. With 112 Illustrations. 8vo., 7s. net.

Petland Revisited. With 33 Illustrations. Cr. 8vo., 3s. 6d.

Out of Doors; a Selection of Original Articles on Practical Natural History. With 11 Illustrations. Cr. 8vo., 3s. 6d.

Wood (Rev. J. G.)—*continued*.

Strange Dwellings: a Description of the Habitations of Animals, abridged from 'Homes without Hands'. With 60 Illustrations. Cr. 8vo., 3s. 6d.

Bird Life of the Bible. 32 Illustrations. Cr. 8vo., 3s. 6d.

Wonderful Nests. 30 Illustrations. Cr. 8vo., 3s. 6d.

Homes under the Ground. 28 Illustrations. Cr. 8vo., 3s. 6d.

Wild Animals of the Bible. 29 Illustrations. Cr. 8vo., 3s. 6d.

Domestic Animals of the Bible. 23 Illustrations. Cr. 8vo., 3s. 6d.

The Branch Builders. 28 Illustrations. Cr. 8vo., 2s. 6d.

Social Habitations and Parasitic Nests. 18 Illustrations. Cr. 8vo., 2s.

Works of Reference.

Longmans' *Gazetteer of the World*. Edited by George G. Chisholm, M.A., B.Sc. Imp. 8vo., £2 2s. cloth, £2 12s. 6d. half-morocco.

Maunder (Samuel).

Biographical Treasury. With Supplement brought down to 1889. By Rev. James Wood. Fcp. 8vo., 6s.

Treasury of Natural History: or, Popular Dictionary of Zoology. With 900 Woodcuts. Fcp. 8vo., 6s.

Treasury of Geography, Physical, Historical, Descriptive, and Political. With 7 Maps and 16 Plates. Fcp. 8vo., 6s.

The Treasury of Bible Knowledge. By the Rev. J. Ayre, M.A. With 5 Maps, 15 Plates, and 300 Woodcuts. Fcp. 8vo., 6s.

Treasury of Knowledge and Library of Reference. Fcp. 8vo., 6s.

Maunder (Samuel)—*continued*.

Historical Treasury. Fcp. 8vo., 6s.

Scientific and Literary Treasury. Fcp. 8vo., 6s.

The Treasury of Botany. Edited by J. Lindley, F.R.S., and T. Moore, F.L.S. With 274 Woodcuts and 20 Steel Plates. 2 vols. Fcp. 8vo., 12s.

Roget.—*Thesaurus of English Words and Phrases*. Classified and Arranged so as to Facilitate the Expression of Ideas and assist in Literary Composition. By Peter Mark Roget, M.D., F.R.S. Recomposed throughout, enlarged and improved, partly from the Author's Notes, and with a full Index, by the Author's Son, John Lewis Roget. Crown 8vo., 10s. 6d.

Willich.—*Popular Tables* for giving information for ascertaining the value of Lifehold, Leasehold, and Church Property, the Public Funds, &c. By Charles M. Willich. Edited by H. Bence Jones. Crown 8vo., 10s. 6d.

Children's Books.

Crake (Rev. A. D.).
- *Edwy the Fair;* or, The First Chronicle of Æscendune. Cr. 8vo., 2s. 6d.
- *Alfgar the Dane;* or, The Second Chronicle of Æscendune. Cr. 8vo. 2s. 6d.
- *The Rival Heirs:* being the Third and Last Chronicle of Æscendune. Cr. 8vo., 2s. 6d.
- *The House of Walderne.* A Tale of the Cloister and the Forest in the Days of the Barons' Wars. Crown 8vo., 2s. 6d.
- *Brian Fitz-Count.* A Story of Wallingford Castle and Dorchester Abbey. Cr. 8vo., 2s. 6d.

Lang (Andrew).—Edited by.
- *The Blue Fairy Book.* With 138 Illustrations. Crown 8vo., 6s.
- *The Red Fairy Book.* With 100 Illustrations. Crown 8vo., 6s.
- *The Green Fairy Book.* With 99 Illustrations. Crown 8vo., 6s.
- *The Yellow Fairy Book.* With 104 Illustrations. Crown 8vo., 6s.
- *The Blue Poetry Book.* With 100 Illustrations. Crown 8vo., 6s.
- *The Blue Poetry Book.* School Edition, without Illustrations. Fcp. 8vo., 2s. 6d.
- *The True Story Book.* With 66 Illustrations. Crown 8vo., 6s.
- *The Red True Story Book.* With 100 Illustrations. Crown 8vo., 6s.
- *The Animal Story Book.* With 67 Illustrations. Crown 8vo., 6s.

Meade (L. T.).
- *Daddy's Boy.* With Illustrations. Crown 8vo., 3s. 6d.
- *Deb and the Duchess.* With Illustrations. Crown 8vo., 3s. 6d.
- *The Beresford Prize.* With Illustrations. Crown 8vo., 3s. 6d.
- *The House of Surprises.* With Illustrations. Crown 8vo., 3s. 6d.

Molesworth—*Silverthorns.* By Mrs. Molesworth. With Illustrations. Cr. 8vo., 5s.

Stevenson.—*A Child's Garden of Verses.* By Robert Louis Stevenson. Fcp. 8vo., 5s.

Upton (Florence K. and Bertha).
- *The Adventures of Two Dutch Dolls and a 'Golliwogg'.* Illustrated by Florence K. Upton, with Words by Bertha Upton. With 31 Coloured Plates and numerous Illustrations in the Text. Oblong 4to., 6s.
- *The Golliwogg's Bicycle Club.* Illustrated by Florence K. Upton, with words by Bertha Upton. With 31 Coloured Plates and numerous Illustrations in the Text. Oblong 4to., 6s.

Wordsworth.—*The Snow Garden, and other Fairy Tales for Children.* By Elizabeth Wordsworth, With 10 Illustrations by Trevor Haddon. Crown 8vo., 5s.

Longmans' Series of Books for Girls.
Price 2s. 6d. each.

Atelier (The) Du Lys: or, an Art Student in the Reign of Terror.

By the same Author.
- *Mademoiselle Mori:* a Tale of Modern Rome.
- *In the Olden Time:* a Tale of the Peasant War in Germany.
- *The Younger Sister.*
- *That Child.*
- *Under a Cloud.*
- *Hester's Venture.*
- *The Fiddler of Lugau.*
- *A Child of the Revolution.*

Atherstone Priory. By L. N. Comyn.

The Story of a Spring Morning, etc. By Mrs. Molesworth. Illustrated.

The Palace in the Garden. By Mrs. Molesworth. Illustrated.

Neighbours. By Mrs. Molesworth.

The Third Miss St. Quentin. By Mrs. Molesworth.

Very Young; and Quite Another Story. Two Stories. By Jean Ingelow.

Can this be Love? By Louisa Parr.

Keith Deramore. By the Author of 'Miss Molly'.

Sidney. By Margaret Deland.

An Arranged Marriage. By Dorothea Gerard.

Last Words to Girls on Life at School and after School. By Maria Grey.

Stray Thoughts for Girls. By Lucy H. M. Soulsby. Head Mistress of Oxford High School. 16mo., 1s. 6d. net.

MESSRS. LONGMANS & CO.'S STANDARD AND GENERAL WORKS. 27

The Silver Library.

CROWN 8VO. 3s. 6d. EACH VOLUME.

Arnold's (Sir Edwin) Seas and Lands. With 71 Illustrations. 3s. 6d.

Bagehot's (W.) Biographical Studies. 3s. 6d.

Bagehot's (W.) Economic Studies. 3s. 6d.

Bagehot's (W.) Literary Studies. With Portrait. 3 vols. 3s. 6d. each.

Baker's (Sir S. W.) Eight Years in Ceylon. With 6 Illustrations. 3s. 6d.

Baker's (Sir S. W.) Rifle and Hound in Ceylon. With 6 Illustrations. 3s. 6d.

Baring-Gould's Rev. S. Curious Myths of the Middle Ages. 3s. 6d.

Baring-Gould's (Rev. S.) Origin and Development of Religious Belief. 2 vols. 3s. 6d. each.

Becker's Prof. Gallus: or, Roman Scenes in the Time of Augustus. Illustrated. 3s. 6d.

Becker's Prof. Charicles: or, Illustrations of the Private Life of the Ancient Greeks. Illustrated. 3s. 6d.

Bent's J. T. The Ruined Cities of Mashonaland. With 117 Illustrations. 3s. 6d.

Brassey's Lady) A Voyage in the 'Sunbeam'. With 66 Illustrations. 3s. 6d.

Butler's Edward A.) Our Household Insects. With 7 Plates and 113 Illustrations in the Text. 3s. 6d.

Clodd's E. Story of Creation: a Plain Account of Evolution. With 77 Illustrations. 3s. 6d.

Conybeare (Rev. W. J.) and Howson's (Very Rev. J. S.) Life and Epistles of St. Paul. 46 Illustrations. 3s. 6d.

Dougall's (L.) Beggars All: a Novel. 3s. 6d.

Doyle's (A. Conan) Micah Clarke. A Tale of Monmouth's Rebellion. 10 Illusts. 3s. 6d.

Doyle's A. Conan) The Captain of the Polestar, and other Tales. 3s. 6d.

Doyle's A. Conan The Refugees: A Tale of Two Continents. With 25 Illustrations. 3s. 6d.

Froude's J. A.) Short Studies on Great Subjects. 4 vols. 3s. 6d. each.

Froude's J. A.) Thomas Carlyle: a History of his Life.

1795-1835, 2 vols. 7s.
1834-1881, 2 vols. 7s.

Froude's (J. A.) Cæsar: a Sketch. 3s. 6d.

Froude's J. A.) The Spanish Story of the Armada, and other Essays. 3s. 6d.

Froude's (J. A.) The Two Chiefs of Dunboy: an Irish Romance of the Last Century. 3s. 6d.

Froude's (J. A.) The History of England, from the Fall of Wolsey to the Defeat of the Spanish Armada. 12 vols. 3s. 6d. each.

Froude's J. A.) The English in Ireland. 3 vols. 10s. 6d.

Gleig's (Rev. G. R.) Life of the Duke of Wellington. With Portrait. 3s. 6d.

Greville's (C. C. F.) Journal of the Reigns of King George IV., King William IV., and Queen Victoria. 8 vols. 3s. 6d. each.

Haggard's (H. R.) She: A History of Adventure. 32 Illustrations. 3s. 6d.

Haggard's (H. R.) Allan Quatermain. With 20 Illustrations. 3s. 6d.

Haggard's (H. R.) Colonel Quaritch, V.C.: a Tale of Country Life. 3s. 6d.

Haggard's (H. R.) Cleopatra. With 29 Illustrations. 3s. 6d.

Haggard's (H. R.) Eric Brighteyes. With 51 Illustrations. 3s. 6d.

Haggard's (H. R.) Beatrice. 3s. 6d.

Haggard's (H. R.) Allan's Wife. With 31 Illustrations. 3s. 6d.

Haggard's (H. R.) Montezuma's Daughter. With 25 Illustrations. 3s. 6d.

Haggard's (H. R.) The Witch's Head. With 16 Illustrations. 3s. 6d.

Haggard's (H. R.) Mr. Meeson's Will. With 16 Illustrations. 3s. 6d.

Haggard's (H. R.) Nada the Lily. With 23 Illustrations. 3s. 6d.

Haggard's (H. R.) Dawn. With 16 Illusts. 3s. 6d.

Haggard's (H. R.) The People of the Mist. With 16 Illustrations. 3s. 6d.

Haggard (H. R.) and Lang's (A.) The World's Desire. With 27 Illustrations. 3s. 6d.

Harte's (Bret) In the Carquinez Woods and other Stories. 3s. 6d.

Helmholtz's (Hermann von) Popular Lectures on Scientific Subjects. With 68 Illustrations. 2 vols. 3s. 6d. each.

Hornung's (E. W.) The Unbidden Guest. 3s. 6d.

Howitt's (W.) Visits to Remarkable Places. 80 Illustrations. 3s. 6d.

Jefferies' (R.) The Story of My Heart: My Autobiography. With Portrait. 3s. 6d.

Jefferies' (R.) Field and Hedgerow. With Portrait. 3s. 6d.

Jefferies' (R.) Red Deer. 17 Illustrations. 3s. 6d.

Jefferies' (R.) Wood Magic: a Fable. With Frontispiece and Vignette by E. V. B. 3s. 6d.

Jefferies (R.) The Toilers of the Field. With Portrait from the Bust in Salisbury Cathedral. 3s. 6d.

Knight's (E. F.) The Cruise of the 'Alerte': the Narrative of a Search for Treasure on the Desert Island of Trinidad. With 2 Maps and 23 Illustrations. 3s. 6d.

Knight's E. F. Where Three Empires Meet: a Narrative of Recent Travel in Kashmir, Western Tibet, Baltistan Gilgit. With a Map and 54 Illustrations. 3s. 6d.

Knight's E. F. The 'Falcon' on the Baltic: a Coasting Voyage from Hammersmith to Copenhagen in a Three-Ton Yacht. With Map and 11 Illustrations. 3s. 6d.

Lang's (A.) Angling Sketches. 20 Illustrations. 3s. 6d.

Lang's A.) Custom and Myth: Studies of Early Usage and Belief. 3s. 6d.

Lang's (Andrew) Cock Lane and Common-Sense. With a New Preface. 3s. 6d.

The Silver Library—*continued.*

Lees (J. A.) and Clutterbuck's (W. J.) B. C. 1887, A Ramble in British Columbia. With Maps and 75 Illustrations. 3*s.* 6*d.*
Macaulay's (Lord) Essays and Lays of Ancient Rome. With Portrait and Illustration. 3*s.* 6*d.*
Macleod's (H. D.) Elements of Banking. 3*s.* 6*d.*
Marshman's (J. C.) Memoirs of Sir Henry Havelock. 3*s.* 6*d.*
Max Müller's (F.) India, what can it teach us? 3*s.* 6*d.*
Max Müller's (F.) Introduction to the Science of Religion. 3*s.* 6*d.*
Merivale's (Dean) History of the Romans under the Empire. 8 vols. 3*s.* 6*d.* each.
Mill's (J. S.) Political Economy. 3*s.* 6*d.*
Mill's (J. S.) System of Logic. 3*s.* 6*d.*
Milner's (Geo.) Country Pleasures: the Chronicle of a Year chiefly in a Garden. 3*s.* 6*d.*
Nansen's (F.) The First Crossing of Greenland. With Illustrations and a Map. 3*s.* 6*d.*
Phillipps-Wolley's (C.) Snap: a Legend of the Lone Mountain. 13 Illustrations. 3*s.* 6*d.*
Proctor's (R. A.) The Orbs Around Us. 3*s.* 6*d.*
Proctor's (R. A.) The Expanse of Heaven. 3*s.* 6*d.*
Proctor's (R. A.) Other Worlds than Ours. 3*s.* 6*d.*
Proctor's (R. A.) Other Suns than Ours. 3*s.* 6*d.*
Proctor's (R. A.) Rough Ways made Smooth. 3*s.* 6*d.*
Proctor's (R. A.) Pleasant Ways in Science. 3*s.* 6*d.*
Proctor's (R. A.) Myths and Marvels of Astronomy. 3*s.* 6*d.*
Proctor's (R. A.) Nature Studies. 3*s.* 6*d.*
Proctor's (R. A.) Leisure Readings. By R. A. Proctor, Edward Clodd, Andrew Wilson, Thomas Foster, and A. C. Ranyard. With Illustrations. 3*s.* 6*d.*
Rhoscomyl's (Owen) The Jewel of Ynys Galon. With 12 Illustrations. 3*s.* 6*d.*
Rossetti's (Maria F.) A Shadow of Dante. 3*s.* 6*d.*
Smith's (R. Bosworth) Carthage and the Carthaginians. With Maps, Plans, &c. 3*s.* 6*d.*
Stanley's (Bishop) Familiar History of Birds. 160 Illustrations. 3*s.* 6*d.*
Stevenson's (R. L.) The Strange Case of Dr. Jekyll and Mr. Hyde; with other Fables. 3*s.* 6*d.*
Stevenson (R. L.) and Osbourne's (Ll.) The Wrong Box. 3*s.* 6*d.*
Stevenson (Robert Louis) and Stevenson's (Fanny van de Grift) More New Arabian Nights.—The Dynamiter. 3*s.* 6*d.*
Weyman's (Stanley J.) The House of the Wolf; a Romance. 3*s.* 6*d.*
Wood's (Rev. J. G.) Petland Revisited. With 33 Illustrations. 3*s.* 6*d.*
Wood's (Rev. J. G.) Strange Dwellings. With 60 Illustrations. 3*s.* 6*d.*
Wood's (Rev. J. G.) Out of Doors. With 11 Illustrations. 3*s.* 6*d.*

Cookery, Domestic Management, Gardening, &c.

Acton.—*Modern Cookery.* By Eliza Acton. With 150 Woodcuts. Fcp. 8vo., 4*s.* 6*d.*

Bull (Thomas, M.D.).

Hints to Mothers on the Management of their Health during the Period of Pregnancy. Fcp. 8vo., 1*s.* 6*d.*

The Maternal Management of Children in Health and Disease. Fcp. 8vo., 1*s.* 6*d.*

De Salis (Mrs.).

Cakes and Confections à la Mode. Fcp. 8vo., 1*s.* 6*d.*

Dogs: A Manual for Amateurs. Fcp. 8vo., 1*s.* 6*d.*

Dressed Game and Poultry à la Mode. Fcp. 8vo., 1*s.* 6*d.*

De Salis (Mrs.).—*continued.*

Dressed Vegetables à la Mode. Fcp. 8vo., 1*s.* 6*d.*

Drinks à la Mode. Fcp. 8vo., 1*s.* 6*d.*

Entrées à la Mode. Fcp. 8vo., 1*s.* 6*d.*

Floral Decorations. Fcp. 8vo., 1*s.* 6*d.*

Gardening à la Mode. Fcp. 8vo. Part I., Vegetables, 1*s.* 6*d.* Part II., Fruits, 1*s.* 6*d.*

National Viands à la Mode. Fcp. 8vo., 1*s.* 6*d.*

New-laid Eggs. Fcp. 8vo., 1*s.* 6*d.*

Oysters à la Mode. Fcp. 8vo., 1*s.* 6*d.*

Cookery, Domestic Management, &c.—*continued.*

De Salis (Mrs.).—*continued.*

PUDDINGS AND PASTRY À LA MODE. Fcp. 8vo., 1s. 6d.

SAVOURIES À LA MODE. Fcp. 8vo., 1s. 6d.

SOUPS AND DRESSED FISH À LA MODE. Fcp. 8vo., 1s. 6d.

SWEETS AND SUPPER DISHES À LA MODE. Fcp. 8vo., 1s. 6d.

TEMPTING DISHES FOR SMALL INCOMES. Fcp. 8vo., 1s. 6d.

WRINKLES AND NOTIONS FOR EVERY HOUSEHOLD. Crown 8vo., 1s. 6d.

Lear.—MAIGRE COOKERY. By H. L. SIDNEY LEAR. 16mo., 2s.

Poole.—COOKERY FOR THE DIABETIC. By W. H. and Mrs. POOLE. With Preface by Dr. PAVY. Fcp. 8vo., 2s. 6d.

Walker (JANE H.).

A BOOK FOR EVERY WOMAN.
Part I., The Management of Children in Health and out of Health. Crown 8vo., 2s. 6d.
Part II. Woman in Health and out of Health.

A HANDBOOK FOR MOTHERS: being being Simple Hints to Women on the Management of their Health during Pregnancy and Confinement, together with Plain Directions as to the Care of Infants. Crown 8vo., 2s. 6d.

Miscellaneous and Critical Works.

Allingham.—VARIETIES IN PROSE. By WILLIAM ALLINGHAM. 3 vols. Cr. 8vo., 18s. (Vols. 1 and 2, Rambles, by PATRICIUS WALKER. Vol. 3, Irish Sketches, etc.)

Armstrong.—ESSAYS AND SKETCHES. By EDMUND J. ARMSTRONG. Fcp. 8vo., 5s.

Bagehot.—LITERARY STUDIES. By WALTER BAGEHOT. With Portrait. 3 vols. Crown 8vo., 3s. 6d. each.

Baring-Gould.—CURIOUS MYTHS OF THE MIDDLE AGES. By Rev. S. BARING-GOULD. Crown 8vo., 3s. 6d.

Baynes.—SHAKESPEARE STUDIES, and other Essays. By the late THOMAS SPENCER BAYNES, LL.B., LL.D. With a Biographical Preface by Professor LEWIS CAMPBELL. Crown 8vo., 7s. 6d.

Boyd (A. K. H.) ('A.K.H.B.').

And see MISCELLANEOUS THEOLOGICAL WORKS, *p.* 32.

AUTUMN HOLIDAYS OF A COUNTRY PARSON. Crown 8vo., 3s. 6d.

COMMONPLACE PHILOSOPHER. Cr. 8vo., 3s. 6d.

CRITICAL ESSAYS OF A COUNTRY PARSON. Crown 8vo., 3s. 6d.

EAST COAST DAYS AND MEMORIES. Crown 8vo., 3s. 6d.

LANDSCAPES, CHURCHES, AND MORALITIES. Crown 8vo., 3s. 6d.

LEISURE HOURS IN TOWN. Crown 8vo., 3s. 6d.

Boyd (A. K. H.) ('A.K.H.B.').—*continued.*

LESSONS OF MIDDLE AGE. Crown 8vo., 3s. 6d.

OUR LITTLE LIFE. Two Series. Crown 8vo., 3s. 6d. each.

OUR HOMELY COMEDY: AND TRAGEDY. Crown 8vo., 3s. 6d.

RECREATIONS OF A COUNTRY PARSON. Three Series. Crown 8vo., 3s. 6d. each. Also First Series. Popular Edition. 8vo., 6d. Sewed.

Butler (SAMUEL).

EREWHON. Crown 8vo., 5s.

THE FAIR HAVEN. A Work in Defence of the Miraculous Element in our Lord's Ministry. Cr. 8vo., 7s. 6d.

LIFE AND HABIT. An Essay after a Completer View of Evolution. Cr. 8vo., 7s. 6d.

EVOLUTION, OLD AND NEW. Cr. 8vo., 10s. 6d.

ALPS AND SANCTUARIES OF PIEDMONT AND CANTON TICINO. Illustrated. Pott 4to., 10s. 6d.

LUCK, OR CUNNING, AS THE MAIN MEANS OF ORGANIC MODIFICATION? Cr. 8vo., 7s. 6d.

EX VOTO. An Account of the Sacro Monte or New Jerusalem at Varallo-Sesia. Crown 8vo., 10s. 6d.

Miscellaneous and Critical Works—*continued.*

Dreyfus. LECTURES ON FRENCH LITERATURE. Delivered in Melbourne by IRMA DREYFUS. With Portrait of the Author. Large crown 8vo., 12s. 6d.

Gwilt.—AN ENCYCLOPÆDIA OF ARCHITECTURE. By JOSEPH GWILT, F.S.A. Illustrated with more than 1100 Engravings on Wood. Revised (1888), with Alterations and Considerable Additions by WYATT PAPWORTH. 8vo., £2 12s. 6d.

Hamlin.—A TEXT-BOOK OF THE HISTORY OF ARCHITECTURE. By A. D. F. HAMLIN, A.M., Adjunct-Professor of Architecture in the School of Mines, Columbia College. With 229 Illustrations. Crown 8vo., 7s. 6d.

Haweis.—MUSIC AND MORALS. By the Rev. H. R. HAWEIS. With Portrait of the Author, and numerous Illustrations, Facsimiles, and Diagrams. Crown 8vo., 7s. 6d.

Indian Ideals (No. 1).

NĀRADA SŪTRA: an Inquiry into Love (Bhakti-Jijnāsā). Translated from the Sanskrit, with an Independent Commentary, by E. T. STURDY. Crown 8vo., 2s. 6d. net.

Jefferies.—(RICHARD).

FIELD AND HEDGEROW: With Portrait. Crown 8vo., 3s. 6d.

THE STORY OF MY HEART: my Autobiography. With Portrait and New Preface by C. J. LONGMAN. Crown 8vo., 3s. 6d.

RED DEER. With 17 Illustrations by J. CHARLTON and H. TUNALY. Crown 8vo., 3s. 6d.

THE TOILERS OF THE FIELD. With Portrait from the Bust in Salisbury Cathedral. Crown 8vo., 3s. 6d.

WOOD MAGIC: a Fable. With Frontispiece and Vignette by E. V. B. Crown 8vo., 3s. 6d.

THOUGHTS FROM THE WRITINGS OF RICHARD JEFFERIES. Selected by H. S. HOOLE WAYLEN. 16mo., 3s. 6d.

Johnson.—THE PATENTEE'S MANUAL: a Treatise on the Law and Practice of Letters Patent. By J. & J. H. JOHNSON, Patent Agents, &c. 8vo., 10s. 6d.

Lang (ANDREW).

LETTERS TO DEAD AUTHORS. Fcp. 8vo., 2s. 6d. net.

BOOKS AND BOOKMEN. With 2 Coloured Plates and 17 Illustrations. Fcp. 8vo., 2s. 6d. net.

OLD FRIENDS. Fcp. 8vo., 2s. 6d. net.

LETTERS ON LITERATURE. Fcp. 8vo., 2s. 6d. net.

COCK LANE AND COMMON SENSE. Crown 8vo., 3s. 6d.

Macfarren.—LECTURES ON HARMONY. By Sir GEORGE A. MACFARREN. 8vo., 12s.

Marquand and Frothingham.—A TEXT-BOOK OF THE HISTORY OF SCULPTURE. By ALLAN MARQUAND, Ph.D., and ARTHUR L. FROTHINGHAM, Junr., Ph.D., Professors of Archæology and the History of Art in Princetown University. With 113 Illustrations. Crown 8vo., 6s.

Max Müller (F).

INDIA: WHAT CAN IT TEACH US? Crown 8vo., 3s. 6d.

CHIPS FROM A GERMAN WORKSHOP.

Vol. I. Recent Essays and Addresses. Crown 8vo., 6s. 6d. net.

Vol. II. Biographical Essays. Crown 8vo., 6s. 6d. net.

Vol. III. Essays on Language and Literature. Crown 8vo., 6s. 6d. net.

Vol. IV. Essays on Mythology and Folk Lore. Crown 8vo, 8s. 6d. net.

CONTRIBUTIONS TO THE SCIENCE OF MYTHOLOGY. 2 vols. 8vo.

Milner.—COUNTRY PLEASURES: the Chronicle of a Year chiefly in a Garden. By GEORGE MILNER. Crown 8vo., 3s. 6d.

Miscellaneous and Critical Works—*continued*.

Morris (WILLIAM).
  SIGNS OF CHANGE. Seven Lectures delivered on various Occasions. Post 8vo., 4s. 6d.
  HOPES AND FEARS FOR ART. Five Lectures delivered in Birmingham, London, &c., in 1878-1881. Crown 8vo., 4s. 6d.

Orchard.—*THE ASTRONOMY OF MILTON'S PARADISE LOST*. By THOMAS N. ORCHARD, M.D., Member of the British Astronomical Association. With 13 Illustrations. 8vo., 15s.

Poore.—*ESSAYS ON RURAL HYGIENE.* By GEORGE VIVIAN POORE, M.D., F.R.C.P. With 13 Illustrations. Crown 8vo., 6s. 6d.

Proctor.—*STRENGTH*: How to get Strong and keep Strong, with Chapters on Rowing and Swimming, Fat, Age, and the Waist. By R. A. PROCTOR. With 9 Illustrations. Crown 8vo., 2s.

Richardson.—*NATIONAL HEALTH.* A Review of the Works of Sir Edwin Chadwick, K.C.B. By Sir B. W. RICHARDSON, M.D. Crown 8vo., 4s. 6d.

Rossetti. *A SHADOW OF DANTE*: being an Essay towards studying Himself, his World and his Pilgrimage. By MARIA FRANCESCA ROSSETTI. With Frontispiece by DANTE GABRIEL ROSSETTI. Crown 8vo., 3s. 6d.

Solovyoff.—*A MODERN PRIESTESS OF ISIS (MADAME BLAVATSKY).* Abridged and Translated on Behalf of the Society for Psychical Research from the Russian of VSEVOLOD SERGYEEVICH SOLOVYOFF. By WALTER LEAF, Litt.D. With Appendices. Crown 8vo., 6s.

Stevens.—*ON THE STOWAGE OF SHIPS AND THEIR CARGOES.* With Information regarding Freights, Charter-Parties, &c. By ROBERT WHITE STEVENS, Associate-Member of the Institute of Naval Architects. 8vo., 21s.

West.—*WILLS, AND HOW NOT TO MAKE THEM.* With a Selection of Leading Cases. By B. B. WEST, Author of "Half-Hours with the Millionaires". Fcp. 8vo., 2s. 6d.

Miscellaneous Theological Works.

For Church of England and Roman Catholic Works see MESSRS. LONGMANS & CO.'s Special Catalogues.

Balfour. — *THE FOUNDATIONS OF BELIEF*: being Notes Introductory to the Study of Theology. By the Right Hon. ARTHUR J. BALFOUR, M.P. 8vo., 12s. 6d.

Bird (ROBERT).
  A CHILD'S RELIGION. Cr. 8vo., 2s.
  JOSEPH, THE DREAMER. Crown 8vo., 5s.
  JESUS, THE CARPENTER OF NAZARETH. Crown 8vo., 5s.
  To be had also in Two Parts, price 2s. 6d. each.
    Part I. GALILEE AND THE LAKE OF GENNESARET.
    Part II. JERUSALEM AND THE PERÆA.

Boyd (A. K. H.) ('A.K.H.B.').
  OCCASIONAL AND IMMEMORIAL DAYS: Discourses. Crown 8vo., 7s. 6d.
  COUNSEL AND COMFORT FROM A CITY PULPIT. Crown 8vo., 3s. 6d.
  SUNDAY AFTERNOONS IN THE PARISH CHURCH OF A SCOTTISH UNIVERSITY CITY. Crown 8vo., 3s. 6d.
  CHANGED ASPECTS OF UNCHANGED TRUTHS. Crown 8vo., 3s. 6d.
  GRAVER THOUGHTS OF A COUNTRY PARSON. Three Series. Crown 8vo., 3s. 6d. each.
  PRESENT DAY THOUGHTS. Crown 8vo., 3s. 6d.
  SEASIDE MUSINGS. Cr. 8vo., 3s. 6d.
  '*TO MEET THE DAY*' through the Christian Year: being a Text of Scripture, with an Original Meditation and a Short Selection in Verse for Every Day. Crown 8vo., 4s. 6d.

Miscellaneous Theological Works—*continued*.

De la Saussaye.—*A Manual of the Science of Religion.* By Professor Chantepie de la Saussaye. Translated by Mrs. Colyer Fergusson (*née* Max Müller). Crown 8vo., 12s. 6d.

Gibson.—*The Abbé de Lamennais, and the Liberal Catholic Movement in France.* By the Hon. W. Gibson. With Portrait. 8vo., 12s. 6d.

Kalisch (M. M., Ph.D.).

Bible Studies. Part I. Prophecies of Balaam. 8vo., 10s. 6d. Part II. The Book of Jonah. 8vo., 10s. 6d.

Commentary on the Old Testament: with a New Translation. Vol. I. Genesis, 8vo., 18s. Or adapted for the General Reader. 12s. Vol. II. Exodus. 15s. Or adapted for the General Reader. 12s. Vol. III. Leviticus, Part I. 15s. Or adapted for the General Reader. 8s. Vol. IV. Leviticus, Part II. 15s. Or adapted for the General Reader. 8s.

Macdonald (George).

Unspoken Sermons. Three Series. Crown 8vo., 3s. 6d. each.

The Miracles of our Lord. Crown 8vo., 3s. 6d.

Martineau (James).

Hours of Thought on Sacred Things: Sermons, 2 vols. Crown 8vo., 3s. 6d. each.

Endeavours after the Christian Life. Discourses. Crown 8vo., 7s. 6d.

The Seat of Authority in Religion. 8vo., 14s.

Essays, Reviews, and Addresses. 4 Vols. Crown 8vo., 7s. 6d. each.
I. Personal; Political. II. Ecclesiastical: Historical. III. Theological; Philosophical. IV. Academical; Religious.

Home Prayers, with *Two Services* for Public Worship. Crown 8vo., 3s. 6d.

Max Müller (F.).

Hibbert Lectures on the Origin and Growth of Religion, as illustrated by the Religions of India. Cr. 8vo., 7s. 6d.

Introduction to the Science of Religion: Four Lectures delivered at the Royal Institution. Crown 8vo., 3s. 6d.

Natural Religion. The Gifford Lectures, delivered before the University of Glasgow in 1888. Crown 8vo., 10s. 6d.

Physical Religion. The Gifford Lectures, delivered before the University of Glasgow in 1890. Crown 8vo., 10s. 6d.

Anthropological Religion. The Gifford Lectures, delivered before the University of Glasgow in 1891. Cr. 8vo., 10s. 6d.

Theosophy, or Psychological Religion. The Gifford Lectures, delivered before the University of Glasgow in 1892. Crown 8vo., 10s. 6d.

Three Lectures on the Vedânta Philosophy, delivered at the Royal Institution in March, 1894. 8vo., 5s.

Phillips.—*The Teaching of the Vedas.* What Light does it Throw on the Origin and Development of Religion? By Maurice Phillips. London Mission, Madras. Crown 8vo., 6s.

Romanes.—*Thoughts on Religion.* By George J. Romanes, LL.D., F.R.S. Crown 8vo., 4s. 6d.

Supernatural Religion: an Inquiry into the Reality of Divine Revelation. 3 vols. 8vo., 36s.

Reply (A) to Dr. Lightfoot's Essays. By the Author of 'Supernatural Religion'. 8vo., 6s.

The Gospel according to St. Peter: a Study. By the Author of 'Supernatural Religion'. 8vo., 6s.

Vivekananda.—*Yoga Philosophy:* Lectures delivered in New York, Winter of 1895-96, by the Swami Vivekananda, on Raja Yoga ; or, Conquering the Internal Nature ; also Patanjali's Yoga Aphorisms, with Commentaries. Crown 8vo., 3s. 6d.

10,000/12/96.

www.ingramcontent.com/pod-product-compliance
Lightning Source LLC
Chambersburg PA
CBHW051742300426
44115CB00007B/664